Irish Drama in Poland

Irish Drama in Poland
Staging and Reception 1900-2000

Barry Keane

intellect Bristol, UK / Chicago, USA

First published in the UK in 2016 by
Intellect, The Mill, Parnall Road, Fishponds, Bristol, BS16 3JG, UK

First published in the USA in 2016 by
Intellect, The University of Chicago Press, 1427 E. 60th Street,
Chicago, IL 60637, USA

A catalogue record for this book is available from the
British Library.

Copy-editor: MPS Technologies
Cover designer: Stephanie Sarlos
Production managers: Jessica Mitchell and Richard Kerr
Typesetting: Contentra Technologies

Print ISBN: 978-1-78320-608-7
ePDF ISBN: 978-1-78320-609-4
ePUB ISBN: 978-1-78320-610-0

Printed and bound by TJ International, UK

Contents

List of Illustrations

Foreword

Translators, in negotiating the rhythms of closure and openness in languages and cultures, both filter and infiltrate the target language and culture. In this respect, it might be opportune to move away from an image that has often been used to capture the task of the translator, the image of the bridge. Translation as a bridge between cultures, translators as bridge-builders, these metaphors are commonplaces of irenic pronouncements on the global importance of translation. However, it may be more useful to look under the bridge and see what is swirling down below. James Joyce opened his hymn to the polyphonic possibilities of modern urban life with this downward gaze:

> riverrun, past Eve and Adam's, from swerve of shore to bend of bay, brings us by a commodius vicus of recirculation back to Howth Castle and Environs.
> Sir Tristram, violer d'amores, fr'over the short sea, had passencore rearrived from North Armorica on this side the scraggy isthmus of Asia Minor to wielderfight his penisolate war.
>
> (Joyce 1939: 1)

The river that runs through *Finnegans Wake* carries with it the multitude of languages and cultures that have passed through the city of Dublin and into the mind and writings of the artist. Without the river, of course, there are no banks and no bridges. It is the river that defines the banks, brings the bridges into being. Rivers both define and ignore boundaries. They gather materials from both banks and bring materials to both banks. If the great civilizations of translation have grown up around rivers – the Nile, the Tigris, the Euphrates – is this not a reminder that translation is better understood not as suspended in the air but as caught up in the living currents of language and cultures that continue to flow through the landscapes of our dwelling places? The riverrun of translation is what both divides and unites us, and if in Heraclitus's words, "no man ever steps in the same river twice", it is because both the river and the man are themselves in endless recirculation, in an endless state of perpetual retranslation.

Moving from the banks of the Liffey to the banks of the Vistula and beyond, Barry Keane's captivating new work explores the dramatic currents of ideas, forms and expressions that have flowed between Irish and Polish cultures for more than two centuries. At different ends of the European geographical compass, fretting at different periods in the shadow of imperial overlords, tracing out the difficult, thankless paths to freedom, negotiating a hospitable relationship with the faiths of Fathers and Mothers, Ireland and Poland have much to talk about, much to engage with on the stage of world literature. As Polish becomes the most widely spoken foreign language in Ireland, *Irish Drama in Poland: Staging and Reception 1900–2000* reminds us of the long literary and dramatic history that has linked the two countries. However, the importance of this book goes beyond the specificity of a relationship between two literary cultures and addresses the wider question of the survival and flourishing of particular cultures in the long European twentieth century. In particular, the work draws our attention to the labour of translation, the constant negotiation and renegotiation that takes place when a work moves in place and time and must be made anew in new places with new words. Nothing can be taken for granted. No assumptions can be made about ready recognition. Line by line, scene by scene, act by act, the translator must engage in that intense form of reimagining and remaking that is translation. In theatre translation, the drama of transformation is collective as directors, actors, set designers translate the text into the live performance of bodies moving and speaking in time. Translation here is not the solitary act of scholarly devotion but a gathering together, a concentration of the metamorphic energies of theatre to bring a character, a scene, a crux into splendid, redemptive life on the boards of a stage a thousand kilometres from the playwright's home. If theatre is, among other things, a kind of protracted dialogue, then translation is an inevitable partner in this dialogue if theatre is to advance beyond the stomping ground of origin.

The translators who feature between the covers of this book are the unaccredited ambassadors, the barely acknowledged plenipotentiaries, who year in, year out, work to keep the communication cords thrumming between different countries, different cultures, different languages. They often work in difficult, hostile circumstances, whether it be the censorious fury of the totalitarian or the blithe indifference of the commercial. They are sustained by a belief in the value of opening up worlds to each other, worlds that reveal how much divides us as much as what unites us. Translation does not provide a short cut to universal epiphanies. It is an apprenticeship of difference, but where difference is an invitation to explore and not a refusal to budge. Too often, translators are missing from literary histories, dictionaries of national biography, newspapers reports, theatre reviews, but they haunt the interstices of any culture that is irrigated by the news from elsewhere. Barry Keane brings to light these largely forgotten histories of linguistic mediation and cultural contact. In doing this he not only offers more complex readings of Irish and Polish cultures, too often beholden to the monocular vision of the monolingual, but he shows the crucial role played by translator-citizens in the construction of a World Republic of Letters.

W. B. Yeats in his poem, 'To Ireland in the Coming Times' (1893) saw literature and history as tied in a mutual knot of self-regard:

Know, that I would accounted be
True brother of a company

That sang, to sweeten Ireland's wrong,
Ballad and story, rann and song;

The poet rights the historical wrongs of an Ireland or a Poland in the measured beats of his songs. The company that features in *Irish Drama in Poland* is at once a company of players and a company of translators that do not so much sweeten as explore, investigate, tease out the recurrent wrongs of what it is to be human. This original and compelling work calls for another kind of accounting, the accounting of the work of the true brothers and sisters of the transformation of the word; those working between Irish literature and the Polish stage that brought whole new worlds into being for the coming times.

Michael Cronin
Dublin, 5 December 2014

Acknowledgements

I would firstly like to thank An Foras Feasa, the Institute for Research in Irish Historical and Cultural Traditions at the National University of Ireland, Maynooth, and SALIS, the School of Applied Language and Intercultural Studies at Dublin City University, for the co-awarding of a postdoctoral fellowship without which I could not have begun this project. Writing this book has been a deeply enriching experience, not least for the interest shown by so many along the way. Principally, I would like to extend my thanks to Michael Cronin who has mentored me in the writing of this book. This heartfelt appreciation also extends to the staff of SALIS, in particular Dorothy Kenny and Jenny Williams. I would also like to express my warmest thanks to Margaret Kelleher and all the team at An Foras Feasa for their generous support and hospitality.

I am particularly grateful to the librarians and archivists who facilitated my research, in particular, Maria Dworakowska of the Theatre Institute of Warsaw, Katarzyna Wodarska-Ogidel of the Polish Theatre Museum of Warsaw, Aleksandra Chrapowicka of the Coastal Theatre of Gdańsk, Jadwiga Adamowicz of the Contemporary Theatre of Warsaw, Barbara Maresz of the Silesian Library, and Diana Poskuta-Włodek of the Archive and Library of the Juliusz Słowacki Theatre of Kraków. And special thanks to Iwona Myszkowska for giving permission to publish a still from the Polish Theatre's 1960-production of Sean O'Casey's *Cock-a-Doodle Dandy*, taken by Franciszek Myszkowski.

I would like to express my thanks to Nicholas Grene for suggesting that Shaw's *Mrs Warren's Profession* was worthier of a deeper exploration than I had originally been inclined to devote to the play. I would also like to extend my warmest thanks to Lauren Arrington who pointed me in the direction of the Irish newspaper reviews of Kazimierz Markiewicz's plays.

I would like to take this opportunity to acknowledge the support and advice extended to me from my colleagues at the University of Warsaw, in particular Aniela Korzeniowska, Agnieszka Piskorska and Izabela Szymańska. I must also thank my fellow travellers in Polish-Irish comparative studies: Michał Lachman, Robert Looby and John Kearns, for their splendid advice and support over the years. I extend this appreciation also to Michael Raab, Jerzy Jarniewicz, Fiorenzo Fantaccini, David Malcolm, Ondřej Pilný and Michel Pharand. A special and heartfelt thanks to my agent, Ewa Ledóchowicz, who has helped me immeasurably in many ways. And to all the team at Intellect, especially Jessica Mitchell and Richard Kerr, who have been wonderful in helping me bring this book to publication.

Parts of the book featuring Shaw's *Mrs Warren's Profession* appeared in *SHAW. The Annual of Bernard Shaw Studies* 33 (2013); Beckett's *Waiting for Godot* in *Translation Ireland* 19/2 (2014); Synge's *Playboy of the Western World* in Polish in *Acta Universitatis Lodziensis. Folia Litteraria Polonica* 2(24) 2014, and Tadeusz Pawlikowski in *Studi irlandesi. A Journal of Irish Studies* (July 2015).

Introduction

This book represents the first attempt to broadly assess Irish drama's impact on both Poland's theatrical world and its cultural and literary heritage from the early part of the twentieth century through to its end. The work incorporates all the great names associated with Irish theatre who enjoyed a theatrical legacy outside of Ireland during their lifetime and beyond.

An intriguing aspect of the study is the extent to which perceived common links with Ireland generated a great deal of anticipation around upcoming theatrical productions. However, in spite of the excitement on the part of audiences and critics at the prospect of witnessing a spectacle that celebrated the fraternal cultures of both Poland and Ireland, very often the same productions only served to confirm that perceptions of national affinity and empathy were somewhat illusory and that the cultural gulf was wider than had previously been thought. What is more, many Irish plays came to Poland years after they had premiered elsewhere, and as a consequence of this tardiness potential dialogue about contemporary issues common to both countries was undermined almost from the outset.

A focal point of this work is the transmission of Irish plays, and so what follows in this narrative is a descriptive and critical look at the actual events and circumstances that led to certain plays being brought to the attention of Polish audiences. This narrative is complemented by an appraisal of the relevant historical and literary backdrops at the time of the productions, which will facilitate any gauging of the extent to which Irish drama contributed to and intersected with Polish history, culture and tradition. Part of the exploration entails assessing the status and roles of some of the Polish translators of Irish drama and looking at the extent to which the translated texts underwent a process of alterity in terms of interpretation, perception and the imagined construct of Ireland. As we shall see, this construct was often strongly influenced by the dialectical characteristics of the translated manuscripts and their relation to Polish regional dialects, or even Polish literary or theatrical works that informed or coloured the critical reception of the staged Irish plays. Interestingly, the efforts of the translators often sparked debate amongst theatre critics pertaining to the acculturation of the plays and their location and association with various regions of Poland, particularly those regions associated with a vibrant peasant culture.

Aside from a pre-history background chapter that focuses on Thomas Moore and nineteenth-century Poland, the scope of the book takes us from the early 1900s, which saw the first Polish productions of George Bernard Shaw, Oscar Wilde and J. M. Synge, toward the cusp of our current century. Somewhere in between, Sean O'Casey went from being lauded for a production of *The Shadow of a Gunman* to being vilified five years later following a highly misunderstood production of *Cock-a-Doodle Dandy*. Shaw is strongly represented in this work, and the scale of his presence testifies to his importance in the history of Polish theatre. Of particular interest should also be the history of Shaw's *Mrs Warren's Profession*, which is a play that explores the causes of prostitution. A number of sub-chapters will show how it was performed variously in different periods, and how the play gave rise to divergent opinions about Poland's own social ills. For the most part, the book focuses on the early impact of plays following their Polish premieres. This approach particularly suits the stories of W. B. Yeats, Synge, O'Casey and Brendan Behan in Poland, as their plays had mostly short runs and were never staged again, whereas the plays of Wilde, Shaw and Samuel Beckett enjoyed enduring popularity and saw numerous revivals. Beckett will be seen, in turn, to have made a hugely important impact in post-war Poland and beyond, principally because his plays, and the interpretations they gave rise to, provided an apolitical space for existentialist and intellectual debate about the place of Polish theatre in modern Europe.

There are more lows than highs in this account, and certainly a late-arriving Friel in the 1990s failed to receive the stellar productions that his works deserved. As we shall see, where Friel's explorations of memory and language seemed heavy-handed to audiences, playwrights Martin McDonagh and Conor McPherson, whose respective plays *The Cripple of Inishmaan* and *The Weir* were performed as the century drew to a close, achieved the kind of notoriety that should have been earlier achieved by Friel. However, these two dramatists had contemporaneity on their side, and perhaps their plays responded to a desire to see 'Polish stories' in 'Polish-like places', where high drama took place in picturesque localities. These plays were eye-openers to the Polish theatrical world both creatively and financially in a way not seen since Shaw, and the current generation of Irish playwrights in the years since the turn of the millennium have also given Polish audiences much to think about, and will surely do so for many generations to come.

Prologue

Thomas Moore: An Early Meeting of the Waters

The third partition of Poland by Prussia, Austria and Russia in 1795 definitively eradicated a power that had held the centre of Europe for eight centuries. Although Poland had disappeared from the map of Europe, the Polish nation had not yet perished, even if the wretched exploits of the Polish legion under General Jan Henryk Dąbrowski made the plight of Poland seem even more desperate. But in the spring of 1812 Napoleon and his army entered Poland, sweeping up legions of Polish men who took a desperate leap of faith and marched against Russia under the French flag, lighter in their step, perhaps, than any of their compatriots had been for a generation or more. These same Polish combatants would taste bitter defeat and find their end either in the environs of Moscow or on the crater-filled fields of Berezina and Mozhaysk. Over the coming months, a newly liberated Europe breathed a sigh of relief. However, soon the empires of continental Europe would exact their vengeance upon errant Poland.

In 1815, when a young Adam Mickiewicz was travelling by cart from Nowogródek in today's Belarus to Vilnius, the Congress of Vienna was busy redrawing the political map of Europe. Russia received the Napoleonic Duchy of Warsaw, which would form the Kingdom of Poland. Other parts of what was formerly Poland were gifted to Prussia and Austria.

At the beginning of the new regime, Tsar Alexander I was conciliatory and made the Polish prince, Adam Czartoryski, his foreign minister. Czartoryski hoped for a union with Russia, wherein he would be made a viceroy of the Polish lands. But soon, the tsar favoured the rule of law over the liberal ideas of his youth, which had envisaged giving Poland some sort of governmental representation. His sea-change may also have been brought about by the poisonous words of his advisors, who possessed a strong anti-Polish bias.[1] The tsar stripped Czartoryski of his office and gave the prince the task of reforming education in the western provinces of Russia. In carrying out his mission, Czartoryski would focus his efforts on reviving the fortunes of Vilnius University. He increased resources and actively recruited new professors from both the former Polish territories and other European countries. The university would educate and inspire a generation of highly gifted and ambitious young Polish men, who were determined that their futures would not be thwarted by occupation and oppression. And indeed, a minor improvement in the economy and a perceptible relaxing of oppressive actions gave many Poles the hope that Russia would loosen the knot.

However, in November 1830 a group of young Polish officers from the military academy in the Russian-occupied Kingdom of Poland staged a *coup d'état* in Warsaw, almost managing to kill the tsar's brother, Grand Duke Constantine.[2] The Russian occupying forces retreated and the other Polish militia joined the rebels. But this was only a temporary victory. The

Russians roundly trounced the valiant Poles in various theatres of battle. Once they had re-established their stranglehold, repressive measures followed. Lands were confiscated and universities were closed. Polish patriots were imprisoned, executed or exiled. Much of Poland's intellectual elite emigrated and chose to settle in France, where they tried to form some sort of resistance amongst Europe's noble classes. But for Adam Mickiewicz and his generation, with their university years ahead of them, these events lay in the future.

Soon after graduating from Vilnius University with a Master's degree in Classical Philology, Mickiewicz debuted in 1822 with the conspiratorial collection *Ballady i romanse* [*Ballads and Romances*], which hailed the beginnings of Polish Romanticism, blending as it did the fantastical of folk motifs with the places of Mickiewicz's childhood, such as the crystal clear lake of Świteź and the fir forests of Nowogródek. Although topographical description is almost totally absent, in its place the reader is given a sense of the starkness and wildness in which the narrated events take place, wherein the rising of a wind or the rustle of a tree branch presage some dark episode. Indeed, a storyteller speaking in whispered undertones of some episode involving murder or outrage narrates many of the ballads in the collection. Prayerful petitions to the Lord, or the Blessed Mary, betray the inner torment of a people whose lives are hard-pressed. Some of the poems are heartbreaking, as when children pray for the return of their father, who has perhaps died defending his family and homestead from unnamed raiders.

Despite being strewn with death and the cries of war-torn lament, Mickiewicz's *Ballads and Romances* were not regarded as seditious. However, even though Mickiewicz's debut directly escaped the ire of the censor, it brought him unwanted attention. In 1823, following a sweeping investigation into secret youth societies operating in Vilnius, Mickiewicz was found to have been in league with a subversive group known as the Philomaths, even though since his graduation he had principally been leading an uneventful and melancholic existence working off his scholarship debt by teaching in the town of Kowno, situated some distance from the conspiratorial hub that was Vilnius. Together with his co-accused, he was arrested and imprisoned in a Basilian monastery and was later found guilty of participating in seditious acts. As a sentence he was ordered to work as a teacher in the Russian provinces. And so Mickiewicz left Lithuania at the end of 1824, and for the next five years he lived between Moscow, Petersburg and Odessa. It was not until 1826–1827, when residing in Odessa, that Mickiewicz translated Thomas Moore's 'The Meeting of The Waters', which had belonged to the slim booklet of words and music that was the first volume of *The Irish Melodies* (1807/1808). As a poem it recalls how the Irish bard admired the scenery afforded by the gloriously picturesque Vale of Avoca in County Wicklow, although the vantage point from which he beheld the scene has always remained the subject of speculation.

Mickiewicz's translation was an isolated endeavor in that Moore did not receive the kind of attention that Mickiewicz was devoting to Byron and Petrarch at this time. However, there is much to suggest that this poem inspired the poet's writing of *Sonety krymskie* [*Crimean Sonnets*] (1826). In May 1828, Mickiewicz wrote to Antoni Odyniec, revealing that the poetry of Moore was principally occupying his thoughts, 'I know nothing sweeter and more delicate, but you have to read it in the original.'[3] Whereas one month later, in another letter to Odyniec, Mickiewicz wrote of the practice and inspiration he derived from translation: 'I have always found in the work a new strength, and have always made great use of it'.[4] And it does seem that the poet modelled a poem featured in *The Crimean Sonnets*, 'Pielgrzym' ['The Pilgrim'], on 'The Meeting of the Waters', particularly in its direct evocation of place and its expression of longing for places close to the poet's heart.

Mickiewicz's actual translation of 'The Meeting of the Waters' imparted the general sentiment of the original. He also achieved a more melancholic note with an exclamatory expression of what for him was a true loss of place.[5] The future provenance of Mickiewicz's translation would prove colourful. For many decades the translation was regarded as an original work principally because Mickiewicz had omitted the place name Avoca, the very invocation of which, according to Moore biographer, Ronan Kelly, 'changed the fortunes of [this] otherwise undistinguished lyric'.[6] Sometime in 1828, Mickiewicz pasted a copy of his translation into an album of friend and fellow exile, Piotr Moszyński, who was also living in Odessa. This album was eventually filled with the pastings of the early versions of Mickiewicz's works, and was later published in 1890 in Kraków.[7]

But if Mickiewicz was corresponding with Odyniec on Moore, Odyniec was also engaged in presenting his work to another burgeoning poet of the Polish Romantic era, Juliusz Słowacki, who, in July 1826, whilst still in his teens and studying at Vilnius, had written two *rifacciamenti* of Moore's: 'Farewell to thee' ['Pożegnanie'] and 'Melody' ['Melodia'] from the French translations of Louise Sw. Belloc entitled *Les Amours des anges et les Melodies irlandaises du Thomas Moore* (Paris, 1823).

Odyniec studied Law at Vilnius University between the years 1820 and 1823, and like Mickiewicz, had been open to conspiratorial debate and patriotic activity, famously providing some rallying songs for the Philomath Society, which featured such lines as 'Begone, begone from us all sadness!'[8] He also shared the same fate as Mickiewicz, in that he was caught up in the crackdown and was initially imprisoned with Mickiewicz and others. However, Odyniec was spared the fate of exile and was allowed to settle in Warsaw, where he remained from 1825 to 1829, following which time he travelled to Petersburg and met up with Mickiewicz. Odyniec would help Mickiewicz to escape arrest following the publication of the allegorical *Konrad Wallenrod* (1828), which told the story of a fourteenth-century Lithuanian pagan knight who enters the order of the occupying Knights of the Holy Cross so as to sow disorder from within – the Lithuania of the poem is associated with Poland and the Holy Cross with Russia.[9] Or so the authorities thought.

This would be the starting point of a two-year odyssey, which saw both men travelling through Germany, Switzerland and Italy. In the years to come, Odyniec would embark on a translation of Moore's *Lalla Rookh* (1817). But at the time of his correspondence with the young Słowacki, it seems as if he was testing the waters and looking for feedback from a literary prodigy – even if Odyniec knew that sweet-talk and star-struck adulation would come his way in abundance no matter what. What transpired was that Odyniec sent to

Słowacki two Polish versions of 'Oh Thou Who Dry'st the Mourner's Tear' and seemingly asked the young poet to guess which version he had written. It is entirely possible that Odyniec was making literary mischief and had produced the two translations himself. However, Słowacki winningly did his best and enjoined older poet, Antoni Gorecki, author of the poem 'Śmierć zdrajcy ojczyzny' ['The Death of the Traitor of the Nation'] (1818), to play a part in the diversion.

In 1837, Moore would come to learn of Odyniec's translations from Count Zygmunt Krasiński,[10] who had himself penned a series of Polish melodies inspired by those of Moore. On being told by Krasiński of the popularity of 'Oh Blame not the Bard' in Poland, Moore later recorded: 'It is a strange fact, that on the banks of the Vistula River the *Irish Melodies* have been translated in a Polish sense, and are adopted by that wronged and gallant people as expressive of their own disastrous fate'.[11] However, 'in a Polish sense' did not mean that Odyniec had tried in his translation to draw overt or covert allusions to Poland, but rather that just as with the Far Eastern tale, which depicts the struggle of the Ghebers against their oppressors, the motif was equally applicable to both Ireland and Poland. Having said that, it is also clear that 'a Polish sense' may be also taken to mean that Odyniec had grafted onto his translation some of Mickiewicz's mastery, metrics and lightness of touch, which goes some way to explaining Mickiewicz's ringing endorsement of Odyniec's translation, so contending that 'The Fire Worshippers' ['Czciciele ognia'] would remain in Polish literature for posterity.[12] The fact that Odyniec's translation reads like a poem by Mickiewicz may also explain the antipathy that the now older Słowacki – a rival of Mickiewicz – held for the poem, so writing to his mother in 1832: 'this strange mosaic; I have no idea why it appeals to him [Odyniec] so'.[13] This is one of the only derisory comments to be found in Polish on the poetry of Moore. But Słowacki had a great deal more to say of a similar tack about Mickiewicz, who at the time was gradually being perceived by Słowacki as his nemesis.

In 1831, Ursyn Niemcewicz, Polish patriot, prose writer, chronicler, poet and occasional translator, accompanied General Władysław Zamoyski to England on a diplomatic mission aimed at garnering political support from the ruling Whigs for the November Uprising of 1830–1831, which had spread revolt throughout the Polish territories. During this time, Niemcewicz played his part as a larger-than-life figure – aided by his corpulence – who dazzled and pressed home his cause to some of the most important men in England. (Although what he thought the English government could or was prepared to do could only have been some illusory expectation.) Niemcewicz would leave England in 1833 and like the majority of his fellow Polish writers and artists, settled in Paris, where he lived in exile until the end of his days.

Despite the weighty burden of their mission, both Niemcewicz and Zamoyski made the most of their time in England. They enjoyed the hospitality of the wealthy and the great, and did a great deal of sightseeing. Niemcewicz formed a close friendship with Henry Petty-Fitzmaurice, the third Marquess of Lansdowne. His family seat was in Bowood, which was situated only three miles from the home of Thomas Moore in Bromham. Chancellor of the

Exchequer at the age of 25, Lansdowne had for some time been 'the best hope of the Whig party in the Commons',[14] but he chose to throw almost all of his reserves of energy into revitalizing Bowood and turning it into a 'crucible of high culture',[15] which hosted some of the most illustrious names of the age. Needless to say, Moore was a frequent guest.

And so, when hosting Niemcewicz in the late summer and early autumn of 1831 and on learning how his Polish guest was a passionate admirer of the Irish bard, Lansdowne made a special point of inviting Moore to dine with them. It was the evening of September 17 and Zamoyski was also in attendance. However, if Niemcewicz, or more pointedly Zamoyski, had expected that Moore would broach the pressing Irish topics of the day, such as Daniel O'Connell and the Repeal of the Union, or that they would get an opportunity to speak on the ghastly course of events unfolding in Poland, they must have been disappointed by the triviality of the evening's conversation, which revolved primarily around some of the arcane aspects of German and French cuisine, and the quality of Edward Gibbon's French. According to diarist, Charles Greville, this kind of literary and miscellaneous talk was simply normal for such occasions, and by his account the evening had been enviably diverting.[16] But the assiduous flapping around the edges of momentous affairs left Zamoyski exasperated. He may also not have been used to being a third wheel, as the two poets parleyed in full flow about artistic matters. Three days later, Zamoyski apprised Prince Czartoryski of the evening. That he does not mention Lansdowne perhaps suggests that he had not got a word in edgeways:

> Niemcewicz is well known in the locality and is loved and respected. Thomas Moore paid a visit in order to make his acquaintance. He is a very short, talkative and good-humoured fellow. He sings his poems on the clavichord with great grace. He sings of the impoverished state of his homeland with great feeling, but it is clear that he prefers to sing of such matters from afar; he lives very well here.[17]

That evening, Niemcewicz arranged to meet Moore once again, as can be seen in his diary account from the following day:

> A famous poet came to dinner, Thomas Moore. A truly tiny figure, since he is even smaller than Mir. He is not at all handsome but the features of his face and his eyes evince a mischievous spark. At the table he was cheerful, amusing, and full of humour. He also related anecdotes, which it seems, he improvises himself. He had learnt that I had translated some of his melodies and requested that I present him with one. He drinks port wine prodigiously. After dinner he sang his *Irish Melodies,* full of mournful sweetness.

> [...] This morning I presented T. Moore with my translation of one of his Melodies 'Remember' etc., placing under each English line a Polish line, since he had wanted it like so. The gift was not unconditional; I asked him in return to write something for my poor country.[18]

Niemcewicz's translation of 'Remember Thee' was only first published in 1908 in the journal *Pamiętnik Literacki* [*The Literary Diary*][19] and it was dated 15 September 1831. This means that Niemcewicz may have set to work on the poem in anticipation of his meeting with Moore. It would certainly have provided a diverting icebreaker and put them on a collegial footing from the outset. Perhaps on this visit to Moore's home Niemcewicz would have spoken in fuller terms about Poland's plight. Perhaps not. But he would almost certainly have read out a back translation to the Irish bard, which would have left Moore in no doubt about the manner in which his poetry sang to Polish hearts. Whereas for Niemcewicz, just like Mickiewicz, the poetry of Moore spoke to his own personal circumstance:

> Remember thee! yes, while there's life in this heart, / It shall never forget thee, all lorn as thou art; / More dear in thy sorrow, thy gloom, and thy showers, / Than the rest of the world in their sunniest hours, …

Moore (1807/1808)

> Nie zapomnę cię, Polsko, póki tylko żyję, / Póki w tych skrzepłych piersiach zwiędłe serce bije. / Przez twój ucisk, łzy, nędze, okropne przygody, / Droższąś mi, niż kwitnące w potędzy narody,…

Niemcewicz (1908)

Back translation:
I will never forget you, o Poland, for as long as I live / For as long as my heart beats / Through your embrace, tears, gloom, and terrible trials, / You are dearer to me than nations blooming in power, …

The day that Niemcewicz visited Moore in Sloperton was 21 September 1831, in the company of Lady Lansdowne and her sister Lady Vallefort, who invited both Moore and Niemcewicz to stay at her home in Lacock. Moore accepted the invitation, and some days later, both he and Niemcewicz spent another evening together as guests in convivial circumstances. Moore would also meet Zamoyski on at least one further occasion, when the general gifted Moore with a Polish folktale.[20] However, in his *Memoirs*, Moore makes no mention of having met or spoken with either of these two distinguished Polish men.[21] Indeed, as far as can be discerned, Niemcewicz and Moore never corresponded with one another thereafter. And so, it may be said that the episode provides anecdotal evidence of the fact that Poland and Ireland would only engage with one another in the coming decades by way of happenstance and through a trickle of works and intermittent correspondence.

Over the next few decades, taking us to the modern era, Moore would be translated by lesser literary figures, although the majority of translations offered subversive commentary on the struggle for Polish independence, all the while providing a shield of protection for the translators to decry their national predicament.

As we have seen, on occasion the sporadic translations of Moore were intended for publication, whereas at other times, they formed a part of the correspondence of the age, which only came to light many decades later when the literary archives and records had been lovingly gathered and compiled. It would be easy to think that the nationalist sentiment of Moore's poetry would have led to it being freely enlisted to the Polish cause through direct cultural transfer. That said, the themes of Moore's poems and airs approximated so closely Polish longings and sufferings that little alteration to the original was ever warranted. Indeed, the very fact that the subject of Moore's poems was so often Erin meant that Polish translators could articulate an insurrectionary outlook while being protected by a poetic translation that sang of a seemingly far-removed experience. And it must also be said that because Moore's *Melodies* struck so many personal chords of loss, grief and the love of place, it is hardly surprising that Polish translators and the readers of Moore could make so many close associations with their own personal trials. It is also undoubtedly the case that the reception of Moore prepared a great deal of the ground for the reception of Irish literature, or more pointedly Irish drama, which began to occupy a prominent place in Poland at the beginning of the twentieth century.

Notes

1 Alina Witkowska and Ryszard Przybylski, *Romantyzm* (Warszawa: Wydawnictwo Naukowe PWN, 1998), 51–52.
2 Czesław Miłosz, *The History of Polish Literature* (Los Angeles: University of California Press, 1983), 197–198.
3 Cited in Edward Balcerzan and Ewa Rajewska (eds), *Pisarze polscy o sztuce przekładu 1440–2005* (Poznań: Wydawnictwo Poznańskie, 2007), 15.
4 'Ja przynajmniej często w tej pracy znajdowałem nowe siły, nowe myśli i lubo nie skończyłem zaczętego tłumaczenia, wielem zawsze z niego korzystał'. Cited in Edward Balcerzan and Ewa Rajewska (eds), *Pisarze polscy o sztuce przekładu 1440–2005,* 18.
5 Ronan Kelly, *The Bard of Erin. The Life of Thomas Moore* (Penguin: Dublin, 2007), 522.
6 Ronan Kelly, *The Bard of Erin,* 522.
7 See Zofia Szmydtowa, *Mickiewicz jako tłumacz z literatur zachodnioeuropejskich* (Warszawa: Państwowy Instytut Wydawniczy, 1955), 44.
8 'Precz, precz od nas smutek wszelki!'
9 See Roman Robert Koropeckyj, *Adam Mickiewicz: The Life of a Romantic* (New York: Cornell University Press, 2008), 93–97.
10 Eoin MacWhite, 'Thomas Moore and Poland', *Proceedings of the Royal Irish Academy,* 3 (1972), 57.
11 Thomas Moore, *The Journal of Thomas Moore: 1836–1842* (ed. Wilfred S. Dowden) (Cranbury: Associated University Presses, 1988), 2001 (e-book).
12 Letter to Romuald Podbereski, as cited in Edward Balcerzan and Ewa Rajewska (eds), *Pisarze polscy o sztuce przekładu 1440–2005,* 13.

13 '... tę dziwną mozaikę; nie wiem skąd ma do niej upodobanie', Paris, 24 January 1832. See Marian Bizan and Paweł Hertz (eds), *Juliusz Słowacki – Liryki* (Warszawa: Państwowy Instytut Wydawniczy, 1959), 229–230.

14 See Ronan Kelly, *The Bard of Erin*, 303.

15 Ronan Kelly, *The Bard of Erin*, 303.

16 'It is a great evil when a single subject of interest takes possession of society; conversation loses all its lightness and variety, and every drawing-room is converted into an arena of political disputation' (Diary entry: 25 June 1820). See Charles Greville, *The Greville Memoirs, A Journal of the Reigns of King George IV and King William IV*, Vol. 1 (London: Longmans, Green, and co., 1874), 31.

17 'Niemcewicz tu w okolicy dawniej już bawi i bardzo go kochają i szanują. Tomasz Moore przybył umyślnie dla poznania go. Człek to maleńki, wiele mówiący i dowcipny, poezye swoje śpiewa przy klawikordzie z wielkim wdziękiem. Swą ojczyznę i jej biedy opiewa z uczuciem, ale widać woli z daleka o nich śpiewać; całkiem tu żyje.' Władysław Zamoyski, *Jenerał Zamoyski*, Vol. III, 1832–1837 (Poznań: Nakładem Biblioteki Kórnickiej, 1914), 49.

18 'Przyjechał na obiad sławny poeta Thomas Moore. Postać prawdziwie maleńka, bo mniejszy od Mira, niepiękny wcale, ale w rysach twarzy i z oczu pryskają iskry dowcipu. – Przy stole wesoły, zabawny, pełen dowcipu i anegdot, które podobno sam improwizuje. Dowiedział się żem przetłumaczył kilka jego melodyi i prosił bym mu dał jednę. Pije portwein wybornie. Po obiedzie śpiewał melodye swoje irlandzkie, pełne smutnej słodyczy. Nuty narodowe mają coś szczególniejszego. [...] Oddałem dziś rano p. Moore tłumaczenie moje jednéj melodyi mojéj, Remember etc. pod każdym wierszem angielskim, kładąc wiersz polski, gdyż tak on życzył, dar ten atoli nie był bez warunku, prosiłem go, by nawzajem napisał co dla biednej mojéj Ojczyzny.' Julian Ursyn Niemcewicz, *Pamiętniki Juliana Ursyna Niemcewicza: dziennik pobytu za granicą od dnia 21 lipca 1831 r. do 20 maja 1841*, Vols. I–II (Poznań: Nakładem Księgarni Jana Konstantego Żupańskiego, 1876), 462–463.

19 Julian Ursyn Niemcewicz, 'Nieznane utwory. Moore's *Melodies* 'Remember Thee', *Pamiętnik Literacki*, 1 (1908), 367–368.

20 The best account of these few days comes from a letter penned by Henrietta Gaisford to her brother, William Talbot, addressed to Laycock Abbey, dated Thursday, 27 September 1831. The letter is to be found in the British Library, London – Fox Talbot Collection, call no. 2425:

> My dear Henry, I hope this letter will have a better fate than that we sent you at Bangor 3 years ago. How came you not to mention Lord Byron's tomb at Newstead – that is what I should have thought the most interesting part. The Galways left us yesterday to go to Melbury – & Harriet & Mr Mundy are just gone to Bowood – They had been here a week, Amandier arrived on Sunday in tolerably good health notwithstanding the cholera – Mr Luttrell came yesterday – Poor old Niemcewicz went away Monday – he said he should never forget the happy days he had passed here. Count Zamoyski is still here, he shewed that Polish fable to Mr Moore, who said he would take the idea & make something of it. Caroline is very well all things considered – Lord V. left her here Sunday & went back to canvass in Cornwall. We had some beautiful tableaux

Saturday last. Lord V. & Gale together constructed a sort of little stage at the end of the South gallery, out of old materials they poked out in the dormitory, & which was a great improvement on the narrow doorway as it admitted of so many more figures. Lord & Lady Lansdowne, Louisa, Mr Rogers & Mr Luttrell came from Bowood to see them & were highly delighted. What are you going to do in Wales? Write me all about it. I think something is going to happen in Europe – the aspect of affairs is warlike – I wish we [text missing] pelt those Russians a little – Addio yr. aff^{te} sister, Horatia.

21 Moore's only mention of social engagement during this period of our narrative is the brief note: 'Slept at Bowood'. See Thomas Moore, *Memoirs, Journal and Correspondence of Thomas Moore* (London: Longman, Green, and Roberts, 1860), 542.

Chapter 1

Compromised Heroes: Irish Drama in the Era of Young Poland
(1900-1918)

Introduction: Art and the Hopes for Polish Nationhood

Coined by critic Artur Górski, in 1898,[1] the term 'Young Poland' came to represent the leading exponents of a generation of writers that emerged at the beginning of the 1890s, who rejected the deterministic values of Positivism, a literary movement that had looked to brush over the disastrous rebellions of the nineteenth century and promote the scientific and social advances made during the partitions of Poland. In doing so, Positivists placed the burden upon the shoulders of the intelligentsia to instruct society in matters of science and modern ideas. Broadly speaking, the generation of Young Poland looked at the world from a more spiritual and metaphysical dimension and embraced the Symbolist ideas of Jean Moréas and the theories of the Belgian poet-playwright, Maurice Maeterlinck, in particular their incorporation of mysticism, mythology and occultism. In fact, during this era, Symbolism was referred to frequently as the 'new art', but it was also understood in tandem with Impressionism,[2] which, together with the 'new art', not only suggested images possessing an esoteric 'other' quality, but also a medium that revealed the psychological state of the artist at the time of writing.[3] In keeping with the times and the situation with regard to the continued partition of Poland, suffering and pessimism were also central motifs – particularly in the 1890s – where death was hailed as a feminine goddess ('death' being feminine 'śmierć') who could liberate people from earthly suffering and raise them up to a Nirvana-like existence.[4] Naturally this quasi-religious outlook did little to move forward the protracted and largely unresolved debate about the thorny issue of art and nationhood in and around the *fin de siècle*. And indeed, the two most high-profile forums who clung to this artistic aloofness, at least in a programmatic sense, were the journals *Życie* [*Life*] of Kraków and *Chimera* of Warsaw.

Życie was founded in 1897 in Kraków by a young journalist called Ludwik Szczepański, and in accordance with its name, it sought to engage in a wide range of issues beyond literature. As a critic, Szczepański rejected utilitarianism and socio-political realism, stating that a national and patriotic literature was a worthy aim, but contended that writers should only look to express themselves, and in a manner that suited their purposes.[5] Steered towards a small elite circle, *Życie* soon met with financial problems and it was taken over by Stanisław Przybyszewski, a prolific literary critic and novelist, who made Herculean attempts to rescue the journal from its financial crisis. Przybyszewski set *Życie* on a different course and proclaimed in his manifesto, 'Confiteor',[6] an era of art for art's sake – separating art from social commitment. In turn, Przybyszewski stated that art remained beyond the parameters of life, and thus, being so inexorably linked with the absolute, it could not be harnessed to serve ideas, which basically meant that the journal would assiduously avoid getting dragged into the nationalist debate and uphold the notion that artists should not get caught up in social causes. However, Przbyszewski's principal achievement during his short tenure as editor of *Życie* was to showcase the art sketches of Stanisław Wyspiański, together with his early dramas, *Warszawianka* [*The Varsovian Anthem*] (1898) and *Klątwa* [*The Curse*] (1899). Although *Życie* had run its course by 1900, the spirit of the journal found its successor in the Warsaw journal, *Chimera*, which was edited and published by Zenon Przesmycki, better known by his pseudonym, 'Miriam'.

From the outset, Przesmycki declared the primacy of art for its own sake,[7] which left him open to accusations by some quarters of having his head in the sand when it came to the nation's continuing bondage. However, highly significant in terms of Polish heritage was Przesmycki's discovery and publication of the works of the late Romantic poet Cyprian Kamil Norwid, who had died in obscurity decades before and whose career had been overshadowed by those of Mickiewicz and Słowacki. Also under Przesmycki's guidance, many Western literary currents were introduced to Poland, with *Chimera* featuring the translation of Western symbolists such as Charles Baudelaire, Paul Verlaine and José-Maria de Hérédia. Also gathered around the journal *Chimera* were many of the most celebrated Polish writers of the age, such as Stefan Żeromski, Wacław Berent, Jan Kasprowicz, Bolesław Leśmian, Władysław St. Reymont, Przybyszewski, and others.

Generally in the Young Poland era reviews of foreign plays did not make mention of the translators, nor indeed did they offer any critical comment on the translations themselves. Having said that, much of Western literature, particularly poems, short stories and prose extracts, were generally translated by Poland's celebrated writers, who left little commentary aside from the work itself. In some respects this is unsurprising, especially given the fact that such translations were often first featured in literary reviews around which closed circles of polyglot writers, critics and literature enthusiasts were gathered. Przesmycki summed up this notion best when he wrote, 'Above all, a perfect thing in a perfect translation is neither what is its own or what is foreign, it is perfect, and that is enough'.[8]

The following chapters will show that the critical reception of Irish plays also drew attention to the Irish aspiration for independence from England and the cultural importance of the Irish Literary Revival at a time when Poland's pantheon of poets and prose writers programmatically avoided incendiary politicking, and who ignored, or were unaware of, what was happening in Ireland. There are always exceptions to every rule, however, and here we may mention the singular efforts of firebrand critic and dramatist Adolf Nowaczyński (1876–1944), who supported the staging of Irish drama in Poland at every turn, and who very much held up the Irish cause as an inspiration for the Polish people, pointing to cultural and technical advancement as being Poland's best means of achieving independence.

At this juncture, it is important to note that the story of Irish drama at the beginning of the twentieth century in Poland is a fairly tangled affair, and this is due to the fact that premieres and other related events were spread over partitioned Poland, and rarely took place concurrently. As a consequence, there will be occasions where our account goes forwards and backwards in order to incorporate as many threads and deviations of the story as possible.

Bunbury Revellers

Leon Winiarski, London correspondent for the socialist gazette *Prawda* [*The Truth*] attended the London premieres of *Lady Windermere's Fan* (1892) and *A Woman of no Importance* (1893), but remained unimpressed by what he had seen. In fact, Winiarski referred to Wilde as a dilettante who had penned plays that only reflected his immorality and cynicism.[9] However, reflecting poorly on the critic himself was his translation of *A Woman of no Importance* as 'A Woman of Little Value / Dubious Reputation' [*Kobieta małej wartości*], although perhaps Winiarski was deliberately emphasizing what he felt to be the 'decadence' of the works, or more pointedly, the 'decadence' of the author. In spite of such strident tones, only a year later, possibly impressed by Wilde's own socialist pamphlets, Winiarski was positively in thrall to the Wildean outlook, stating that the artistic age belonged to the aesthetes, 'who do not want to be taken seriously',[10] and this was more an expression of concern than criticism. Here Winiarski proclaimed Wilde the leading exponent of the movement, whom 'only fools would call a charlatan'.[11] This *volte-face* on the part of the *Prawda* correspondent took on a deeper dimension with the trial and imprisonment of Wilde. In particular, Winiarski took exception to the universal rejection of prisoner-Wilde as an artist, and the critic reserved his ire for the French journal *Revue des Deux Monde*,[12] which had described Wilde's dramatic works as insignificant. He went on to say that it was just as well that Wilde's career had been interrupted, the suggestion being that the public had been spared more of the same. Incensed as he clearly was at this good riddance'ing of the disgraced Irishman, Winiarski could not help agreeing with a widely held view that Wilde had diminished his art by having looked to flourish in the commercial world; something which had both compromised and somehow precipitated his downfall. And here one gets the sense that Winiarski was grabbing at a unique opportunity to firstly stand against what was at the time a fairly universal rejection of Wilde, and secondly, to champion his importance as an artist, going so far as to describe Wilde as the greatest creative talent from amongst the youngest generation of English-language writers.[13] Here, with this article, the era of 'Winiarski on Wilde' ended, but the Irish writer soon found a place in the most prestigious artistic journal of the era.

In 1898, Wilde's essay, *The Critic as Artist* [*Krytyk jako artysta*] (1891), was serialized in *Życie*, translated by an initialled R.W., and uniquely came with an introductory footnote referring to Wilde as a theoretician completely unknown in Poland, who had conceived the notion of a refined art that would exist in an ivory tower, inaccessible to the masses[14] – a view which is certainly at odds with the accessibility of Wilde's work. Notable also was the inclusion of Wilde's poetic vignette, *The Disciple* (1894), the following year.[15] However, this small entry would mark the beginning of a short hiatus when it came to the translation of Wilde in Poland, explainable in some part by the closure of *Życie* in 1900. *Życie's* cessation also meant that there was no literary forum in Poland at the time that felt a need to provide the recently deceased Wilde with a suitable obituary. For example, all that the weekly newspaper *Prawda* announced was that Oscar Wilde, 'the English writer' had died in Paris.[16] Only the newspaper *Kurier Warszawski* [*The Warsaw Courier*] would provide a longer obituary of some eight lines, but managed to mistranslate *The Importance of Being Earnest* (1895) as *Nieszczęście Ernesta* [*The Misfortune of Ernest*], which illustrates the extent to which Oscar Wilde was largely unknown in Poland at the time of his death.[17]

In 1903 the success of the stage adaptation of *Salome* (1894) in Berlin at the Neues Theatre marked a resurgence of interest in Wilde on the Continent, while in Poland the publication of anonymous translations of his children's stories in various newspapers and journals also did much to cement his reputation. But precisely why so many of his stories were translated anonymously remains puzzling, and here we can only hazard a guess that the translators were simply enthusiasts writing on editorial initiatives. At any rate, Wilde's first book publication in Poland, the same *Salome*,[18] did appear with the name of the translator, Władysław Fromowicz, printed on the inside title page. But the translation itself was met with a mixed reception, with the anonymous literary critic for Warsaw's *Tygodnik Ilustrowany* [*The Illustrated Weekly*][19] disapproving of its coarse style and language, whilst praising the literary merits of a competing translation that had been penned by Jadwiga Gąsowska, the ex-wife of the poet and dramatist Jan Kasprowicz.[20]

Salome would have its premiere in Kraków's Teatr Miejski [Municipal Theatre] on 13 May 1905, and it followed a recent performance of Jan Kasprowicz's *Uczta Herodiady* [*Herod's Feast*] (1905), which also represented a luscious treatment of the infamous Biblical episode. In contrast with Wilde's female protagonist, Kasprowicz's heroine wholly dominated the proceedings, so much so that reviewer, Konrad Rakowski, 'remembered only Salome'.[21] Coming to the production of Wilde's play, Rakowski praised its sweeping mosaic and the way in which the tension mounted towards its inevitable dénouement: 'Oscar Wilde's *Salome* is a rare and unique example of a work whose soul, whose expression, the author was able to artificially construct and artificially adorn with the appearance of life and poetry. It is a work of high culture […]'.[22] Inspired greatly by the Neues Theatre's production of *Salome*, and in particular what had been its opulent, palatial stage design, the director, Józef Kotarbiński, seeing an opportunity to really make a mark on the season, spared no expense on the costumes and stage design. But ultimately, it was a standout performance that delivered the desired theatrical triumph. The actress playing Salome, Jadwiga Mrozowska, gave one of the great performances of the era, throwing her all into the part by addressing the character's complexities through subtle movements and gestures. Indeed, judging by the way in which Rakowski wrote of Mrozowska's performance, he could have been waxing lyrical about a master class in method acting. Sadly, however, the play was not performed contemporaneously in Warsaw, as the Russian censors kept the play from being performed in the city for another ten years.

In 1905, the first translation of *The Picture of Dorian Gray* (1891) was rendered by Maria Feldmanowa, the wife of literary critic Wilhelm Feldman, who had blamed the closure of *Życie* on the fact that it had featured a litany of decadent and satanic writers – and in particular the one who had recently got his comeuppance in Britain.[23] Feldmanowa's translation was published by *Przegląd Tygodniowy* [*The Weekly Review*] but was republished a year later by the publishing house of Feliks West. This second edition was a great improvement on the first, with many of the linguistic errors corrected, and it also included the epigrams at the beginning, which had been strangely omitted in the earlier work. This work cleared the waters for many when it came to giving them an understanding of Wilde as both man and artist, as is particularly evident in the reviews of the later stage adaptation of the novel, which premiered in Warsaw on 2 August 1916. Here the critics rounded universally on the adaptation, contending with some justification that if Wilde had wished for the book to be a play, then he would have written it as one, and they recommended that only those who had not read the novel should go and see the play, whereas the rest were advised to spare themselves a distressing experience. But for all the warnings, critic Stanisław Noyszewski maintained that Wilde the novelist was so little known in Poland that the galleries were sure to fill to capacity.[24]

Wilde, in fact, made his Polish theatrical premiere on Friday 22 January 1904 in Kraków's Municipal Theatre with *A Woman of no Importance*. The play was greeted by Rakowski as a shameless melodrama, which did not betray an ounce of artistic effort on the part of the playwright.[25] He and other critics were particularly irritated by Wilde's boasts that the writing of his plays took days, a criticism that bluntly implied that praise must not be given to those who had not earned their theatrical stripes. Perhaps unbeknownst to Rakowski, he was anticipating a debate that would take place some years later in the newly independent Poland, which, following T. S. Eliot's contentions in *Tradition and the Individual Talent* (1919), focused on the artistic division between inspiration, craft and hard work. But certainly in the early part of the twentieth century, Polish critics would not forgive Wilde the absence of what they considered to be the third component. That said, Rakowski greatly admired the silky tones of the salon dialogue, with its flirtations and unspoken *intimité*, although he was disappointed that the cast had pitched its performance echelons below the perceived watermark of aristocratic *habitué*. Making recourse to large swathes of his previous review, Rakowski had the same things to say when it came to the staging of *An Ideal Husband* (1895), a play that premiered in Kraków on 14 December 1907, and one that he himself had translated. In what must be described as an auto-review of sorts, the critic reiterated the importance of capturing the quintessence of the English aristocracy, with their nonchalant air, diction and delivery.[26] But this time around, much to the satisfaction of the critic, the cast had managed to deliver the kind of stellar ensemble performance that had been lacking on their first outing. Although not directly stated, it is evident that Rakowski had made some forceful points to the director and cast during the read through, and that consequently he was pleased when his instructions had been followed. His most fulsome praise was reserved for Stanisława Wysocka, playing the role of *la dame d'intrigue*, who, for Rakowski, had brought more life to the role than Wilde had brought to the entire play, expressing his incredulity once again at the speed with which the play had been written. Years later, as a mature actress and celebrated exponent of theatre in Kiev during World War I, Wysocka would nurture the next generation of Kiev literati and actors, and the plays *Salome* and *A Florentine Tragedy* (1893) would form a fixed part of her theatrical repertoire.[27]

Like Rakowski, Warsaw-based theatre critic, Jan Lorentowicz, was also critical of Wilde and thought that his plays had been the great failings of the writer's oeuvre. In truth, the critic had formed a poor opinion of Wilde because of the debacle that was the Warsaw premiere of *A Woman of no Importance* in the Teatr Rozmaitości [Variety Theatre]. Indeed, Lorentowicz was annoyed with all parties associated with the performance.[28] He was particularly piqued by the publicity posters, which had declared that the play's dialogues had been fashioned for the benefit of the poor. It had been a rather mangled way of stating that the proceeds of the first night were to go to the Association of Good Works, an association that had also been charged with selling cheap tickets to those who would not normally be able to afford such entertainment (presumably some commission arrangement had been put in place). But Lorentowicz's chagrin pertaining to this matter was small-tat when compared to his frustration at having to sit through what was an excruciatingly long performance that saw the final curtain falling well after midnight. To compound his ire, he had hated the play and thought it nothing other than an example of Wilde's expression of contempt for the English theatregoing public, and an unintended exposure of their inability to tell good plays from bad. The cast, who had placed too strong an accent on their delivery of Wilde's aphorisms and paradoxes, had also done much to diminish the evening's performance.

Certainly the Warsaw production of *The Importance of Being Earnest* only contributed to Lorentowicz's incredulity. Although Wilde's most beloved comedy had not been published in book form at this time, the play did have something of a colourful history. It was first translated in 1905 by an unknown translator based in Lwów, who gave it the title of *Birbant*, meaning 'Reveller', which, though intended to onomatopoeically resonate with Bunbury, sounds more Euripidean than Wildean. Also, the fact that Algernon's friend's name was Reveller must have thrown out of kilter the very notion that Algernon was able to excuse his absences to the countryside in order to visit his invalid friend Bunbury. This translation was either co-opted or commissioned by Ludwik Śliwiński, the director of Warsaw's Teatr Nowości [The New Theatre], but he deemed the work to be of such poor quality, so Lorentowicz tells us, that Adolf Nowaczyński was engaged to redraft it.[29] However, it was a task that was beyond even Nowaczyński himself. The cast did not help matters either, disgruntled with the fact that the cash-strapped city theatres failed to pay wages, they peppered the performance with irreverent allusions to postal strikes and the city's financial crisis. Unsurprisingly, critics and audiences were uniformly unimpressed. However, Lorentowicz's tortured memories belie the fact that the play enjoyed contemporaneous success in Kraków and Lwów.

Rakowski admired *The Importance of Being Earnest* greatly when it was staged in Kraków and looked to defend it against accusations of it having been farcical for the sake of farce, maintaining that the play was an 'unpretentious and enjoyable trifle'.[30] We can see from the surviving and maddeningly unsigned manuscript that Lwów had sourced the manuscript directly from Kraków, which means that it was free of Nowaczyński's embellishments. The Lwów premiere took place on Monday 23 October 1905, with a repeat performance on the Wednesday. The review, featured in *Gazeta Lwowska* [*The Lwów Gazette*][31] and penned by Adam Krechowiecki, reveals just how the long shadow of Wilde's fall from grace and early death continued to cast a pall over the way in which his works were perceived. For Krechowiecki, indeed, the play was like laughter through gritted teeth, and whilst acknowledging its farcical characteristics, he was much more struck by the mendaciousness that lay at the heart of the play, uttering simultaneously his disbelief that people could lie with such ease: 'who was leading who?' ['qui trompe-t-on ici?']. The critic also accepted that the converse of this puzzlement – which obtained also for the play – was that lies are taken as truths because it is the most expedient thing to do. In turn, Krechowiecki felt that Wilde's fall made for extra-textual poignancy, and he recalled that as the curtain was falling he had seen in his mind's eye a bloodied Wilde, undone by his own Bunburying, and trusting to the fates that things would come right in the end. Wilde's tragic fate was also a subject for discussion in Lwów that same year with the Polish publication of Wilde's *Intentions* (1891) [*Dialogi o sztuce*], which featured an extensive introduction by Nowaczyński, who rued the fact that Wilde had moved away from his mother's patriotic activities, and maintained that Wilde's pinning of his artistic colours to English culture had precipitated his fall.[32] In a later essay, where he provided an introduction to his selection of Wilde's aphorisms, Nowaczyński attacked the French for having deserted Wilde, and warned Poles that the Irishman's dilettante ways and his lack of application to his art should be seen as a cautionary tale. Here Nowaczyński painted Wilde's downfall in terms of the lyrical-Romantic Celtic imagination being trampled upon by the dullard imperiousness of the English establishment, but he also spoke of a shared love that the Irish and Poles had for French culture at the expense of what English social culture had to offer, hinting in the process at the establishment of some social contacts that had arisen between Polish and Irish writers as a result of their Parisian pilgrimages: 'The Irish as a rule are very similar to us Poles. They travel to Paris like to Mecca once a year in a festive mood so as to reinvigorate human progress.'[33]

Asking Big Questions

Echoing the exasperation of theatre critics such as William Archer, in 1889, London correspondent Edmund Naganowski for the journal *Biblioteka Warszawska* [*The Warsaw Library*] lamented the fact that English theatregoers were irredeemably attached to their melodramas and farcical comedies, which were, he argued, little more than *rifacciamenti* of triumphs from the previous season.[34] For the next fifteen years this would remain a fixed criticism of English theatre from the Polish standpoint,[35] that is to say, until the arrival of Shaw. One of the earliest mentions of Shaw in Poland came in 1898, when Jerzy Płoński commended the Irish writer in *Życie* for having by-passed the mediocrity of London so as to stage his plays in America and the provinces. Later that year Ludwik Szczepański remarked in a review of the Kraków staging of Arthur Pinero's *The Princess and the Butterfly* (1897) that Shaw's reformist plays and criticism had marked the arrival of Ibsenesque drama in England.[36]

Over the next decade many of Shaw's plays were staged in the cities of partitioned Poland, and it could be said that the accessibility of the plays themselves, together with their depiction of the familiar realities of a struggling populace, struck a chord with Polish critics and theatregoers.[37] All of these plays were translated with varying degrees of success on commission for their theatrical staging. The manuscripts that have been preserved are without the insightful and entertaining prefaces that Shaw had provided for his plays, albeit that is not to say that fragments of these prefaces were not sometimes published in the theatre programmes.

Unbeknownst to Shaw, the playwright had his Polish premiere on Friday 27 November 1903 in Lwów with the unauthorized staging of *The Devil's Disciple* (1897), only a couple of months after its continental debut in Vienna's Raimund Theatre, and with a theatre script that, according to Klemens Kołakowski of the *Dziennik Polski* [*The Polish Daily*], had been translated directly from the English by an initialled 'B-é', widely thought to have been Barbara Beaupré.

Shaw's first commercially successful play, *The Devil's Disciple,* is set in the time of the American Revolution, which pitches an uncompromising life-force in the figure of Richard 'Dick' Dudgeon firstly against puritanical religiosity, and secondly against the injustice of the occupying British. It is a play that could have been readily associated with Poland's own national bondage. But whilst *The Devil's Disciple* boasted a happy and romantic ending, the prospects that the same were true for Poland in 1903 were still a long way off.

The production came at a time when the cast was juggling as many as three plays per week, this policy being part of managing director Tadeusz Pawlikowski's plan to flood the city of Lwów with drama.[38] And this ambition entailed quick run-throughs and the shortening of texts in order to facilitate the rapid learning of lines: and indeed the surviving theatre manuscript provides evidence of this. However, often there must have been little time for work on characterization, which must have become glaringly evident whenever a challenging piece came along.[39] As a result, many of the plays were described as 'naturalistic', which was a term chosen to describe instinctive and improvised performances. This approach, as it was all too often pointed out, was not enough to bridge the cultural gap where a foreign piece was concerned, and the shortfall was often exposed. Though Shaw's premiere evening passed off without any glitches, there were no fireworks, and the general sentiment that lingered long after the premiere was that both the play and the playwright had deserved a better first outing.

Reviews followed the next day, with the most informative provided by Kołakowski,[40] who described the cast as having played naturalistically without having understood the delivery of the British military inquisitors and the contexts necessary to hold the play together. That said, contrary to Shaw's contention that Dick's bravery derives from pure selflessness, the critic thought that feelings of ardent love made Dick's actions much more explicable, a conviction asserted by critic Władysław Rabski years later following the play's Warsaw premiere.[41] Kołakowski discerned, however, that this was a new play, the like of which Poland had never seen before.[42] He saw in the play a chaotic coming together of emotions and impressions, which ultimately unveiled the nobility of the soul, the beauty of self-sacrifice and freedom of thought, all of which together signify the aspirations of burgeoning nations. He only greatly regretted that in the actors' hands the play had descended into a farcical free-for-all ending with the regretful conclusion that if Shaw's play cannot be understood, then it should be 'best left alone'.[43] Adam Krechowiecki[44] also pointed to the flawed performance of the cast, but at the same time adjudged that the play should be retained as part of the theatre's repertoire, as the actors needed time to understand their roles better, particularly as each act represented a plethora of dramatic genres. Stanisław Knake-Zawadzki, playing Richard, came in for the harshest criticism, even though at certain times in the play he was deemed to have acted well. In the first act, so Krechowiecki wrote, Knake-Zawadzki had not been demonic enough, whereas in the third act he had come across as far too noble, and lacked the sarcastic wit that the character calls upon in order to parry the military tribunal. Another problem was with Ludwik Solski's interpretation of the parson Anthony Anderson, wherein Solski played the role as an old man whose conspiratorial side was kept completely hidden from view. Here the critic would have preferred to see a warrior priest, perhaps after the fashion of Father Robak in Adam Mickiewicz's *Pan Tadeusz* [*Master Tadeusz*] (1834), which would have better explained how Anderson had managed to end up reappearing at the head of a militia army. That said, the critic felt that the production was deserving of praise, and that it had really only been let down by the fact that some of the supporting actors had forgotten their lines, a glaring flaw in the production not mentioned elsewhere. But instead of excoriating the cast for committing what is a cardinal sin, the critic just mildly recommended that the minor actors needed to do better in future performances. On the very same page in the theatre repertoire column it was announced that the next performance would take place on the following Tuesday, and that the previous night's performance had been generally liked. And so, if the performance was not wildly successful, it was also far from a fiasco, in spite of Warsaw's *Tygodnik Ilustrowany* reporting that it had been an outright failure.[45]

Kraków's Municipal Theatre had its first taste of Shaw with its production of *Arms and the Man* (1894) on 15 October 1904. The translation was made by Konrad Rakowski, in what was hailed as a rendering from the English, although the actual title of the Polish translation, *Bohaterowie* [*Heroes*], hints strongly that the German translation of the play had been the principal source.

Set in the time of the Serbo-Bulgarian war, which ended in 1855, a young Bulgarian girl, Raina, waits for the return of her betrothed, Major Sergius Saranoff, who had just headed a successful cavalry charge. But into her room steals Captain Bluntschli, a Swiss mercenary who is fleeing the Bulgarian forces. She agrees to let him rest awhile and covers for him when a Russian soldier knocks on her bedroom door and asks about a man who had been seen climbing up the water pipe into her balcony. When Raina hands back the gun that the captain had carelessly left on her bed, he bluntly reveals that it is not loaded because he carries chocolates in his ammunition belt. What follows is a playful series of events that contrasts a childish view of war with the deconstruction of conventional heroism.

The play had its first performance on 21 April 1894, in London's Avenue Theatre. It was attended by Shaw himself, along with other great literary luminaries of the era; Wilde, George Moore and W.B Yeats were all in attendance. The latter's own play *The Land of Heart's Desire* (1894) had been the evening's *lever de rideau*. Yeats described the venture as the 'first contest between the old commercial school of theatrical folk and the new artistic school'.[46] The play brought Shaw instant financial rewards with a run of fifty performances, followed by a successful run stateside on Broadway a few months later.

The most unusual aspect of the Kraków production was perhaps the fact that the translator, Rakowski, was also afforded the opportunity to review the play.[47] In his review, featured in *Czas* [*Time*], Rakowski could not hide his frustration that the production had not achieved the standards that he had been hoping for. Again, as in Lwów, according to the critic, the problem lay in the fact that the actors could not get to grips with the delivery necessary to impart the humour and the irony underpinning so much of the dialogue. Rakowski's article, which occupied the bottom third of the first page of the Tuesday afternoon edition,[48] came three days after its Saturday premiere, and the article was both a celebration of the author and the play itself, which for the critic hailed a new form of theatre that brought together both the tragic and comic aspects of life, not to mention all that happens in between. The key challenge for the Polish actors, Rakowski maintained, had been to find the humoresque in the melodramatic. But this they had failed to achieve. Rakowski did not blame the cast outright for the play's failure, but he did maintain that not enough time had been allocated for rehearsals, and as a result the production had only scratched the surface in terms of the play's comic and dramatic potential. Elsewhere, Feliks Koneczny pointed to the same problems, saying that each member of the cast had 'performed like an island', which seems to suggest that none of the actors had had the time to get comfortable with what was an ensemble work.[49] In spite of the fact that it was greeted as a landmark piece, *Arms and the Man* only enjoyed two performances, and it was widely agreed that blame for the failure of the production must be affixed to the host theatre. Kraków's Municipal Theatre certainly made a better job of staging Shaw's comedy *You Never Can Tell* (1897), even though Tadeusz Konczyński, the translator of the play, had, following the German translation, rendered *Der Verlorene Vater* [*The Lost Father*] as *Ojciec marnotrawny* [*The Prodigal Father*], which in terms of the plot of the play, could not have been wider of the mark. This fact was noted by at least one critic.[50] Konczyński is an interesting figure and emblematic of the pool of potential translators whom theatre directors of the day could call upon. Like some of his fellow translators, Konczyński was active on the fringes of the theatrical and literary world, although later his work as both a dramatist and director brought him to greater prominence and ultimately led to his leaving a theatrical legacy of some note.

Shaw wrote this whimsical play as a response to the success of Wilde's *The Importance of Being Earnest*, and as such the play only concerns itself with the immediate world that it presents. The plot is a rather genial comedy of domestic crisis, and pits the mother of grown children, a woman who is of the progressive school, against her ex-husband, who had never seen anything wrong with taking the whip to their children, particularly as the whip had been taken to him as a child. What follows sees the now wealthy father re-entering the lives of his wife and grown children and a concord being established. A penniless dentist, Valentine, also enters what is essentially a family drama. Valentine falls in love with one of the daughters, Gloria, who, in contrast to her mother, lacks worldliness and is conflicted about the rightness or suitability of plunging into a whirlwind romance. The end of the play alludes to the ending of Shakespeare's *A Midsummer Night's Dream*, as the action draws to a close in the middle of a fancy ball, signifying a dissipation of all discord.

The Kraków premiere of the play, which took place on 31 November 1906, and the seven performances that followed, proved to be a critical success, with actors Józef Węgrzyn and Aleksander Zelwerowicz shining in the respective roles of Crampton, the father, and Bohun, the legal counsel. Konrad Rakowski heaped praise also on the actress, Natalia Pomian-Borodzicz, playing Gloria, who, appearing on the Kraków stage for the first time, had managed to combine the pleasantness of her delivery with suitable movements and gestures.[51] Rakowski could find few faults with the production, only saying that the cast should in future be less respectful and lighter in their delivery in order to keep the play on its toes. However, it seems that the director's excisions undermined the production's potential for being a top-rate comedy. As Rakowski argued, Shaw's dialogues were so finely constructed that the excision of even short sentences could throw the plot out of kilter. But the perceived success was unquestionable and Rakowski was sure that more of Shaw's plays would follow. Amazingly, the same play and with the same translation, but with a different cast, failed miserably when it opened in Warsaw almost one year later. It seems that where the actors in Kraków had contributed much to the production, the cast in Warsaw did precisely the opposite. Polish actors had often fallen victim to the mystifications of the Irish playwright, but for Lorentowicz the acting company of Warsaw's Variety Theatre, which produced the play, was always going to fail. Indeed, he went so far as to say that when it comes to their general performances, 'you simply never can tell!'[52] Lorentowicz was so appalled by the production that he went straight to the director, Władysław Jastrzębiec-Zalewski, in order to express his outrage and frustration. But all that Jastrzębiec-Zalewski could find for a riposte was, 'Fine, give me different actors!'[53] This excuse didn't wash with Lorentowicz, who insisted that such a play needed great acting, and therefore the director should have had the good sense not to stage it in the first place. But that is not to say that the critic was gushing about the play's potential. Indeed, Lorentowicz was sure that Shaw had intended for something to happen over the course of the play, but nothing had.[54] For critic Władysław Rabski, the play simply went a long way to confirming why Shaw was an overrated playwright.[55]

As a more accessible form of Ibsenesque drama, Lorentowicz considered *Candida* (1894) as having arrived just in time to save theatrical life in Poland.[56] And more important for the critic was the fact that the audience had also seemed to understand the significance of the play in terms of what had gone before:

> [...] there was a great sense of atmosphere in the theatre, testifying to the fact that not only were the audience members enjoying themselves, but they were also getting a sense

of the basis of the comedy. [...] And because of *Candida* Shaw enjoyed with us a moment of true European popularity.[57]

Shaw's moment of 'true popularity' came in Warsaw, which in many ways would henceforth become the principal home of Shaw in Poland in terms of the number of premieres and theatrical successes that followed. *Candida* had its premiere in Warsaw's Variety Theatre on 13 March 1907, with yet again a translation provided by Rakowski, who, at least this time around, had little cause for complaint. What was for Lorentowicz a sudden flash of recognition on the part of the public was also partly accredited to the efforts of Adolf Nowaczyński, who, prior to the raising of the curtain, had given a lengthy but riveting talk entitled 'O młodej Anglii i Bernardzie Shaw' ['On Young England and Bernard Shaw'], wherein he presented Shaw as having stripped the English of their mystique, and in so doing advancing the Irish cause immeasurably. One way or another, Nowaczyński must have been in his element. But apart from the actual reception of *Candida* at this time, it is also possible to discern amongst critics a growing awareness that Shaw had become, or was in the process of becoming, one of the towering figures of the age. And nowhere is this more perceptible than in an article written by Tadeusz Rittner, which anticipated the premiere of *Candida*. Here also, the critic seemed to get to the nub of the problem as to why Shaw's plays were often misinterpreted in performance.

> With him [Shaw] people are neither bad nor good [...] people in his plays gradually 'find themselves'. Just as in life, and in his plays, we can see how a man can seem totally different from the time of our first meeting, and later, when we have come to know him well. In fact, he is the same person as earlier, but now he is without his toilette, where earlier he was dressed. The audience is then surprised and then accuses the author of being inconsistent ('after all this man was different in the first act'). But the meaning of comedy and life is that a person is always the same and always different (and this is always a surprise for both himself and those close to him).[58]

Candida in Warsaw succeeded in spite of the cast, of which Lorentowicz spoke scathingly, 'artistic concerns would not cost them so much as a night's sleep'.[59] But the general excitement that the play had generated came to the attention of Ludwik Heller in Lwów, who was just embarking on a new tenure as theatre manager. However, Lwów would once again refuse to fall in love with Shaw and the performance proved to be an even more disastrous affair than the ill-fated *The Devil's Disciple*. Alfred Wysocki seemed to think that the problem with the staging of *Candida* lay in the fact that the actors had been unsure about the cultural milieu of the play, and consequently had been unable to interpret their roles; so much so that the cast had ended up playing to the gallery and looking for cheap laughs.[60] But the gallery, as the critic wrote, was not for turning: 'at the beginning they laughed at a few funny and original jokes, but they never took to the whole, and in the end they were visibly bored'.[61] Writing in *Krytyka* [*Critic*], Juliusz Tenner teased out the extent to which the theatre had compromised itself with this production.[62] He also looked to provide the backstory to Heller's recent elevation to theatre manager, and Tenner's criticisms in this respect were very much in keeping with what was described as an orgy of disgruntlement.[63]

Like many of his fellow critics, Tenner felt that Heller's humdrum competence fared badly against the unbridled, if controversial, genius of Tadeusz Pawlikowski, who had excelled in developing an ensemble cast and cultivating audiences without kowtowing to popular tastes. (We shall speak more about Pawlikowski later when discussing his staging of J. M. Synge's *The Well of the Saints*.) As soon as Heller took the reins, a perceived rot had set in. The most troubling issue was a crisis of discipline amongst the actors, which had given rise to a number of bloodcurdling situations onstage, where actors were sniggering at each other's non-scripted jokes. One such episode occurred during the staging of Wyspiański's *The Varsovian Anthem*, where, when the actors present onstage were accepting news from a messenger-soldier that was mortally wounded, they chose to greet him with smiles and giggles. This was described by Tenner as a descent into the kind of anarchy that gathered momentum with each production. The most unforgivable development was Heller's heavy-handedness with manuscripts. With Jan Kasprowicz's *Uczta Herodiady* [*Herod's Feast*], which was poetic verse, the director did away with the poetry and put large fragments to the music of German opera. It was not received well, and by the third performance the play was performing to an empty house. For Tenner, however, Heller's cultural vandalism scaled new heights with the staging of *Candida* when he advertised the production as a comedy, which would explain why so many jokes had been 'mis'-fired in the audience's direction. The sudden and frequent leaps from drama to farce befuddled the actors and either left audiences laughing or thinking, but seemingly not both. However, for all the problems entailed in staging Shaw, he had never been seen as a playwright who courted controversy … but that was all soon to change.

Mrs Warren's Profession (1893) is both drama and crypto-pamphlet, wherein high-pitched disputes morph into hyperbole speech asking about prostitution and its causes: the capitalist foundations upon which prostitution is organized, and the rights of women to earn a liveable wage. The play's eponymous heroine is a Madame of several continental brothels who began at the inauspicious bottom of society's ladder. The self-management of her business affairs, however, is a Victorian success story, built as it was on the virtues of industriousness, astuteness, thrift and the ability to make good connections and surround oneself with the right sort of people. What is more, Mrs Warren has selflessly tended to the upbringing of her only daughter, Vivie, who has grown up to become a brilliant mathematician and who, as the play begins, is contemplating a bright future after having achieved top honours at Cambridge. But if the play commences where mother and daughter have every reason for self-congratulation, their felicity is short-lived. Both are due to spend a pleasant weekend together in their country cottage, but as events transpire the house ends up playing host to a gathering of Mrs Warren's associates and admirers, both past and present, whose loose-tongued ways will reveal to Vivie the truth about her mother's ill-gotten wealth. However, it is not so much Mrs Warren's past, as her refusal to give up her business interests, which will fatally compromise her in the eyes of her daughter.

Shaw wrote this, his self-professed greatest play, in 1893 at the outset of his career as a dramatist. Nevertheless, hardly before the ink had dried on the manuscript, it was refused a licence for performance by the Lord Chancellor. The play mostly remained in the drawer for another decade before it was briefly staged to a mixed reception at the New Lyric Club in London on 5 January 1901. The first night's performance was triumphant, whereas the second and last performance the following afternoon, staged for the benefit of critics and luminaries of the theatrical world, was largely denounced for having attacked the ideals upon which British society was built. *Mrs Warren's Profession* had its first public performance in the United States on 27 October 1905, in the Hyperion Theatre of New Haven, but the production was immediately closed down, having been described as a whole rotten mess of immoral suggestions, and was wished a speedy exit from the boards there and elsewhere.[64] While *Mrs Warren's Profession* was receiving such negative banner headlines stateside, in partitioned Poland the early critical response to the play was entirely positive. And while an errant production almost irreparably distorted this fact, as we shall see presently and later on, the play would continue to hold a fascination for Poland's theatrical world, which attempted to grapple with both the issues that underpinned the play and the motivations of its lead characters.

Pre-empting the play's German premiere by several months, *Mrs Warren's Profession* had its Polish premiere on 2 August 1907 in Warsaw's Teatr Mały [Little Theatre], the city's first private theatre of the new century. Run by Marian Gawalewicz, the theatre itself had no permanent home but took the chamber room of Warsaw's Philharmonic, which could seat four hundred patrons.[65] With the translated manuscript provided by Wiktor Popławski, the play opened to largely favourable reviews. However, Lorentowicz suggested that the play could have been cut down from four to two acts and should have focused entirely on how Vivie absorbs the truth about her origins and upbringing.[66] In turn, Lorentowicz felt that Shaw might have better explored the dogged reasoning behind Mrs Warren's decision to carry on running her business, particularly when she realizes that this decision will definitively end her relationship with her daughter. The critic regarded these preponderances as largely unanswerable and concluded that both mother and daughter were in fact archetypes of intransigence in a melodrama that was simply hard to fathom. In this respect, Lorentowicz thought that the public had been fed laughter and intrigue, when in fact they had been seeking to be better informed by the issues that Shaw had been looking to raise.[67] Yet, for all the expressed doubts as to the perceived inconsistencies of the play, Lorentowicz did contend that its realism would ensure it a long life in Poland, and at least in the immediate term his prediction proved correct. Elsewhere, Jan Kleczyński for *Tygodnik Ilustrowany* hailed the premiere as a de-masking of England's puritanical mores and an exposure of its amoral capitalist practices. Indeed, the critic was not surprised in the slightest that the play had been banned in Shaw's adopted homeland, as few in England, he assumed, would have been prepared to hear that they would move heaven and earth to 'sell to the highest bidder'.[68]

Mrs Warren's Profession was soon taken up by Tadeusz Pawlikowski, who first staged the play in Kraków's Municipal Theatre. Pawlikowski's Kraków production, which premiered on

5 October 1907, boasted a new translation (although the preserved manuscript is unsigned). It was unquestionably the most successful of the three performances of the play in Poland during this era, and the run was extended for a number of performances due to popular demand. Even though in reviewing the play Konrad Rakowski expressed his admiration for both the play and the Kraków production, he was keen to impress upon readers that the play's loose ends should be put down to the fact that it was not a new play, but a precursor to greater works by Shaw.[69] What is more, Rakowski contended that in their condemnation of the play, the English had only exposed their ignorance of continental courtesan drama. Here he gave as an example Victorien Sardou's *Odette* (1881), although one wonders if Rakowski was aware that Shaw had dismissed the French playwright years earlier with the coined term 'Sardoodledom',[70] implying that his plays were empty of ideas.

Two years later, Pawlikowski brought the play to Lwów, where its two performances turned out to be memorable for all the wrong reasons. A late and colourful recounting of the Lwów production can be found in an article that was featured in theatre programs from productions of the play staged in the cities of Wrocław (in 1952) and Elbląg (in 1954). The author of this account was actor and director Wiktor Biegański, who at the time of the Lwów premiere had been an apprentice member of the cast.[71] Interestingly, Biegański thought that the Lwów performance had been the Polish premiere, indicating either the extent to which Gawalewicz's 1907 production had perhaps already become a forgotten event, or simply the degree to which it was unknown to a wider audience at the time.

The premiere of the play took place on 17 February 1909, and it seems that problems began with the cast, who took a very burlesque approach to their characterizations. Ferdynand Feldman, who played Crofts, Mrs Warren's business partner, conceived his character as a coarse, larger-than-life pimp. Indeed, Biegański suggested that such low-life was all too common on the streets of the city at the time, and that some people in the audience assumed that Feldman had been trying to make an unsubtle point. Indeed, everything the play offered grated on the sensibilities of sections of the audience, who were in any case generally disgruntled about what they regarded as Pawlikowski's hitherto decadent French-leaning repertoire.[72] The audience was unsettled by the way that Frank addressed his father, and also by the fact that the play impugned the reputation of a man of the cloth. All in all, Biegański thought that Pawlikowski had failed to come to grips with the play and, by giving his actors free rein, had lost sight of the values or challenging issues that were central to the play.

The tumult that ensued during the second performance two days later stemmed principally from the fact that some sections of the audience had been spoiling for a fight, particularly right-wing sympathizers who had been stirred up by a review of the play in the conservative newspaper *Słowo Polskie* [*The Polish Word*], which had decried the play's immorality.[73] This same group grew noisy and agitated in the third act when Mrs Warren and Crofts pay the pastor a visit to his home, and are then guided towards the church. This trampling over sacred ground proved too much for a schoolteacher, a certain Michalski: sitting in the front row, he stood up and demanded that the curtain be brought down on a play that was an offence to the most basic notions of human decency, so shouting, 'It is a disgrace that such plays are performed on a Polish stage.[74] Others in the rows immediately behind Michalski soon joined him in facing down the stage. But these protesters were not to have it all their way, as students from the university and the polytechnic located in the galleries came to the defence of the play and were joined in their out-shouting of the protesters by a strong Jewish contingent associated with the newspaper *Dziennik Polski* [*The Polish Daily*], and who were members of socialist organizations.[75] The commotion that followed lasted twenty minutes and pitched 'respect for freedom and free thought'[76] against a determination to defend social norms at all costs. By the time the police had arrived, agitators and defenders were squaring up to each other in isolated pockets of the theatre. The police somehow managed to quell the protests and remove Michalski from the premises. As a gesture of solidarity, some of his supporters followed him out of the theatre. However, once order had been restored, the actors carried on in defiance of a request by the police that the performance be terminated.

The cast threw their all into the final act, and Biegański fondly remembered the night as a great piece of theatre in every respect. In spite of a full house, with many more having sought entry, the city authorities demanded that all performances cease. Nobody could have predicted that this mini riot would bring the curtain down on *Mrs Warren's Profession* in Poland for the next thirty years.

Blindness and Upstarts

First staged in 1901, Stanisław Wyspiański's drama *Wesele* [*The Wedding*] depicted the inertia of a nation that had suffered for too long under the yoke of foreign rule. Much in the same way that J. M. Synge's play *The Playboy of the Western World* (1907) was vilified and considered by many at the time of its premiere to have libelled the Irish nation, Wyspiański's characterizations in *The Wedding* also became the subject of a contentious debate, particularly in relation to the absence in the play of a heroic figure around which the Polish nation could draw inspiration. In 1908, one year after Wyspiański's premature death – a demise that also draws a sad biographical parallel with that of Synge – Bolesław Prus chided the recently deceased writer for not having given the Polish dream a leg to stand on, something Prus regarded firstly as a betrayal of the Romantic dream, and secondly as a slander upon the whole nation.[77] Both dramatists, it seems, were destined to be misunderstood and revered by their contemporaries in equal measure.

Wyspiański was born in Kraków in 1869 to an acclaimed sculptor who had his white-vaulted workshop at the foot of Wawel.[78] He studied Fine Arts at the Jagiellonian University where he was greatly influenced by Jan Matejko, the painter of giant historical canvases laden with the finest detail. Scholarships followed, and Wyspiański had an opportunity to study in Germany, Italy and France: principally in Paris at the Académie Colarossi. Fascinated with theatre since childhood, it was here in Paris, inspired by the many plays that his sojourn had afforded him the opportunity of seeing, that he sat down to write his first dramatic piece, the previously mentioned *The Varsovian Anthem*, a play which like others that followed expressed his discontent at Kraków's status as a fiefdom of the Hapsburg Empire. Wyspiański spent a number of years reworking the play, and in 1897, on establishing himself as illustrator for *Życie*, he submitted it to Tadeusz Pawlikowski.

Hailing from a famous aristocratic family of artists, writers and patriots, Pawlikowski understudied in some of the great theatres of Austria and Germany. In the early 1890s he wrote theatre reviews for the Kraków journal, *Nowa Reforma* [*New Reform*], which sought to showcase new trends in art and literature. Like many of his generation, Pawlikowski fell under the spell of Edward Gordon Craig, and he translated for *Nowa Reforma* a number of extracts from Craig's *On the Art of Theatre*, which extolled the communicative function of theatre, 'to spit it out laddie, and fling it at the back of the theatre [...] all stage action, all stage words must first of all be clearly seen; must be clearly heard',[79] a contention that mirrors, as we shall see anon, what Pawlikowski tried to achieve when it came to the adaptation of foreign plays.

Pawlikowski was appointed director of Kraków's Municipal Theatre in 1893 and there followed seven tempestuous years where he was forced to grapple with an interfering city council, which frequently left the theatre short of allocated funds, while his enemies made much of the fact that he was a married man romantically involved with an actress in the company.[80] Very often, Pawlikowski was forced to subsidize the running of the company out of his own pocket, and matters came to a head when the theatre entered into protracted negotiations with a belligerent theatrical agent who held the rights to many contemporary foreign dramas.[81] It was in the context of these rather fraught times that Pawlikowski, whilst accepting *The Varsovian Anthem*, could not provide a concrete date for the premiere and was compelled to string Wyspiański along with pep talks and recommendations for further rewrites.[82] In the autumn of 1898, an understandably impatient and frustrated Wyspiański sent to Pawlikowski an envoy in the figure of Alfred Wysocki (also previously mentioned in this narrative), an expert in Scandinavian culture, who was cutting his journalistic teeth as a staff writer for *Życie*. Wysocki also failed to make any headway, and so adopted a different strategy by looking to convince actress Wanda Siemaszkowa that one of the play's leading roles had been written with her in mind. Wysocki accompanied Wyspiański to the actress's apartment where the playwright in a trembling voice read through the part. Recognizing that this was more than just an exercise in flattery, she undertook to take the dramatist's part and petitioned Pawlikowski directly. Wysocki's intrigues reaped dividends when Pawlikowski committed to a date for the premiere and assigned directorial duties to Ludwik Solski. However, preparations on the play were soured somewhat by Siemaszkowa's gossipy assertions that Wyspiański had had the gumption to demand artistic control over both the manuscript and rehearsals. Whatever the truth about this matter, Pawlikowski certainly did Wyspiański a great disservice when he inappropriately staged the play together with two rather ephemeral and unimportant one-act works, particularly when he had originally planned to stage *The Varsovian Anthem* in a more suitable pairing with Maeterlinck's *Intérieur*. But Solski oversaw what was hailed as a flawless production, having also commissioned Wyspiański to provide the stage design. In spite of the play's arduous road, *The Varsovian Anthem* had its premiere on 26 November 1898. It would mark the beginning of a new era in Polish drama.

A number of months earlier, in June 1898, the Kraków Municipal Theatre company had visited Lwów for a month, and its performances were met with great acclaim and enthusiasm.[83] There can be little doubt that this visit laid the groundwork for Pawlikowski's later move to Lwów. Despite running Kraków's Municipal Theatre for one more successful season, he considered his chances of re-election as slim, and so entered into the open competition for the manager of the fledgling Lwów Municipal Theatre, which meant running against the acting manager, Ludwik Heller. Following a highly successful public relations campaign, which garnered support from theatrical critics throughout partitioned Poland, Pawlikowski was elected to the position. The unseated Heller was much chagrined, perhaps rightly feeling that the Pawlikowski name had unduly swayed the decision of those who had cast their votes.[84]

From the outset, Pawlikowski looked to establish a European repertoire that would be performed alongside Polish drama. With this aim in mind, whenever a new play made an impact, Pawlikowski sent a scout at his own expense to assess its merits. He would then oversee all the steps involved in bringing the play before the theatregoers of Lwów, which included his close involvement in the translation of the manuscript. One translator whom he came to work closely with was Alfred Wysocki, who had left Kraków following the closure of the previously mentioned journal *Życie* in order to take up a journalistic career as theatrical reviewer for *Gazeta Lwowska* [*Lwów Gazette*]. Intrigued by the fact that Wysocki knew Ibsen personally, Pawlikowski wined and dined with the journalist one evening in a top restaurant, which ended in the early hours of the morning.[85] Relations quickly progressed from a social to a professional basis, and Wysocki went on to translate for the Lwów Municipal Theatre: Ibsen, Bjørnson, and most notably for our story, Synge's *The Well of the Saints* (1905), which had had its Abbey premiere just three years earlier, in 1905. Wysocki would translate the title *The Well of the Saints* as *Cudowne źródło* [*The Miraculous Spring*].

Synge's play presents the story of a married couple who are blind beggars living on the roadside. Martin and Mary Doul are chthonic figures at a oneness with the landscape. They are content to believe, contrary to the truth, that they are both fine-looking individuals. When a saint carrying a flask of miraculous holy water restores their eyesight, they are left in despair at the sight of each other and prove incapable of adjusting from a life of the mind to the ugliness of reality.

Wysocki only briefly mentioned his translation of Synge in his memoir *Sprzed pół wieku* [*Looking back on Half a Century*], but in doing so, he recalled how his translations in general were carefully read over by Pawlikowski, who, following Craig, wanted for a text to facilitate a strong emotional and right-sounding delivery:

> When writing, I repeated aloud every sentence. In spite of this, when I read out my translation to Pawlikowski, he would often interrupt me and in a quiet voice say, 'Perhaps that word should be changed, or moved, or removed altogether.' And he was always right.[86]

In Wysocki's translation, Synge's reality can be beheld in all its beauty and bitterness. What is more, Wysocki rendered a rustic world in thrall to saints and superstitions that is recognizably Irish in origin. But equally, the translator found a Polish speech filled with its own strong rural and religious traditions. In Wysocki's manuscript the exchanges between blind Martin and Mary Doul are suitably affectionate and filled with pathos when they are ignorant of each other's unsightliness, whereas the bitter exchanges that take place once their sight is restored retain plenty of the sharpness and barbed wit of the original. It would be easy to suspect that much of Synge's theatrical West-of-Ireland dialect could have led the translator astray, but that was not the case. However, a lot of the sentences were trimmed, and as can be seen from the surviving manuscript, Pawlikowski also made cuts in favour of both moving the action along, shortening the play from three acts to two, and achieving a directness of speech.

The Well of the Saints was staged on Friday 11 November 1908 as the second play in a double bill with Wyspiański's *Sędziowie* [*The Judges*] (1907), which was a vengeful tale of ethnic conflict between a Jewish and Hutsul family that had actually taken place near Lwów in the early nineteenth century. It was an episode involving murder, infanticide and other unspeakable crimes. Whatever the remoteness of the plays to one another, the staging of the two playwrights together was clearly a signalling of their comparable stature in their respective national theatres. The plays were performed on the Wednesday and Friday, alternating with *Madame Butterfly*, which was performed on the Thursday and Saturday.

The theatre review column of the Lwów newspaper *Gazeta Narodowa* [*The National Gazette*][87] spoke highly of Synge's play as compared to what had been perceived as the strangeness of Wyspiański's drama. Although the unsigned review provided little more than a summary of the play, it did show a clear understanding of the poetic theme at the heart of the play, wherein 'sometimes blindness is best'.[88] Wysocki also wrote a review of the evening's theatrical fare, although he made no mention of his own particular involvement.[89] His review, in fact, devoted more space to Wyspiański's play, although Wysocki did emphasize that both plays depicted reality as a point of departure from the unpleasantness of life so as to take flight into the world of the imagination. However, the reviewer did have his doubts about Synge's loose treatment of religious beliefs, and was particularly troubled by the idea that Martin Doul could be so removed from a state of blessedness and yet be deemed worthy of having God's grace bestowed upon him a second time.

On reassuming his post in 1913 as head of the Kraków Municipal Theatre, which had recently been renamed as the Teatr im. Juliusza Słowackiego [Juliusz Słowacki Theatre], Pawlikowski actively sought to stage dramas that were making an impact on the world stage, and he tried to balance high-end drama with more popular offerings suited to the tastes of Kraków's notoriously difficult-to-please audiences. He showed his faith in *The Well of the Saints* by staging it again, handing the directorial reins over to Andrzej Mielewski. The play's Kraków premiere took place on Saturday 31 January 1914, with two more performances the following week. Once again, the play served as a second helping, but this time it strangely followed an adapted Latin work by the late Polish Renaissance dramatist Szymon Szymonowic, entitled *Castus Joseph* (1578). Pawlikowski either must have felt that

Synge's play would not enjoy success in its own right, or he was simply wedded to the idea of presenting the play as part of a double bill.

Zygmunt Rosner, writing for *Gazeta Poniedziałkowa* [*The Monday Gazette*], provided a brief summary of the play and was complimentary about the production.[90] In turn, Władysław Prokesch reviewing the play for *Czas*[91] lamented the fact that Synge's play had not been given an evening all to itself, and particularly because the evening had been brimming with quality and burdened by quantity. In relation to the play itself, the reviewer thought that Synge's work was highly evocative of Maeterlinck's play, *The Miracle of Saint Anthony* (1904), recently blacklisted by the Vatican. The reviewer also showed a great understanding of its underlying themes: 'having gone through the hell of life, and blind once again, they reunite in their shared pain, a blindness which hides their ugliness from one another. Not for the entire world do they wish for another miracle....'[92] Indeed, for the reviewer, Synge's play was filled with intelligent ironies, which, in turn, had many delicate things to say about the human condition. Great praise was bestowed upon the actors Antoni Siemaszko and Zofia Czaplińska, who had played the Douls and who had been fully committed to portraying the delirious delight of expectation only to be matched by the anguish of the blind couple's thwarted dreams. Warm words were reserved in turn for the way in which the actors had portrayed the abject fear that the Douls had at the prospect of their sight being restored a second time. The reviewer ended by complimenting both the stage design and the choreography of the collective scenes, whilst also applauding Pawlikowski for having brought to the public's attention the 'talent of a [highly] original poet'.[93] But once again, as something of a parting rebuke, it was reiterated that both plays should have been staged in their own right.[94]

A Playboy's Carpathian Shades

In 1936 in an article for the journal *Teatr* [*Theatre*], which had put together an issue dedicated to Shaw, Florian Sobieniowski recalled his trip to London in 1912 in order to meet the great dramatist. Sobieniowski had hoped to win from Shaw the rights to translate his plays into Polish and what followed was an awkward meeting that lasted three hours, whereby Shaw pressed Sobieniowski on his literary qualifications and suitability for the task of translating his plays.[95] Shaw should have been impressed with Sobieniowski's educational path, having earned a degree in Fine Arts from Kraków's Jagiellonian University and having completed postgraduate stints in both Vienna and Paris. Whether or not Shaw thought he was taking a gamble on a translator with no significant successes to his name, at the end of the interview he presented Sobieniowski with wrapped proofs of the as-yet unpublished plays of *Pygmalion* (1913) and *Androcles and the Lion* (1912). But although Shaw was handing the keys to Sobieniowski's future, he would never warm to his Polish translator. Indeed, if we are to wholly believe Shaw, Sobieniowski was a thoroughly unpleasant sort: 'the most incapable, incorrigible, impecunious, always-borrowing, never-paying victim of a craze for literature at present alive in London'.[96] That said, their collaborative relationship would continue smoothly for the next thirty-five years or so, and Shaw clearly thought highly of Sobieniowski's abilities: 'a man of genuine literary vocation and talent'.[97] Sobieniowski, in turn, would give Shaw some of his most spectacular theatrical successes in Europe.

It is not certain whether Shaw had seen a penny from the early Polish enactments of his work, but by the time of his first meeting with Sobieniowski, Shaw was comfortably settled in a profitable collaborative arrangement with his German translator, Siegfried Trebitsch, even though some Austrian and German critics were up in arms about the quality of the translator's work. Indeed, one critic had been so outraged that he turned up at Shaw's home in London and presented him with a list of errata. There would be little fear of such disconcerting feedback when it came to his newly found Polish translator. But interestingly, from Sobieniowski's same account, we learn that he did not start straight away on Shaw's plays. Weighing up commercial possibilities, he was swayed by his circle of Irish and English literary friends centred around the Oxford literary review, *Rhythm*, to take on what he described as the untranslatable play of Synge's *The Playboy of the Western World*. Immediately discerning a kindred link with Wyspiański's *The Wedding*, he wrote six drafts, and sent his final effort to Arnold Szyfman at the Teatr Polski [Polish Theatre] of Warsaw, who on reading the manuscript promptly decided to stage the play at the earliest possible opportunity.[98]

Certainly in terms of what both plays came to represent, *The Playboy* and *The Wedding* have much in common. They depict generally implausible situations wherein falseness and fantasy reflect on harder realities, and where national identity is intertwined with the world of the peasantry, whether evoked as an Arcadian perception of reality, or simply as a social cradle of language and memory – or indeed, half-eluded to on at least one occasion in both plays as pike-wielding, front-line cannon fodder in countless failed insurrections.

The setting of the three-act play is the coast of County Mayo in the public house of Michael James Flaherty, and the action takes place at the turn of the twentieth century. It tells the story of young Christy Mahon who has run away from his farm, greatly convinced that he has struck his father, Old Mahon, and killed him. The locals have great sport listening to the minutiae of the deed, which Christy relates after the fashion of a heroic tale and with great bardic power. None of the villagers are at all disturbed by the fact that the deed he boasts of was an act of cold-blooded murder. Christy achieves even greater status amongst the people of the village due to the poetic beauty of his speech and his physical prowess, triumphing as he does in the sporting games held on the strand. Completing his elevation, Christy captures the romantic attention of barmaid Pegeen Mike, who accepts his proposal of marriage. These are merry and felicitous times, it seems, and there is an inebriation of joy and expectation of prosperous days to come. However, Christy's father, severely wounded but not dead, arrives in the village and asks for his son. When the villagers see that Christy has in fact failed in his heroic deed, they turn against him. In order to salvage his reputation, he strikes his father once again, and it looks as if this time he has succeeded in killing him.

The villagers, on seeing the viciousness of the act with their own eyes, harangue Christy, bind him with rope and subject him to torture. He is in danger of being hanged from the nearest tree when Old Mahon revives in time to intervene and save his son. They leave the village in haste, buoyed by the renewal of their old relationship, vowing to never return, and from this day forth, to tell 'stories of the villainy of Mayo, and the fools is here'. Even though she had egged on the haranguing and even burnt Christy's flesh with a cinder, Pegeen is left desolate at the departure of her playboy, 'Oh, my grief. I've lost him surely'.

In order to re-create the style of Synge's work, Sobieniowski looked to subtly acculturate his piece in the world of the Tatra peasantry. Aside from adopting the Carpathian dialect featured in *The Wedding*, which clashed in the play with the literary Polish as spoken by poets and noblemen, for the purposes of research, Sobieniowski would most certainly have found inspiration in the mountain folktales of Kazimierz Przerwa-Tetmajer, *Na Skalnym Podhalu* [*On the Rocky Peak of Podhale*], published as a series of five volumes between the years 1903 and 1910. These tales were written in the Podhale dialect of the Tatra Mountains and were accompanied by a comprehensive glossary of words and phrases. But equally so, Sobieniowski may have looked at the Polish legends and folkloric tales to be found in Jan Kasprowicz's *Bajki, klechdy i baśnie* [*Fairytales, Tales of the Peasantry, and Folktales*] (1902). What is more, Sobieniowski chose to excise all direct mentions of Munster in favour of allusions to 'wide open spaces, mountains and valleys' ['obszary, góry, doliny'].

When Szyfman received Sobieniowski's manuscript of *The Playboy of the Western World*, he was several months into his tenure as director of the Polish Theatre, which aimed to usher in a new era for the staging of drama in Poland. Having secured investment from businessmen, philanthropists and small shareholders, Szyfman hoped that the theatre would be able to function free of municipal subventions and operate in a similar manner to that of Berlin's Deutsches Theatre, which was managed at the time by Max Reinhardt.[99] The building of the new theatre had got underway in 1912, and both construction and rehearsals had proceeded simultaneously. As the roof was being both metaphorically and actually placed on the new building, Szyfman was joined by top actors, stage designers and directors from Kraków and Łódź, all of whom were anxious to take advantage of the artistic and career opportunities that the new project afforded. According to theatre director and theoretician Leon Schiller, the Polish Theatre had two principal aims in its opening season: to stage productions in keeping with the most modern postulates pertaining to acting, stage design and direction, and to lay foundations for the development of a new style of national theatre that aspired to bring about a resurgence in the classical repertoire.[100] Szyfman laid great emphasis on the uniqueness of each production, which should stem from the director's reading of the play, interpretation of the roles, and following from this, consultation with the set designers on the stage settings.[101] The stage settings and costume details of the new theatre were widely hailed as wonders of their time.

Translated as *Kresowy Rycerz-Wesołek*, *The Playboy of the Western World* had its Polish premiere on 12 November 1913. Before the curtain was raised for the commencement of the first act, the audience may have suspected that it would be an evening of tragedy and not comedy – and certainly not anything in between – particularly in the light of the introductory speech given by Adolf Nowaczyński, who declared that Ireland's cultural revival represented the best possible model for the refashioning of a unified Polish identity. However, where Ireland was concerned, Nowaczyński tended to indulge in hyperbole and stereotype. Indeed, only a couple of years previously, Nowaczyński had greatly under-represented his own country's calamitous misfortunes in respect of Ireland's, so writing:

> Let us picture a nation, numerically three times smaller than our own, and with three times fewer people – the ridiculousness, sins and eyesores; let us remember that for seven centuries the Irish have suffered the kind of persecution and torture that make our own nineteenth century seem like a wisp of cloud that will quickly cross the horizon and disappear.[102]

And that evening, as Nowaczyński stood on the stage prior to the raising of the curtain, he looked to make the same alternate comparisons, all the while emphasizing that Synge's Irish peasant was emblematic of the quasi-Romantic paralysis that Wyspiański had also discerned and chosen to dramatize: 'his [Synge's] peasant cannot handle a fishing net, a compass, or a mechanical sower'.[103]

The most heated critical response to the play came from Stanisław Pieńkowski, a self-declared detractor of both Shaw and experimental literature, who wrote two extensive reviews of the play.[104] The first was an enthusiastic summary of the plot but what followed after that was an unbridled rant against Józef Węgrzyn, the actor who had played Christy Mahon. Pieńkowski felt that Christy's tragedy, and indeed the tragedy that lay at the heart of the play, had been to try and to fail. Reading *The Playboy* from the bardic perspective of *The Wedding*, wherein the Romanticism of mighty talk and deeds was trampled on by the glib reality of continued national bondage, the critic had no truck with any notion of the play being interpreted as a comedy. Pieńkowski took Węgrzyn to task for having played Christy as 'a fool and a degenerate'[105] who was not in the least bit conflicted about the crime that he had perpetrated. What should have been foregrounded, so maintained the critic, was that the son had performed an extraordinary, and not ordinary, feat of patricide, and that the horror of this same fact should have tormented him like the furies had Orestes. Pieńkowski was so exercised on this point that he called for the Polish Theatre to host a public debate on the interpretation of Christy Mahon. It was a summons that fell upon deaf ears.

Where Pieńkowski saw tragedy, and the potential for heaps more, Lorentowicz thought that the play had been far too bleak and unforgiving.[106] For this he principally laid the blame at the feet of Sobieniowski for having made too many phraseological borrowings from Wyspiański, which meant that the actors had performed after the fashion of Wyspiański – understandable, given that much of the cast had either cut their teeth, or in some instances made their acting reputations on the back of having performed in Wyspiański's plays. Many other critics felt that Sobieniowski had gone too far in respect of his having 'Wyspiańskized' the play, and indeed this neologism occurs so often amongst the post-premiere press reviews that there must have been a general discussion on the point immediately following the performance. Kazimierz Wroczyński for *Tydzień Teatralny* [*Theatre Weekly*], for example, thought that representative allusions to Polish speech and reality should have sufficed: 'Synge's work has so many elements that are not alien to us, it would have been enough to simply Polonize it. Whereas the translator's zealous excess succeeded in "Wyspiańskizing" the play.'[107]

Not all critics registered a close national affinity with the play, with Wiktor Popławski suggesting that *The Playboy* was so far removed from Polish aesthetics and values that it was impossible to pass judgement on it. The play did solidify, however, a number of prejudicial views that he had held of Ireland: 'I know from Synge that the Irish Nation is not a fallen one. It is only rotten and disgraced.' And here the critic added, 'One can feel sorry for Synge but we cannot understand him.'[108]

If Warsaw theatregoers emerged from the Polish Theatre following the premiere feeling as Lorentowicz stated 'highly disturbed',[109] it is likely that attitudes remained divided over the course of the play's following eight performances. Indeed, even though it was later praised in the newspaper *Nowa Gazeta* [*New Gazette*] by one of the central figures of the next generation of Polish poets, Jan Lechoń, he referred to Synge's play as Ireland's national tragedy, which is a comment that perhaps supports Lorentowicz's contention that the play had been variously interpreted. And indeed, when we take the reviews as a whole, it seems that the play as it was performed not only reinforced cultural stereotypes pertaining to the excessive stylization of folk culture, but that the acculturated translation of Sobieniowski had inspired debate that took the legacy of Wyspiański beyond the parochial and beyond the aspirant Polish cause. Whilst critics often felt that Sobieniowski had been too willing to over-egg the parallels, their entire appreciation of the play had been ironically based on analogous dichotomizing with a Polish playwright whom they had been more familiar with.

In spite of his detractors and the general hue and cry surrounding his translation of Synge's *The Playboy of the Western World*, Florian Sobieniowski had launched his career in a way that drew a great deal of attention to himself as the translator of a dramatic work. It was an unprecedented feat. But more importantly, he had proven himself with Arnold Szyfman, who must have been happy with the respectable run and strong critical reception of the play. Even more felicitously, their first collaboration would soon be followed by a more profitable venture, that of Shaw's *Pygmalion*.

A Flower Girl Tries Her Hand at the Vistulan Dialect

When Shaw handed Sobieniowski the unpublished manuscript of *Pygmalion*, he was surely hoping to offset, if not put an end to, the practice of Polish theatres staging his plays based on the retranslations of Trebitsch's German versions. Shaw bemoaned the practice to Trebitsch in a letter from November 1913: 'I am told the Polish and Russian theatres procure, through agents, copies of German translations from the Viennese & Berlin theatres, which greatly complicates matters of rights and royalties' and in artistic terms, 'will not only extend the alteration but may pick up the blunders of the earlier translator'.[110] Shaw may have been even more chagrined to know that his efforts to prevent this happening to his new play were still being rudely flaunted in Poland, almost concomitantly with his penning of this letter – something we will come to presently.

The play *Pygmalion* was first published in book form by Trebitsch in German, and then the translator looked to ensure that the play would have its premiere in his home city of Vienna, where it was staged in the Imperial Hofburg Theatre on 16 October 1913. However, where Shaw had wanted to use the play as a means of goading the English into respecting their language and, what is more, into teaching their children to speak properly, Trebitsch sought to please the theatregoers of Vienna and Berlin with a winning romance. To this end, he cleansed the text of racier phrases and avoided dialect altogether, which meant that Eliza's cockney was impeccable German, which of course undermined 'a sizable' – Shaw may have said 'the entire' – premise of the play by having placed a greater emphasis on the romantic plot.[111] Unsurprisingly, the absence of the play's reforming agenda did not unduly upset German critics and audiences, who saw much to take delight in.

Shaw based his premise of the play on the belief that the acquisition of correct pronunciation on the part of everyone would lead to a much more egalitarian society, where advancement could not be hindered by any perceived stigma of class. To this end, the play's hero, celebrated phonetician, Professor Higgins of Wimpole Street, following a chance meeting in the flower market of Covent Garden, agrees to bring a cockney-speaking wretch of a flower girl, Eliza Doolittle, into his house so as to teach her to speak properly. He makes a bet in the process with his fellow bachelor companion, Colonel Pickering, that he will eventually be able to pass her off as someone of high birth at the Embassy Ball that is to take place six months hence. This is an experiment that will be conducted onstage, but there is little of the egalitarian spirit in evidence as Higgins treats Eliza like a lackey, and has her fetching his slippers and the like. His engagement with Eliza never goes beyond the science. And for this reason, the fundamental question, or rather concern, about 'what will become of Eliza?' is one of the play's most compelling sub-themes. With relentless tutelage, and with many comic moments along the way, Eliza becomes a pedantic but perfectly correct speaker of received English. Given her mistreatment at his hands, some may describe Eliza's deepening feelings for Higgins as an example of Stockholm syndrome, but in a definitive divergence of the Pygmalion myth, where a yearning to marry lies at its heart, Higgins is seemingly unmoved by such sentiment. However, in the fifth and final act, Eliza demands to know where she stands, whereas Higgins, although wanting things to remain the same between them, is incredulous at the prospect of her leaving him to either marry Freddy, the unsuitable suitor, or, as she threatens, to strike out on her own and set herself up as a teacher of phonetics, applying to her new profession all the knowledge that she has learnt from her erstwhile tutor. Tempers fray towards the end. There is much screaming, scratching and man-handling, indicative of the passion that is bubbling beneath the surface. When Eliza storms out, it is unclear whether romance will blossom, or not. Shaw was happy to have it said in a later version that Eliza would marry Freddy, but at some stage early on in the play's life, popular opinion had ceased to heed Shaw's opinion on the matter. And as it happens, the first production of *Pygmalion* in Poland was also determined to deliver a happy ending.

Whilst Sobieniowski was working on his translation of the play in the winter of 1913–1914, the march was rudely stolen on him by Ryszard Ordyński, a highly acclaimed Polish theatrical director working at the time in Berlin's Deutsches Theatre. Despite his being an acquaintance of Shaw, the evidence suggests that Ordyński undertook the translation without the playwright's knowledge.[112]

Ordyński had studied librarianship in London in 1908, and, as part of the wider student program, he had also undertaken volunteer work in poorer areas such as Whitechapel, an activity that would by and large involve participating in public library gatherings where over tea and biscuits people enthusiastically asked the foreign students about social, political and cultural issues in their home countries.[113]

During this period, Ordyński often marvelled at the Salvation Army standing and singing on street corners, and it was perhaps a case of serendipity when in 1910, Ludwik Solski of Kraków's Municipal Theatre sent him a manuscript of Shaw's *Major Barbara* (1907), with a request to provide a translation for performance. It is not clear whether Ordyński worked from the English original or not – although it rather seems that he did – but his most difficult challenge was the characterization of arch-capitalist Undershaft, as neither Ordyński, nor, as he assumed, the cast, had ever met his like before. Realizing that many issues needed to be teased out, Solski invited Ordyński to provide assistance with rehearsals in the run-up to its premiere, which took place on 19 February 1910.

When in 1911 Ordyński took Max Reinhardt's pantomime play *Sumurun* (1910) to London's Coliseum Theatre, he had the opportunity to meet and talk with Shaw in person at an informal gathering of writers and cast, which had been organized by Granville Barker. Initially, Ordyński served as an interpreter between Reinhardt and Shaw, with the Irish playwright jesting that Reinhardt could quite conceivably knock him off his perch in terms of potential box-office receipts. Having paid the compliment, however, Shaw proceeded to talk of the need for a dramatic work to be more than a crowd-pleaser, and for it to tackle social issues and reverberate beyond the immediacy of the performance and the theatre itself. Ordyński remained in London for several weeks as a guest of Barker's, and found himself being invited to Shaw's house, where Mrs Shaw served non-vegetarian meals for this meat-eating Polish guest. Back in Germany, Reinhardt handed Ordyński the directorial reins for Shaw's *Misalliance* (1909/1910), and Ordyński took this opportunity to travel back to London to discuss with Shaw some of the work's many difficult aspects, and hoping at the same time to secure permission from him to make cuts that would aid clarification. Shaw politely listened to Ordyński argue passionately that non-English productions of the play needed interpretative room. However, when Ordyński actually took his pencil out and showed where he wanted to make the cuts, Shaw, always smiling, responded by pointing out the problems that would arise from such excisions. Once Shaw had given his opinion on the matter, he told Ordyński that he was free to do what he liked with the play, remarking that he had long made peace with the fact that foreign productions were always going to take liberties. But Ordyński realized that he had asked Shaw and been rebuffed. It is for this reason, I believe, that he did not mention *Pygmalion* to Shaw when he travelled to meet the Irish author in London, in October 1913, in order to seek his advice for the Deutsches Theatre's upcoming production of *Androcles and the Lion* with respect to the costumes and stage design.[114]

Basing his work on Trebitsch's German translation, Ordyński produced a shortened version of *Pygmalion* and then sought to have it staged in Kraków's Juliusz Słowacki Theatre, which, as we have mentioned already, was once again under the directorship of Tadeusz Pawlikowski. Ordyński's unpublished manuscript has been preserved in the archive of the theatre and a very interesting instruction from the translator is provided on the page with the list of characters: 'Eliza in the first and second act speaks the dialect of a street merchant. The actress playing this role must be consistent with this dialect, especially in tone and the exaggerated extension and shortening of vowels.'[115] On reading the manuscript, one immediately notices that Eliza's Polish accent and annunciations before the transformation are not incorrect or wayward in any way, and as such her accent and speech do not signify an impoverished background. In fact, her disadvantaged state is only made more discernible by Higgins' allusions to the unpleasant high-pitched sounds that she is making: 'Don't be screeching in our ears.'[116] Throughout the Polish adaptation, the emphasis was less on phonetics and more on the tempestuous relationship between Higgins and Eliza. Indeed, a crucial interpolation is to be found at the very end of the Polish manuscript, where it is made clear that Eliza will remain with Higgins, and that her decision to stay is very much his triumph.

The play had its premiere on 24 January 1914 in the middle of a tough winter for Pawlikowski, who was fast losing patrons to the cinemas that had recently opened in the city, and also due to the fact that this was a transformative period during which tastes were changing.[117] But *Pygmalion* proved to be the hit of the season, with critics applauding both the production and the play itself.[118] It is clear, though, that the acquisition of correct speech and accent was less foregrounded than the notion that kindness and good breeding can work their magic on any disadvantaged person. Mirroring the perspicacity of an alert German reviewer, who had pointed out the similarity of the play to the episode with a sixteen-year-old beggar girl in chapter 87 of Tobias Smollett's novel *The Adventures of Peregrine Pickle* (1751), one Polish reviewer thought that the play must have been inspired in part by Sardou's *Madames Sans-Gêne* (1893), which told the story of a laundress that marries a soldier, who is himself subsequently elevated by Napoleon to the rank of Duke of Danzig.[119] However, the heroine's newly found fortune and position does not smooth out her rough edges, and she continues to behave in a raucous manner at court, thus earning for herself the name of Madame Sans-Gêne, meaning Mrs No-Embarrassment. It is an important observation, particularly given the fact that English critics would gleefully speculate that Shaw had agreed to have the play staged in Germany, as a pall of plagiarism hung over the play with respect to Smollett. Of course, Shaw provided himself with an inimitable defence: 'Do not scorn to be derivative.'[120] The performances of Leonard Bończa-Stępiński playing Higgins and Irena Solska playing Eliza were hailed as career-topping turns, with the same reviewer stating 'I couldn't imagine better performers of these two roles.'[121] It seems that Bończa-Stępiński had brought great charm and authenticity to Higgins' quirky and gesticulating character, whereas Solska was praised for having understood the psychology that underpinned Eliza's transformation.[122] Perhaps the only criticism that was made of the production was the sound of the rain in the first act that drowned out the exchanges and made the entire scene inaudible, a problem that recurred when the play with Ordyński's translation was performed on 13 February 1914, in Lwów's Municipal Theatre. The review in *Gazeta Lwowska*[123] presents some intriguing possibilities in terms of how the plot had been reworked, the crux of the divergence being that Freddy was excised from the plot and that Eliza had the prospect of marrying Pickering. When Higgins learns of the depths of her feelings in the showdown, which takes place at the end of the play, he takes her as his wife. The reviewer speculated, however, that Eliza's life would not be easy with her chosen love. The production was only a qualified success, with Zofia Dobrzańska and Gustaw Rasiński, playing Eliza and Higgins respectively, exaggerating in the violence of their mutual exchanges wherein they tended to boom, roar and screech through the scenes, eventually losing the run of themselves in the final act.

There are many aspects that distinguish Sobieniowski's translation of *Pygmalion*, not least the translator's use of what Lorentowicz described as a Warsaw city-Vistulan uneducated dialect, most readily associated with Warsaw's east-bank district of Praga. When it came to Eliza's father, Sobieniowski's dialect achieved macabre proportions, although here the critic added that the actor Maksymilian Węgrzyn had managed to bring the right amount of noble realism to the role of the raconteur dustman. With few instances of city dialect in Polish literature to draw on, it could be said that Sobieniowski was charting new territory. Here the translator provided a mixture of changed word endings – which superficially, at least, accorded with the Pragan dialect. The translator also looked to emulate Shaw's determination to make every joke and humorous exchange count. This was not lost on Lorentowicz, who, following the play's opening night on 10 March 1914, wrote, '(Shaw) is looking to entertain with the most sought-after joke.'[124] But what occupied Lorentowicz's attentions most in his review was the play's non-romantic ending, and even in this matter the critic revealed an anti-English bias. Here in this extract he is almost writing on behalf of Shaw: 'I showed in Higgins a new me and a new expression of my contempt for English hypocrisy, I flung into your palms fresh thoughts of brilliant paradoxes, and surprise situations – what more do you need?'[125] What is more, many today would be surprised by the extent to which Polish critical reflections on *Pygmalion* gave rise to musings on the Irish nationalist question. But we can guess that following the performance of *The Playboy of the Western World*, Ireland had remained something of a current topic:

> With Synge, Warsaw critics had searched for an allegory or symbol of the island of Erin, but these are so much more vividly drawn in Shaw's *Pygmalion*. Synge was the song of the

poet about the birth and emergence of a hero – and the same can be said of *Pygmalion*. Only with Synge the hero grew more out of himself (in a more manly way), whereas here the hero develops in a more feminine way – since Eliza is the hero.[126]

The staging of *Pygmalion*, which had its premiere on 10 March 1914, cemented Shaw's stellar reputation in Poland, and the play enjoyed an unprecedented run of eighty performances, by the end of which Sobieniowski had firmly established himself as Shaw's man in Poland.

Finding Markiewicz

Perhaps the most intriguing episode of this era from the Irish perspective features Kazimierz (Casimir) Markiewicz, who on leaving Ireland in 1913 turned up in Poland a short time later and embarked on an extraordinary career in theatre, which after a number of years fizzled out quite suddenly. His story, as revealed by the Polish sources, began at the annual costume ball of the Vitti Academy in Paris in 1900, where he first met Constance Gore-Booth. At some time during the course of the evening, future dramatist and close friend of Markiewicz, Stefan Krzywoszewski – who provided an account of this evening – struck up a conversation in French with Constance, who was attending the ball with Eva, her elder sister.[127] Constance had not been dancing, and remarked ruefully to Krzywoszewski that so few of the eligible attendees came up to her height, hinting none too subtly that she wished to be introduced to his more-than-suitably tall friend. Stopping Kazimierz as he was passing by, Krzywoszewski suggested that he ask Constance to dance. Markiewicz obligingly did so, and these two towering figures literally waltzed into history.

Kazimierz and Constance left the ball together early that evening and Krzywoszewski did not see his friend for another two weeks; and when they eventually did meet, it was only by chance in a café, where Kazimierz gushed about his new paramour and the regular cycling excursions that they had been taking together. As Krzywoszewski marvelled, it seemed that in their short time together Kazimierz and Constance had already arrived at the intimacy of an old friendship.[128]

Soon the couple were to be seen around Paris engaged in endless conversation and high-spirited debate. However, Krzywoszewski got a taste of Constance's incendiary character when he sat down with her one day for coffee in the Café Vachette on the Boul'Mich. Aiming to be polite, no doubt, Krzywoszewski mentioned how the Polish people sympathized with the Irish cause for independence. But Constance turned on him straightaway, retorting in a shrill voice that shocked the café's clientele into a momentary silence: 'The Irish are not capable of appreciating all the good that England has done for them. They are not deserving of such benevolence.'[129] And then in a direct put-down of Krzywoszewski himself, Constance exclaimed: 'A gentleman should not take an interest in such shameful nonsense.'[130]

When it comes to the future doubts surrounding Markiewicz's claim of nobility, it is most certain that he revived an ancient link that his family may have had with high aristocracy in order to ingratiate himself with Constance's sceptical parents. As it has come to light in recent years, Constance's family did make enquiries in both Moscow and Paris, learned the truth of his fraudulence, and seemingly chose to keep quiet on the matter. Markiewicz gave an alternative account of this matter to his friend Krzywoszewski, which, depending on one's perspective either exonerates him of duplicity or makes Constance complicit in the sham. And so, according to Krzywoszewski, for his wedding day – which took place in London – Markiewicz chose to dress in the attire of a Ukrainian aristocrat, and dazzled the British press into bestowing upon the groom the title of count. On the insistence of Constance, the young couple accepted what must have been a convenient and flattering appellation. An interesting and little-referred-to slant on this matter comes from Warre B. Wells, an American chronicler of Irish history at the turn of the twentieth century, and an acquaintance of the Markiewiczes. Wells was convinced that in Ireland Constance had insisted on her title, whereas Kazimierz had 'always rebutted the accusation of nobility'.[131]

For the first few months after their marriage, the newlyweds remained in Paris, hosting an international bohemian set in a rented studio. Whiskey and soda flowed, or at least that is until Constance's parents coaxed them back to Ireland, tempting Markiewicz with portraiture commissions.[132] In November 1901, Constance gave birth to their first and only child, Maeve. The Markiewiczes moved permanently to Ireland in 1903 and brought back from Ukraine Kazimierz's son from his first marriage, Stanislaus, his first wife having died sometime after his meeting Constance.

In the immediate years that followed, Kazimierz and Constance moved easily between the Dublin Castle set and the city's literary and artistic circles. As part of Ireland's school of Young Artists, both Constance and Kazimierz placed their works in various exhibitions and collections with the likes of George William (AE) Russell. In 1904 they also threw their weight behind the campaign to permanently house the Hugh Lane collection in Dublin, with Kazimierz writing in the *Irish Times* in November that the new gallery could be procured along the lines of the Petit Palais. As part of a series of lectures organized to raise funds for the planned gallery, Kazimierz chaired a lecture by George Moore, who argued persuasively that the opening of a gallery such as the one envisioned would only inspire Irish artists to travel to Paris, where they would inevitably end up painting like the French.

It was in 1908 that Markiewicz began to write plays, inspired in no small part by his involvement as one of the founders of the Independent Dramatic Company and the Theatre of Ireland, which would go on to stage plays for the Abbey and Gaiety theatres. The plays he produced at this time were regarded as more society events than socially relevant theatre.[133] In terms of their plot and general tone, a number of his plays suggest that Shaw's *The Philanderer* (1893) was very much a prototype piece for Markiewicz. His first play was entitled *Seymour's Redemption* (1908), whose plot faintly echoes the saga of Charles Stewart Parnell and Kitty O'Shea. The play's hero is Walter Seymour, an MP who has cast aside his true love, Daphne, in favour of a marriage more befitting his political ambitions. However, Seymour meets his former lover in the first act and their romance is rekindled. Swept up by the power of his recaptured feelings, Seymour makes speeches in parliament on free love, the abolition of marriage and relief for the unemployed. Not surprisingly, Seymour is deemed by his peers to not be 'playing the game'. Seymour's advisor, Morley, writes to Daphne demanding that she end the relationship before Seymour utters something that will potentially ruin his career. Daphne complies, and Seymour is left a broken man. However, Mrs Seymour is not happy to see her husband so dejected, and she ends up summoning Daphne. The play ends with the lovers determining that love, or rather an amiable *ménage à trois*, will conquer all.

Whilst critics pointed to its need for polishing, the play was welcomed in some quarters for giving the Irish theatregoing public a welcome respite from the Abbey's peasant plays. Such talk was of course anathema to W. B. Yeats, who resented distractions from the Abbey project. Indeed, petty quarrels between Markiewicz and Yeats were ongoing in those years, despite their both being members of the United Arts Club, which was 'a meeting-place for the city's respectable bohemians'.[134] For example, when *The Leader* newspaper accused Yeats in September 1908 of having attended a 'God Save the King' dinner at the Corinthian Club, Markiewicz gleefully chose to gossip widely about 'the poet's delight at meeting the Viceroy'.[135]

Nevertheless, Yeats, who was convinced that the fervent nationalism of the Markiewiczes stemmed from the fact that the count's rowdy behaviour had led to him being banned from the Castle's functions (although his banishment had almost certainly more to do with Constance's recent decision to throw herself wholeheartedly behind the nationalist cause), agreed to hire the Abbey out to the Independent Dramatic Company and the Theatre of Ireland for a joint production in December 1908 of Markiewicz's *The Dilettante* and a one-act farce, which Markiewicz had co-written with Nora Fitzpatrick, entitled *Home, Sweet Home. The Irish Times* described these plays as complementary to, and a welcome respite from, the Abbey fare, but then went on to mistakenly say that Markiewicz had 'written several plays in Polish, which had been performed with considerable success in his own country'.[136]

Towards the end of his life, Markiewicz recounted to friend and collaborator, Mieczysław Fijałkowski, that more than anything else, his commemorative play of the 1798 Irish rebellion, *The Memory of the Dead*, which had premiered in the Abbey on 8 March 1908, had inspired Constance to embark on a revolutionary path that within a few short years would lead to the disintegration of their marriage.[137] It is perhaps his finest play. What is more, it was the only one of his plays to have received a contemporaneous review back in Poland, courtesy of Krzywoszewski, who penned the piece for his Warsaw weekly newspaper *Świat* [*The World*],[138] which he signed under his pseudonym, Gordon. Krzywoszewski described the play as having been conceived both to help Constance in her patriotic activities and to parallel the national struggles of both Ireland and Poland.

The play, described as a romantic drama, tells the story of heroic Dermod O'Dowd, who leaves his wife Nora (played by Constance), and in the company of his friend, James Gavan, sets off to meet up with the French army, recently landed at Kinsale, in order to both inform them of the English army's movements and to join in the fight. Following the

English defeat of the French army and their routing of the Irish militia, Dermod carries a wounded James home to his house and leaves him with Nora, while he sets out once again in order to lead a French captain along secret trails to a safe rendezvous point. But Dermod is captured by the English and tortured. Somehow he manages to escape and lead a counter insurgency against the English, becoming in the process a celebrated brigand who goes by the single name of Dermod. However, none from his locality know that the illustrious outlaw is in fact the same Dermod who had disappeared some months previously. Indeed, all, including James, believe that Dermod has betrayed his people to the English. Only his wife, Nora, refuses to believe that her husband is a traitor. One day, Dermod, pursued by the English, makes it to his old home, and through the window hears James complaining bitterly to Nora about the treachery of her husband. Dermod is understandably distraught to have been suspected of such villainy. Tragically, he does not get the opportunity to declare his return and act to restore his reputation, as an English patrol approaches the cottage and positions itself to attack. Dermod stands in the doorway so as to shield those inside from the volley of bullets and is subsequently shot and killed. Nora rushes out to her mortally wounded husband. Only when they behold the woman holding her dying husband in her arms do the locals realize the extent of Dermod's heroism and self-sacrifice. The play ends with Nora declaring that their children will be brought up with the ideal of laying down their lives for Irish freedom. It is a declaration that surely must have inspired Constance to establish the scouting movement Fianna na hÉireann, which would nurture the next generation of Irish revolutionaries. Indeed, although it is a play, which, like Markiewicz's other plays, is today a largely forgotten piece, it has been accredited with having inspired the idea of blood sacrifice, which saw its dénouement with the events of Easter 1916, and with the executions that followed.[139]

If Constance had been hitherto swept up by the cause, it was her playing the role of Nora that brought her fervour to unmet levels. However, the rallying call that *The Memory of the Dead* represented was the high watermark of Kazimierz's involvement in the cause of Ireland's freedom. Whilst he was prepared to tolerate Constance's firebrand views, Kazimierz had no interest in accompanying her to conspiratorial meetings and political rallies. Indeed, in every respect, Constance's activities had for some time begun to run contrary to Kazimierz's expectations of a congenial life in Ireland spent landscape painting, dabbling in drama and impressing all and sundry with his fencing prowess and fondness for scotch and soda.

An episode that brought matters to a head took place during the summer of 1913. Constance left early one day to attend a meeting and Kazimierz decided to retire early to bed. However, he could not get comfortable and quickly realized that something hard under the bed was pressing against the springs. On further exploration, he discovered a wooden chest with numbered markings. To his horror, when he opened the chest he found himself staring at a cachet of bombs and dynamite. He let fly a philippic at the walls, which he must have repeated in full to Constance on her return: 'Was it for this that I severed ties with Poland, to marry an English aristocrat only to find that a few years after our wedding I end up sleeping on dynamite!?'[140] Little wonder, it seems, that Kazimierz packed his bags and left the country before the month was out. What is ironic, though, is that Kazimierz rejected out of hand a potential Irish conflict only to throw himself into an unfolding conflict in far-off Albania.

It is a Byronic episode that remains clouded in mystery, but circumstances suggest that he may have been acting as a secret agent, somewhat after the fashion of Sidney Reilly. Markiewicz ended up becoming a close advisor to Austria's prince William of Wied, and played a central role in placing him upon what was a contested throne.[141] However, the new king proved not to be of kingly mettle and soon found a ready escape from the pressures of the new office in his cups. With generations of hardiness, and decades of practice to call upon, Kazimierz proved to be a convivial – and manipulative – companion for the prince.[142] But whatever the intended outcome, this Albanian adventure came to an abrupt end at the beginning of 1914, when Kazimierz had to absent himself from the country at a moment's notice.

Kazimierz turned up in Warsaw in early April, and took a room in the plush Bristol Hotel (was he in funds following Albania?), which was just the shortest of walks to the Polish Theatre. He soon made the acquaintance of Arnold Szyfman, who was at the time basking in the crowd-pleaser that was Shaw's *Pygmalion*. And having also enjoyed critical success with Synge's *The Playboy of the Western World* only four months previously, Szyfman was charmed to meet someone of almost mythical status who could claim an intimacy with the world of the Irish Literary Revival. The director knew of Markiewicz's celebrated marriage, his reputation as an artist, and had almost certainly read of his theatrical successes in Ireland. In turn, the playwright would presumably have had a number of items to show Szyfman, such as cuttings, reviews, perhaps manuscripts of his Irish staged plays, and a published copy of *The Memory of the Dead*.

Szyfman must have been extremely impressed by Markiewicz, as not only did he commission a play but settled on having it staged by the end of May. An obvious choice of plays would have been *The Memory of the Dead*, but Markiewicz was a good way along with a Polish reworking of his play, *The Dilettante*, which entailed the creation of a new title *Dzikie Pola* [*Wild Fields*], and an introduction of minor alterations to the plot, including the relocation of the setting from rural Scotland to a rustic Ukraine. In keeping with a fascination for regional dialects, as had been exemplified in recent years by Wyspiański and Kasprowicz, the Polish play featured a strong local dialect spoken by servants and the local villagers. The play was also replete with the relaying back and forth of the minutiae of local happenings. Indeed, when Markiewicz had written *The Dilettante* he was surely thinking of his own life back in Ukraine, and in this sense, his reworking of the play could be said to have been an exercise in reclaiming and reimagining a familiar world.

The Dilettante had achieved considerable notoriety when it was first performed in the Abbey on 3 December 1908.[143] Set in a shooting lodge in the Scottish Highlands, the play begins with Lady Althea Dering declaring her love to Archibald Longhurst. When her husband, Lord Dering, dies, there is seemingly nothing to prevent Althea and Archibald from being together. However, Archibald reveals that he is romantically involved with

Ella Wat, the daughter of the estate steward. To add to her sense of bitterness, Lady Althea discovers that Ella has been compromised and demands of Archibald that he does the honourable thing. The two women strike up a friendship and their feelings for Archibald turn to derision when they learn that Archibald has discovered a Gainsborough in the lodge of Ella's father and has fooled the old man into selling him the painting for a paltry 50 pounds. The play ends with Archibald running off with the intention of selling the painting for ten times the price he had paid for it.

If Dublin theatregoers had conjectured that the play was not entirely fictional, knowledge of the Polish *rifacciamento* would have confirmed any suspicions they had had. In *Wild Fields* the bounder is Count Józef Przedmilski, the son of a widow who owns a gentry lodge mansion near Humań and Zaporoże, which was an area historically known as *Dzikie Pola*. His mother is blind, having lost her sight in an accident that also claimed the life of her husband. The first love interest is Roma Splawa Podlipska, a young woman, recently married, who has brought a large dowry to the union. However, she has fallen head over heels in love with Józef and the intensity of her passion makes her incapable of hiding this fact from her husband. Her husband remains unperturbed by this infatuation and assures Roma that it will soon pass, telling her that she may love as much as she wants, provided that she goes to bed early and gets her beauty sleep. Another paramour is Hela Rzepkiewiczówna, the young daughter of the estate steward, whose family have served the Przedmilskis for generations. Józef's third love interest is Ciupa Topnicka, a widow who makes no claim on him and like a Marquise de Merteuil is interested in the salacious details of his other dalliances. Józef's comfortably manageable love-life begins to unravel when Roma divorces her husband. Being the guilty party, she ends up surrendering much of her money to her cuckolded husband. Having sacrificed so much, she presses Józef to marry her. Józef has no wish to get married, however, and cruelly reveals his involvement with Hela, who also may be with child. Playing out a romantic fantasy where she takes on the role of selfless lover, Roma then decides that Hela should marry Józef. However, when Józef visits the house of Hela's father, he sees a bucolic painting on the wall and is convinced that it is the work of Jean-Antoine Watteau. He offers to buy the painting for 500 rubles, all the while hoping to sell it for 10,000 rubles. Taking his fraudulence beyond the pale, Józef offers to settle matters with a promissory note. In the third and final act, Hela and Roma meet up and 'swap notes'. When they realize what Józef is up to, they come to despise him. However, Józef is not even slightly concerned about either his tarnished reputation or his standing with his lovers. On the advice of Ciupa, who admires and defends his cunning to Hieronim, 'So he is not quite the dilettante we all thought him to be',[144] Józef ends up taking the painting and setting off to Warsaw with the intention of selling it.

Markiewicz completed his manuscript of *Wild Fields* on 21 April, signing it K-Ma, although in typed letters below he wrote 'Bristol Hotel / Copyright by Casimir Dunin-Markiewicz'. It is perhaps the most tangible piece of evidence that places Markiewicz at a particular place and time at this point in his life. Directed by Józef Sosnowski, who had also directed *The*

Playboy of the Western World, *Wild Fields* had its premiere on 30 May 1914. Although much was made of Markiewicz's Polish debut, with Warsaw's press only too happy to welcome him into the theatrical fold, the play ended up having a short run. However, reviews universally praised the production, the performance of the cast and the play's unconventional setting. A particularly enthusiastic report was to be found in *Tygodnik Ilustrowany*, with the critic Ignacy Baliński expressing the wish that the playwright contribute more to Polish drama.[145] In turn, Krzywoszewski in *Świat* loyally declared that the play represented a late flowering and the promise of greater things to come.[146] Little did he realize, however, that plays by Markiewicz would never again grace the boards of such an esteemed theatre, with Szyfman having adjudged that his friend's plays were more suited to the intimate settings of Warsaw's smaller theatres.

The Perishing World of the Countess Cathleen

Hailing from a Polish peasant background, the poetry of Jan Kasprowicz was infused with folkloric and peasant motifs, whereas his first folkloric play, *Świat się kończy* [*The World is Coming to an End*] (1891) was written in a Kujawy peasant dialect and themed the encroachment of industrialization on village life, although in depicting murder and degeneracy in abundance, the play could quite easily be regarded as being closely linked with Synge's and Yeats's seemingly prejudicial depiction of the Irish peasantry. What is more, Kasprowicz's most celebrated poetry collections, *Ginącemu światu* [*To a Perishing World*] (1901) and *Salve Regina* (1902), which were both infused with highland folkloric motifs, and which combined religious lament with existential musings, may have directly coincided with his work on *The Countess Cathleen* (1892). The poem 'Święty Boże! Święty Mocny! ['Holy Lord! God of Power and Might!'] from *Salve Regina*, for example, echoes the sentiment expressed in *The Countess Cathleen* that God has allowed evil to run amok: 'Satan crawls the earth / through the generations / casting his treacherous net / he shall turn son against father / and brother shall twist knife into brother.'[147] For Kasprowicz, both the workings of Satan and earthly misery were constants in people's lives and that it was only through recognition of this fact that people could contemplate flight to an alternative realm of spiritual and Nirvana-like peace: 'You flee so as to seek the silence which your heart will hear. Misery is everywhere.'[148] This escape, in turn, could best be achieved through metaphysical contemplation of the wondrousness of nature, which albeit was not assumed to be a straightforward thing, particularly given the harshness of what the poet knew to be the realities of peasant life. As Kasprowicz wrote, 'Every painful symptom of a peasant's life gives rise to a sense of longing in his soul … he lives for water and bread, and dreams of the wings of a butterfly',[149] which is a sentiment that could quite easily be taken as a Yeatsian summation of *The Countess Cathleen*.

Whether it was simply a case of having a copy of Yeats's 1895 *Poems* to hand or not, Kasprowicz chose to translate the heavily rewritten 1895 edition of *The Countess Cathleen*, although the original 1892 manuscript could possibly have represented a better choice of versions in terms of its clarity of plot, and the absence of over-worked symbolism synonymous with the later rewrites.

The play itself presents a stark vision of a people suffering biting famine and, feeling forsaken by God and God's mother 'who nod and sleep', invoke Satan to deliver them from their suffering. Thus called upon, devils veiled as merchants travel through the land and offer to purchase people's souls. This motif is to be found in many European traditions and Poles would have quickly linked this motif with their own legend of Master Twardowski – most famously recorded by the Romantic poet Józef Ignacy Kraszewski (1840) – who sold his soul to the devil in exchange for knowledge and magical powers. This motif had also been reworked more recently by Wyspiański in *The Wedding*, wherein a spectral Hetman (l. 678–682) tells of his infernal torments for having taken the collaborator's gold from the Muscovite powers.

First performed in 1899 at a time when the Irish Land League was campaigning for the three F's of Fair Rent, Fixity of Tenure and Free Sale on behalf of Ireland's landless classes, this play was not only considered as heretical, but also a piece of ascendancy propaganda that had portrayed the Irish peasantry as 'degraded idiots'[150]… 'being not [so] near to God' (l. 729, 1892 manuscript); whereas in choosing to ignore the Christ-like nature of Cathleen's sacrifice, some detractors wondered openly how it was that one Protestant soul could so tip the scales. But it is doubtful whether Kasprowicz would have discerned such historical sensitivities.

Kasprowicz's translation is a powerful rendition of the original play wherein all Irish elements are kept in their entirety, including names, places, customs and mythological references. Without any doubt, the most interesting aspect of the translation was Kasprowicz's decision to translate all Celtic mythological references as literally as possible, all the while presumably suspecting – as indeed did Yeats – that many of the mythological references would be lost on theatregoers, and that it would be more a case of soaking up the wonder of the unknown.[151]

Some ten years would pass before *The Countess Cathleen* had its Polish premiere.[152] It would be staged on 14 December 1914, in Warsaw's Variety Theatre under the direction of Konstanty Tatarkiewicz. The Variety Theatre generally staged plays that ran for between thirty and fifty performances, and given the fact that *The Countess Cathleen* had only two performances – and that the theatre was only half full on the first night – something disastrous must have gone wrong with either the publicizing of the play or the production itself. Lorentowicz thought the play's theatre poster, describing the play as a folktale in verse ('baśń wierszem') must have been partly to blame, which, as the critic contended, had surely kept Warsaw's bourgeois classes away in their droves.

Lorentowicz,[153] in turn, recalled how, when watching the play, he had thought of Yeats's poem 'The Sad Shepherd' – a number of poems that had been translated by Kasprowicz – which relates how a shepherd sings gently his sorrows into a shell only for his words to be changed by the 'lone sea-dweller' into an 'inarticulate moan'. And what the critic seems to have been alluding to was the lack of musicality, 'a graceless prose'[154] on the part of the actors when it came to the delivery of their lines, which suggests that the critic may have known that Yeats considered chanting as being integral to the performance of his plays.[155] In particular, Lorentowicz was quick to praise the theatre for having taken on such a play, comparing the significance of the work to the legend-filled plays of Wyspiański. Of course, the fact that he did not highlight the similarity of Yeats to the work of the actual translator of the play indicates the extent to which Wyspiański had come to dominate the imagination of the age.[156]

Significantly, the failure of this production of *The Countess Cathleen* adversely impacted on Yeats's theatrical legacy in Poland. His close association with Wyspiański and Kasprowicz also meant that in the era of inter-war Poland, he was never perceived as a modern poet, and this uninformed position must also have extended to Synge, as was evidenced by the total absence of his plays from Polish theatres for many decades to follow.

Notes

1   Artur Górski (Quasimodo), 'Młoda Polska', *Życie*, 15 (1898), 170.

2   See Maria Podraza-Kwiatkowska, *Programy i dyskusje literackie okresu Młodej Polski* (Wrocław: Ossolineum, 2000), 22–29.

3   See Maria Podraza-Kwiatkowska, *Programy i dyskusje literackie okresu Młodej Polski*, 63–64.

4   See Czesław Miłosz, *The History of Polish Literature*, 327–328.

5   See Ludwik Szczepański, 'Sztuka narodowa', *Życie*, 9 (1898), 97–98; 10 (1898), 109–110.

6   Stanisław Przybyszewski, 'Confiteor', *Życie*, 1 (1899), 1–4.

7   See Maria Podraza-Kwiatkowska, *Literatura Młodej Polski* (Warszawa: Wydawnictwo Naukowe PWN, 1992), 14.

8   'Przede wszystkim, rzecz doskonała w doskonałym przekładzie nie jest ani swoja, ani obca, jest doskonała, a to Wystarczy.' Zenon Przesmycki, 'Po półtoraroczu', *Chimera*, 6 (1902), 474.

9   Leon Winiarski, 'Estetyzm – Oskar Wilde: *Wachlarz Lady Windermere i Kobieta małej wartości*', *Prawda*, 27 (1893), 315–316.

10 Leon Winiarski, 'Czynniki etniczne w sztuce i poezji z drugiej połowy naszego stulecia', *Prawda*, 10 (1894), 112.

11 '… którego tylko głupcy uważają za szarlatana.' Leon Winiarski, *Prawda*, 10 (1894), 112.

12 Wanda Krajewska, *Recepcja literatury angielskiej w Polsce w okresie modernizmu (1887–1918)* (Warszawa: Wydawnictwo Polskiej Akademii Nauk, 1972), 93.

13 Wanda Krajewska, *Recepcja literatury angielskiej w Polsce w okresie modernizmu (1887–1918)*, 93.

14 '… może być uważany za teoretyka sztuki wyrafinowanej, zamkniętej w >>wieży z kości słoniowej<<, nieprzystępnej dla szerokiej masy', R.W., *Życie*, 7 (1898), 76.

15 Unsigned, 'Uczeń', *Życie*, 13 (1899).

16 'Zmarli: Oskar Wilde, pisarz angielski, w Paryżu', *Prawda*, 50 (1900), 603.

17 Unsigned. 'Nekrologia', *Kurier Warszawski*, 334 (1900), 6. See Wanda Krajewska, *Recepcja literatury angielskiej w Polsce w okresie modernizmu (1887–1918)*, 95.

18 Oscar Wilde, *Salome* (Kraków: Stanisław Fromowicz 1904), trans., Władysław Fromowicz.

19 *Tygodnik Ilustrowany*, 38 (1904), 731.

20 Oscar Wilde, *Salome* (Lwów: Księgarnia H. Altenberga, 1904), trans. Jadwiga Gąsowska.

21 '...pamięta się w dramacie ją tylko i ją tylko jedną'. Konrad Rakowski, 'Z teatru. *Salome, tragedya w jednym akcie Oskara Wilde'a*', *Czas*, 112 (1905), 1.

22 '*Salome* Oskara Wilde'a wydaje mi się rzadkim, wyjątkowym przykładem dzieła, którego duszę, którego wyraz umiał autor sztucznie skonstruować, sztucznie ozdobić pozorami życia i poezyi. Jest dziełem kultury wysokiej'. Konrad Rakowski, *Czas*, 112 (1905), 1–2.

23 Wilhelm Feldman, *Piśmiennictwo polskie ostatnich lat dwudziestu* (Lwów: Ksiegarnia H. Altenberga, 1902), 149.

24 *Przegląd Poranny* (4 August 1916).

25 'Z teatru. *Kobieta bez znaczenia*, komedya w 4 aktach Oskara Wilde'a', *Czas*, 19 (1904), 1–2.

26 Konrad Rakowski, 'Z teatru. *Mąż idealny*, sztuka w 4 aktach Oskara Wilde'a', *Czas*, 289 (1907), 3.

27 See Marek Radziwon, *Iwaszkiewicz. Pisarz po katastrofie* (Warszawa: Wydawnictwo W.A.B., 2010), 43; see also Jarosław Iwaszkiewicz, *Stanisława Wysocka i jej kijowski teatr 'Studya': wspomnienie* (Warszawa: Wydawnictwo artystyczne i filmowe, 1963).

28 See Jan Lorentowicz, *Dwadzieścia lat teatru*, Vol. II (Warszawa: Nakładem Księgarni F. Hoesicka, 1930), 112–116.

29 Jan Lorentowicz, *Dwadzieścia lat teatru*, Vol. II, 108–110.

30 Konrad Rakowski, 'Z teatru. *Birbant*. Trywialna komedya w 4 aktach Oskara Wilde'a', *Czas*, 218 (1905), 1.

31 Adam Krechowiecki, 'Z teatru. *Birbant*. Trywialna komedya w 4 aktach Oskara Wilde'a', *Gazeta Lwowska*, 244 (1905), 4.

32 See Wanda Krajewska, *Recepcja literatury angielskiej w Polsce w okresie modernizmu (1887–1918)*, 10.

33 'Irlandczycy prawie w regule są w tem umiłowaniu galizmu łudząco podobni do nas Polaków, do Paryża jadą jak do Mekki raz na rok, ale w odświętnym nastroju po pokrzepienie się w progressy ludzkie'. Adolf Nowaczyński, *Oskar Wilde. Studium, Aforyzmy, Nowela* (Warszawa: W. Wiediger, 1906), 15.

34 See Wanda Krajewska, *Recepcja literatury angielskiej w Polsce w okresie modernizmu (1887–1918)*, 190.

35 Ludwik Szczepański, 'Teatr Krakowski', *Życie*, 21 (1898), 247. See also Wanda Krajewska, *Recepcja literatury angielskiej w Polsce w okresie modernizmu (1887–1918)*, 190.

36 Wanda Krajewska, *Recepcja literatury angielskiej w Polsce w okresie modernizmu (1887–1918)*, 193.

37 See Antoni Dębnicki and Ryszard Górski, 'Bernard Shaw na scenach polskich. Okres pierwszy 1903–1913', *Pamiętnik Teatralny*, 2 (22) (1957), 232–233.

38 See Wanda Krajewska, *Recepcja literatury angielskiej w Polsce w okresie modernizmu (1887–1918)*, 58; see also Franciszek Pajączkowski, *Teatr lwowski pod dyrekcją Tadeusza Pawlikowskiego, 1900–1906* (Kraków: Wydawnictwo Literackie, 1961), 51–57.

39　It is important to note that at the beginning of the twentieth century, municipal theatres in cities like Warsaw, Kraków and Lwów were subsidized by the city, and very often their remit or program, as defined by the theatre manager, was to present as many plays as possible. As a consequence, this meant that theatres would very often stage up to three plays a week, which placed almost impossible demands on the actors and often impacted negatively on the quality of their performance. See Adam Grzymała-Siedlecki, *Tadeusz Pawlikowski i jego krakowscy aktorzy* (Kraków: Wydawnictwo Literackie, 1971), 153–160.

40　Klemens Kołakowski, '*Uczeń Szatana*', *Dziennik Polski*, 557 (1903), 2.

41　Władysław Rabski, '*Uczeń Szatana*', *Kurier Warszawski*, 23 (1912), 3.

42　'Nie ulega wątpliwości, że mało u nas znany pisarz albioński znalazł nowy wyraz dramatyczny dla swej twórczości; wyraz jakiego nie mieliśmy dotychczas.' Klemens Kołakowski. *Dziennik Polski*, 557 (1903), 2.

43　'dajmy jej zatem spokój!' Klemens Kołakowski, *Dziennik Polski*, 557 (1903), 2.

44　Adam Krechowiecki, 'Syn Szatana', *Gazeta Lwowska*, 274 (1903), 4.

45　Unnamed Review, *Tygodnik Ilustrowany*, 50 (1903), 966.

46　Michael Holroyd, *Bernard Shaw* (London and New York: Vintage, 1998), 171. See also Roy Foster, *W. B. Yeats: A Life – The Apprentice Mage, 1865–1914* (Oxford: Oxford University Press, 1997), 141–142.

47　Konrad Rakowski, 'Z teatru. *Bohaterowie*, komedya w 3 aktach Bernarda Shaw'a, *Czas*, 239 (1904), 1–2.

48　Konrad Rakowski, *Czas*, 239 (1904), 1–2.

49　Feliks Koneczny, 'Teatr Krakowski', *Przegląd* Polski, 154 (1904), 367.

50　See Zast. (stand-in reviewer), '*Marnotrawny ojciec*, komedya w 4 aktach Bernarda Shawa', *Głos Narodu*, 455 (1906), 3–5.

51　Konrad Rakowski, 'Z teatru. *Marnotrawny ojciec*, komedya w czterech aktach Bernarda Shaw'a, przekład T. Konczyńskiego', *Czas*, 224 (1906), 1.

52　Jan Lorentowicz, '*Nie można przewidzieć*', *Dwadzieścia lat teatru*, Vol. II, 153.

53　'Dobrze, dajcie mi innych aktorów', *Dwadzieścia lat teatru*, Vol. II, 153.

54　'ale w rzeczywistości – nic się nie działo', *Dwadzieścia lat teatru*, Vol. II, 154.

55　Władysław Rabski, 'Z teatru. *Nie można przewidzieć*', *Kurier Warszawski*, 291 (1907), 3.

56　'... chciałem cię zawiadomić o drobnem, bardzo dodatniem, bo rzadkiem zjawisku artystycznym, jakie na kilka dni nawiedziło twą ukochaną Warszawę [I wanted to inform you about a small, but meaningful and rare artistic phenomenon, which for a few short days held sway in your beloved Warsaw]'. Jan Lorentowicz, *Dwadzieścia lat teatru*, Vol. II, 130.

57　'... I w teatrze powstał szczególny nastrój świadczący, że widzowie nie tylko się bawią doskonale, ale i odczuwają jako tako istotę komedii. [...] A przecież z powodu *Candidy* miał u nas Shaw chwilę całkiem europejskiej popularności', Jan Lorentowicz. *Dwadzieścia lat teatru*, Vol. II, 124–125.

58　'U niego ludzie nie są ani źli, ani dobrzy, tylko są – ludźmi [...] ludzie u niego stopniowo 'się odkrywają'. Jak w życiu, tak i w jego sztukach widzimy przy pierwszym spotkaniu całkiem innego człowieka, aniżeli później, po zawarciu z nim bliżej znajomości. W istocie jest ten sam człowiek, co przedtem, ale teraz jest bez toalety, a przedtem był ubrany. Publiczność się dziwi i publiczność zarzuca autorowi brak konsekwencji ("bo przecież ten człowiek był w pierwszym akcie inny"). Ale sens komedyj i życia jest zawsze ten sam i zawsze inny (i zawsze jest dla siebie i bliźnich Niespodzianką)'. Tadeusz Rittner, 'Przed premierą *Candidy* – Bernard Shaw', *Świat*, 9 (1906).

59 'Żadna troska artystyczna snu im nie zakłóca', Jan Lorentowicz, *Dwadzieścia lat teatru*, Vol. II, 130.

60 Alfred Wysocki, '*Candida* Shawa', *Gazeta Lwowska*, 216 (1906), 4.

61 Alfred Wysocki, *Gazeta Lwowska*, 216 (1906), 4. '... nasza publiczność została zimna; z początku śmiała się z paru udanych i oryginalnych dowcipów, całość jednak nie zajęła i pod koniec widocznie się nudziła.'

62 See Juliusz Tenner, 'Teatr Lwowski', *Krytyka*, Vol. II (1906), 471–477.

63 Edward Webersfeld, *Teatr Miejski w Lwowie za dyrekcji Luwika Hellera 1906–1918* (Drukarnia W. A. Szyjkowskiego: Lwów, 1917), 50.

64 See Leonard W. Connolly (ed.), *Bernard Shaw. Mrs Warren's Profession* (Peterborough, Ontario: Broadview Press 2005), 13–17.

65 The Little Theatre actually managed to turn a tidy profit in its first season and enjoyed a reputation for serious theatre with productions of Ibsen, Goethe and Polish dramatists. Gawalewicz took much personal credit for the theatre's achievements, so stating, 'Jeżeli się teatr dobrze prowadzi, to powodzenie jest niewątpliwe [if a theatre is well run, then success is assured]'. See *Kurier Warszawski* 134 (1907), cited in Roman Taborski, *Warszawskie teatry prywatne w okresie Młodej Polski* (Warszawa: Wydawnictwo Naukowe PWN, 1980), 38.

66 Jan Lorentowicz, *Dwadzieścia lat teatru*, Vol. II, 194–196.

67 Jan Lorentowicz, *Dwadzieścia lat teatru*, Vol. II, 194.

68 'Sprzedawać temu, kto da najwięcej'. J. Kl. (Jan Kleczyński), 'Z teatru', *Tygodnik Ilustrowany*, 32 (1907), 658.

69 'Pani Warren [...] ulega jeszcze w znacznej części wymaganiom współczesnego sobie teatru, jest niejako surowym dopiero materiałem prawdziwej rzeczywistej komedyi, której stylu mianem, jest: Bernard Shaw' ['Mrs. Warren [...] whilst conforming to the requirements of modern theatreer, is still raw material for the kind of comedy whose style is: Bernard Shaw']. Konrad Rakowski, 'Z teatru. *Profesja pani Warren*, komedya w 4 aktach Bernarda Shawa' ['From the Theatre. *The Profession of Mrs Warren* a comedy in 4 acts by Bernard Shaw'], *Czas*, 230 (1907), 1.

70 G. B. Shaw, 'Sardoodledom', *The Saturday Review* (1 June 1895).

71 Here I cite from Wiktor Biegański, 'Polska Prapremiera Profesji Pani Warren' ['The Polish Premiere of *Mrs Warren's Profession*']. Theatre Programme for *Profesja Pani Warren*. The Theatre of Stefan Jaracz. Olsztyn – Elbląg (1954), 12–14. Available at: http://dlibra. bibliotekaelblaska.pl/dlibra/docmetadata?id=124&dirids=6&ver_id=. Accessed 14 August 2012.

72 See Alfred Wysocki, 'Tadeusza Pawlikowskiego czasy lwowskie', *Pamiętnik Teatralny*, 1 (5) (1953), 145; see also Antoni Dębnicki and Ryszard Górski, 'Bernard Shaw na scenach polskich. Okres Pierwszy 1903–1913', *Pamiętnik Teatralny*, 2 (22) (1957), 232–233.

73 See Zygmunt Wasilewski, '*Demonstracja w teatrze miejskim we Lwowie*', *Słowo Polskie* 84, (1909), 3. Dr M. Thullie summarized Wasilewski's standpoint as follows: 'Więc sztuka o treści zbyt drażliwej, aby o niej napisać w gazecie, napisana w sposób cyniczny, ale z

wielkim talentem, może ona działać umoralniająco na audytorium teatralne?' ['And so the play is too awful to be written about in the newspaper, it's been written in a cynical manner, but with great talent, may affect the morals of those in the theatre auditorium?'] 'Tumult w Teatrze Miejskim we Lwowie', *Przegląd Powszechny*, 101 (1909), 482–483.

74 ['Wstyd, że takie sztuki przedstawia się na scenie polskiej'.] See Dr M. Thullie, *Przegląd Powszechny* 101 (1909), 482–483; and Wiktor Biegański, Olsztyn – Elbląg (1954), 14. See also Stanisława Kumor, *Polskie debiuty Bernarda Shaw* (Warszawa: Wydawnictwo Uniwersytetu Warszawskiego, 1971), 135–136.

75 See Wiktor Biegański, Olsztyn – Elbląg (1954), 14; and Dr M. Thullie, *Przegląd Powszechny*, 101 (1909), 483.

76 Wiktor Biegański, 'wzywające do poszanowania wolności i swobody myśli', Olsztyn – Elbląg (1954), 14.

77 Bolesław Prus, 'Kronika Tygodniowa. Poezja i Poeci', *Tygodnik Ilustrowany*, 23 (1909), 456–457.

78 Czesław Miłosz, *The History of Polish Literature*, 352.

79 Edward Gordon Craig, *On the Art of Theatre* (London: Heinemann, 1911), 18.

80 Edward Webersfeld, *Teatr Miejski we Lwowie za dyrekcji Luwika Hellera 1906–1918*, 13.

81 Jan Michalik, *Dzieje teatru w Krakowie w latach 1893–1915. Teatr Miejski*, Vol. V (Kraków: Wydawnictwo Literackie, 1985), 77.

82 This entire episode is recounted in Adam Grzymała-Siedlecki, *Tadeusz Pawlikowski i jego krakowscy aktorzy*, 275–278.

83 Adam Grzymała-Siedlecki, *Tadeusz Pawlikowski i jego krakowscy aktorzy*, 298–299.

84 Edward Webersfeld, *Teatr Miejski w Lwowie za dyrekcji Luwika Hellera 1906–1918*, 15.

85 Alfred Wysocki, *Sprzed pół wieku* (Warszawa: Wydawnictwo Literackie, 1974), 221.

86 'Pisząc powtarzałem sobie głośno każde zdanie. Mimo to, Pawlikowski przerywał co chwila czytanie mego przekładu, mówiąc cichym głosem: 'Zdaje mi się, że to a to słowo trzeba przestawić, albo zmienić, albo cały zwrot wyrzucić'. I zawsze miał rację', Alfred Wysocki, *Sprzed pół wieku*, 222.

87 Unnamed reviewer, 'Ruch artystyczno-literacki. Z teatru. *Cudowne źródło*, legenda irlandzka w 3 aktach J.M. Synge'a', *Gazeta Narodowa*, 262 (1908).

88 '…lepsza jest czasem ślepota', *Gazeta Narodowa*, 262 (1908).

89 Alfred Wysocki, 'Z teatru. *Cudowne źródło* J. M. Synge'a', *Gazeta Lwowska*, 262 (1908), 4.

90 Z. R. (Zygmunt Rosner), '*Castus Joseph* Szymonowica', *Gazeta Poniedziałkowa*, 5 (1914), 4.

91 Władysław Prokesch, 'Teatr Miejski', *Czas*, 26 (1914), 4.

92 '… a gdy przeszedłszy całe piekło życia, znowu oślepli i zbliżyli się do siebie we wspólnej doli, która im ich brzydotę zasłoniła. Nie chcą już za nic w świece drugiego cudu […]'. *Czas*, 26 (1914), 4.

93 '… z talentem oryginalnego poety', *Czas*, 26 (1914), 4.

94 Józef Flach would support this judgement, remarking that the audience had been too exhausted, given the lateness to really enjoy the play. See Józef Flach, 'Teatr Krakowski', *Literatura i Sztuka*. Supplement to *Dziennik Poznański*, 8 (1914), 118. Danuta Poskuta-Włodek also speculates that the dialect of the translation, which had been spoken by the cast in a poetic delivery replete with pauses, had fatally undermined the production. See Danuta

Poskuta-Włodek, *Trzy dekady z dziejów sceny. Teatr im. Juliusza Słowackiego w Krakowie w latach 1914–1945* (Kraków: Teatr im. Juliusza Słowackiego w Krakowie, 2001), 54.

95 Florian Sobieniowski, 'Wspomnienia tłumacza.' *Miesięcznik*, 9–10 (1936), 17–18.

96 ALS, 19 February 1924. Berg Collection, NYPL. See Fred. D. Crawford. 'Shaw in Translation. Part 1: The Translators.' *SHAW. The Annual of Bernard Shaw Studies*, 20 (2000), 177–196.

97 Shaw to T. J. Wise, TLS, 29 September 1933. Ashley Library, bl, b4019, f. 115.

98 Florian Sobieniowski, *Miesięcznik*, 9–10 (1936), 18.

99 Jan Michalik, *Dzieje teatru w Krakowie w latach 1893–1915. Teatr Miejski*, Vol. V (Kraków: RSS–G, 1996), 82–83.

100 Leon Schiller, *Teatr Ogromny* (Warszawa: Czytelnik, 1961), 27. See also Edward Krasiński, *Teatr Polski Arnolda Szyfmana 1913–1939* (Warszawa: Wydawnictwo Naukowe PWN, 1991).

101 Edward Csato, *The Polish Theatre* (Warszawa: Polonia Publishing House, 1963), 42–43.

102 'Wyobraźmy sobie naród, liczebnie trzy razy przeszło mniejszy od naszego, a naszych wad, śmieszności, grzechów i brzydactw spotęgowanie; przypomnijmy sobie, że Irlandowie od siedmiu wieków cierpią prześladowania i tortury, wobec których nasz wiek XIX zmniejsza się do rozmiarów obłoku, który szybko horyzont przemierzy i zniknie.' Adolf Nowaczyński, 'Odrodzenie Erynu', *Co czasy niosą* (Warszawa-Lwów: Księgarnia St. Sadowskiego, 1909), 69–70.

103 '[…] jego chłop nie umie sobie poradzić z siatką rybacką, kompasem, busolą, z mechanicznym siewnikiem.' 'Przed premierą irlandzką', Loose Leaf. Polish Theatre Museum of Warsaw.

104 Stanisław Pieńkowski, 'Z powodu dramatu Synge'a', *Gazeta Warszawska* (18–19 November 1913), 5.

105 '…jako głuptasek i degenerat…', *Gazeta Warszawska* (18–19 November 1913), 5.

106 Jan Lorentowicz, *Dwadzieścia lat teatru,* Vol. II, 196–202.

107 'Utwór Synge'a ma jak widzimy tyle elementów nam nie obcych, że wystarczyło go jedynie spolszczyć. Tłumacz zaś przez zbytek snadź gorliwości – sztukę 'zwyspiańszczył'.' Kazimierz Wroczyński, 'Kresowy Rycerz', *Tydzień Teatralny*, 43 (1913), 12.

108 Wiktor Popławski, 'Współczuć Synge'owi możemy, nie potrafimy jednak go Zrozumieć.' 'Kresowy Rycerz-Wesołek', *Gazeta Poranna, Dwa Grosze* (21 November 1913), 3–4.

109 '…z uczuciem zupełnie zmąconem'. Jan Lorentowicz, *Dwadzieścia lat teatru,* Vol. II, 197.

110 See Peter Conolly-Smith, 'Shades Of Local Color: *Pygmalion* and its Translation and Reception in Central Europe, 1913–1914', *Shaw*, 29 (2009), 134.

111 See Michael Holroyd, *Bernard Shaw*, 435–440.

112 See Ryszard Ordyński, *Z mojej włóczęgi* (Kraków: Wydawnictwo Literackie, 1956), 261–262.

113 Ryszard Ordyński, *Z mojej włóczęgi*, 262–263.

114 Ryszard Ordyński, *Z mojej włóczęgi*, 359–360.

115 'Liza w akcie pierwszym i drugim mówi gwarą ordynarną uliczną. Przedstawicielka tej roli musi przeprowadzić ten dialekt konsekwentnie, zwłaszcza w tonie i przedłużeniu i skracaniu samogłosek bardzo dosadnie.'

116 'Nie jęcz nam nad uszami.' Unnamed reviewer, 'Z teatru', Loose-leaf, The Juliusz Słowacki Theatre Archive.

117 See Jan Michalik, *Dzieje teatru w Krakowie w latach 1893–1915. Teatr Miejski*, Vol. V, 361.

118 As Konrad Rakowski wrote, '*Pygmalion* Shaw'a na sobotniem przedstawieniu po swych europejskich sukcesach, zdobył sobie i publiczność krakowską i powodzenie w repertaurze ma zapewnione.' ['The Saturday performance of Shaw's *Pygmalion* following its European triumphs won over Kraków's theatregoing public and its success in the repertoire is assured.'] 'Z Teatru Miejskiego w Krakowie. *Pygmalion*. Komedya w 5 aktach Bernarda Shaw'a', *Czas*, 18 (1914).

119 Unnamed reviewer, 'Z teatru', *Pygmalion*. Komedya w 5 aktach Bernarda Shaw'a. Z oryginału przełożył Ryszard Ordyński, Loose-leaf. The Juliusz Słowacki Theatre Archive.

120 Cited in Michael Holroyd, *Bernard Shaw*, 441.

121 'Nie mogę sobie wyobrazić lepszych wykonawców tych dwu ról.' Unnamed reviewer, 'Z teatru', *Pygmalion*. Komedya w 5 aktach Bernarda Shaw'a. Z oryginału przełożył Ryszard Ordyński', Loose-leaf. The Juliusz Słowacki Theatre Archive.

122 Jan Pietrycki, 'Z teatru', *Gazeta Narodowa* (14 February 1914), 2.

123 Gbr (Bolesław Gubrynowicz), 'Z teatru. *Pygmalion*, komedya w 5 aktach Bernarda Shawa, przekład Ryszarda Ordyńskiego', *Gazeta Lwowska*, 32 (1914) 4–5.

124 '…rozbawi najbardziej wyszukanym dowcipem', Jan Lorentowicz, *Dwadzieścia lat teatru*, Vol. II, 145.

125 '…pokazałem wam w Higginsie nową odmianę mnie samego i nowy wyraz mojej pogardy dla angielskiej obłudy, rzuciłem garść myśli świeżych, paradoksów błyskotliwych, sytuacyj niespodzianek – czegoż potrzeba?' *Dwadzieścia lat teatru*, Vol. II, 150.

126 'W Syngu szukała krytyka warszawska alegorii czy symbolów wyspy Erynu, które bez kropek nad i, a jednak więcej niż przejrzyście rysują się w *Pygmalionie* Shawa. *Wesołek* Synge'a był pieśnią poety o narodzeniu się i zmaganiu się bohatera, tem samym jest *Pygmalion*. Tylko u Synge'a bohater wyrastał bardziej ze siebie i przez siebie (bardziej po męsku), tu zaś wyrasta on bardziej po kobiecemu, skoro bohaterem jest Eliza.' Mieczysław Limanowski, '*Pygmalion*', *Prawda* (13 March 1914), 9.

127 See Stefan Krzywoszewski, *Długie życie. Wspomnienie* (Warszawa: Księgarnia Biblioteka Polska, 1947), 120–123.

128 Stefan Krzywoszewski, *Długie życie. Wspomnienie*, 121.

129 Stefan Krzywoszewski, 'Irlandczycy, wołała, to wałkonie i niewdzięcznicy. Nie potrafią ocenić dobrodziejstw, jakimi obdarzyła ich Anglia.' *Długie życie. Wspomnienie*, 122.

130 Stefan Krzywoszewski, 'Dżentelmen nie powinien zajmować się taką hałastrą!', *Długie życie. Wspomnienie*, 122.

131 Warre B. Wells, *Irish Indiscretions* (London: George Allen & Unwin Ltd. Ruskin House, 1922), 30–31.

132 Stefan Krzywoszewski, *Długie życie. Wspomnienie*, 131.

133 See Mary Trotter, *Modern Irish Theatre* (Cambridge: Polity Press, 2001), 129.

134 See Roy Foster, *W. B. Yeats: A Life – The Apprentice Mage, 1865–1914*, 375.

135 Roy Foster, *W. B. Yeats: A Life – The Apprentice Mage, 1865–1914*, 375.

136 'Count Markievicz's New Play', *Irish Times* (3 December 1908).

137 See Mieczysław Fijałkowski, *Uśmiechy lat minionych* (Katowice: Śląsk, 1969), 262–269.

138 Gordon (Stefan Krzywoszewski), 'Patriotyczna sztuka irlandzka – utwór Polaka', *Świat* 35 (1910), reprinted in *Dialog*, 2 (1975), 107–108.

139 Christopher Morash, *A History of Irish Theatre 1601–2000* (Cambridge: Cambridge University Press, 2001), 152.

140 Mieczysław Fijałkowski, 'Więc po to zerwałem z Polską, ożeniłem sie z arystokratką angielską, żeby w parę lat po ślubie spać samemu na dynamicie?!' *Uśmiechy lat minionych,* 266.

141 Kornel Makuszyński, 'Jak w romansie Stevensona', *Kurier Warszawski* 198 (1935). Available at: http://biblioteka.kijowski.pl/makuszynski%20kornel/kartki/jak.htm. Accessed 14 September 2013. See also Patrick Quigley, *The Polish Irishman. The Life and Times of Count Casimir Markiewicz* (Dublin: The Liffey Press, 2012), 155–156.

142 Mieczysław Fijałkowski, *Uśmiechy lat minionych,* 266.

143 See J. H. Cox, 'Two New Plays', *Irish Independent* (4 December 1908), 4. See also, Lauren Arrington. *Revolutionary Lives: Constance and Casimir Markiewicz* (Princeton, New Jersey: Princeton University Press 2016), 42–44.

144 '... nie taki dyletant, jakby się zdawało znów z niego.'

145 Ignacy Baliński, 'Rozmowy o Teatrze', *Tygodnik Ilustrowany,* 23 (1914), 449.

146 S. K. [Stefan Krzywoszewski], 'Teatr Polski. *Dzikie Pola*', Loose-leaf. The Polish Theatre Museum of Warsaw.

147 'Szatan po ziemi tej krąży, / na pokolenia / zarzuca zdradną sieć, / w synu na ojca zapalczywość budzi (…) bratu na brata wciska krwawy nóż ....'

148 'Uciekasz przed siebie, aby szukać ciszy, która twe serce usłyszy. Nędza jest Wszędzie.' Cited in Jan Lorentowicz, *Młoda Polska*, Vol. 1 (Warszawa: Księgarnia S. Sadowskiego 1908), 129.

149 'Każdy bolesny objaw życia chłopskiego wywołuje w jego duszy ten szmer tęsknoty ... o wodzie i chlebie żyje, a marzy o skrzydłach motyla', Jan Lorentowicz, *Młoda Polska*, Vol. 1, 129.

150 So described by Frank Hugh O'Donnell in his anti-Yeats protest pamphlet *Souls for Gold*, see Roy Foster, *W. B. Yeats: A Life – The Apprentice Mage, 1865–1914*, 209–210.

151 Kasprowicz did make an effort at cultural assimilation when it came to the various otherworldly spirits that are mentioned in the play, and here I particularly refer to the wondrous shee dwellers of the tumulus, and the outcast, spritely and evil-working sheogue. Unfortunately, Kasprowicz bunched the shee and sheogues together as 'chochlicy' (sing. 'chochlik') who were the devilish goblin-like monsters of Polish folklore, who notably turned up in Juliusz Słowacki's *Balladyna* (1842). Consequently, the shee are somewhat misrepresented in the Polish version, and where the countess, suffering a crisis of *taedium vitae*, so says: 'I could go down and dwell among the shee / In their ever-busy honeyed land', what we have in Polish ... 'Chciałabym dzisiaj […] zejść między chochlików' ['I could go down and dwell amongst the goblins'] comes across as an expression of forsakenness and abandonment. However, by Cathleen referring to the wanderings of her mind as 'wicked words', translated in more hyperbolic terms by Kasprowicz as 'bezbożne słowa' ['Godless words'], narrative coherence is just about retained.

152 But that is not to say that in the interim *The Countess Cathleen* of (*Chimera*, 7 (20/2) (1904), 17–84) may not have made something of a cultural mark. Intriguingly in 1908 the Polish Association of Theatres hosted a conference that focused on the place of folk drama in

Polish theatre, among which Kasprowicz's *The World is Coming to an End* and Yeats were keynote topics – though specific plays were not given in the prospectus.

153 Jan Lorentowicz, *Dzwadzieścia lat teatru*, 192–195.

154 'bezwdzięczna proza …'

155 For further reading, see Ronald Schuchard, *The Last Minstrels. Yeats and the Revival of the Bardic Arts* (Oxford: Oxford University Press, 2008).

156 See Arnold Szyfman, *Labyrint teatru* [*The Theatre Labyrinth*] (Warszawa: Wydawnictwo Artystyczne i Filmowe, 1964), 278. We also have a short theatre report from Wiktor Popławski, who praised the highly poetic nature of the play, which treats 'the tragedy of the soul', and the quality of the performances, although he did express doubt about the costumes and general pacing of the play. Somewhat exceptionally, he also made mention of Kasprowicz as translator, praising the poet for having achieved the kind of strong language and spirit of the original that people had come to expect from his literary translations. See Wiktor Popławski, 'Teatr Rozmaitości', *Gazeta Poranna Dwa Grosze*, 52 (1914), 3.

Chapter 2

A Fall from Grace: Irish Drama During the Inter-War Years (1918–1939)

Introduction: Out in the Cold

Although surely pleased with the moderate success of *Wild Fields*, Markiewicz may not have remained in Warsaw for the end of the play's theatrical run. Inspired by Tsar Nicholas's proclamation that promised freedom to the Poles, he joined the ranks of the Imperial Huzar regiment. From a publicity photograph for *Wild Fields*, published in the Warsaw newspapers, it is clear that the grey-haired Markiewicz was at this time well past the flush of youth. But just as he had excelled in espionage, Kazimierz earned a reputation as a formidable and fearsome cavalry officer who made a point of enumerating his many kills. When he entered Lwów at the beginning of 1915, following the routing of Austro-Hungarian forces at the Battle of Galicia, Kazimierz sought out Kornel Makuszyński, who was astounded by the imposing sight of Markiewicz on his heavily laden horse.[1] That evening the friends drank a small cask of wine and Markiewicz recounted his exploits with relish and merriment. Later Markiewicz rode with his Huzars to Carpathia and was shot several times and left for dead in the snow, his heavy frame hindering his own chances of being dragged to safety. A fellow soldier somehow got him to a railway line, and there Kazimierz waited for a transport with other wounded men, many of whom died of exposure. Markiewicz was subsequently taken to a hospital in Lwów but contracted typhus. There followed weeks of agony as his wounds healed. He then moved back to Kiev where he spent several months recuperating.

Adjudged to have suitably recovered, Markiewicz may have been sent back to the front at this time. However, his lungs had been compromised and so he was duly decorated for bravery and discharged. As Makuszyński humorously suggested, the likely reason for his being discharged was that the Russians feared Markiewicz's martial prowess could have singlehandedly brought the war to a premature end.[2] When Makuszyński was himself resettled in Kiev from Lwów, he was amazed to see Markiewicz back in civilian clothes, and busying himself with painting and the completion of two plays: *Marta wychodzi za mąż* [*Marta is Getting Married*] and *Lilie polne* [*Wild Lilies*], the latter of which was produced by Makuszyński in Kiev's Polish Theatre on 4 November 1915.

The most detailed account of Markiewicz's life in this period comes from Arnold Szyfman. A year earlier, in the August of 1914, the finances of the Polish Theatre, together with the rest of Warsaw, had been in a precarious state. With credit lines exhausted, Szyfman was at his wits end trying to match expenditure with shrinking takings. Miraculously, the theatre was saved from the brink of closure by a sagacious decision to stage *Alsace*, a hyper-patriotic

French play that had been penned by Lucien Camille and Gaston Leroux the previous year. Indeed, so marvellous was the turnaround that whilst other theatres in Warsaw were playing to empty houses, *Alsace* was packing in audiences taken with the play's nationalist fervour, and delighting in the opportunity to stand for 'La Marseillaise' and sing their hearts out.[3] And yet, fervour and hope could do nothing to alter the fact that the German army was steadily advancing, although no one could be sure if it would be a week, a month or a year before they breached the city limits. Szyfman, who hailed from Ulanów in the Austrian partitioned part of Poland, realized that both he and his fellow Austrian actors, not to mention those from the German-occupied part of Poland, could face internment or conscription. With such a fate predominantly occupying his thoughts, Szyfman decided to accept a longstanding invitation to take his company to Kiev to perform at the Municipal Theatre. And in October 1914, having prepared a number of plays, such as *Pygmalion* and *Alsace*, Szyfman embarked on a journey to Kiev together with those actors whom he considered to be in a perilous position.[4] (It is telling, perhaps, that Szyfman chose to omit Markiewicz's Ukrainian play from the repertoire.) Having been warmly received by both the Polish and Russian press, the performances were extended from two weeks to three. So successful was this tour that an invitation was extended from Moscow's Polish Theatre. However, Szyfman had to decline, saying that transport difficulties and pressing matters back in Warsaw warranted their immediate return. Szyfman and his company of actors returned home in November with the theatre's finances in a healthier state. However, for the next two months, audience numbers were down and plays were performed to half-empty houses. Events took a sinister turn at the beginning of December, when Szyfman was arrested in the middle of the night and imprisoned for a month, having only been questioned once during the time of his incarceration. He was released in the New Year on the day of the Epiphany.[5]

It would not be until August of 1915 that the Russians evacuated Warsaw and the Germans entered the city. Like many citizens of occupied Warsaw, Szyfman hoped to wait out the war in the relatively peaceful provinces, but this meant having to be able to drum up the funds for such an evacuation. Markiewicz sent the director a formal invitation to his estate outside of Kiev as early as May, whereas friends in Warsaw helped Szyfman to secure a travel permit. Having invested everything he had in the theatre, Szyfman had no funds for the journey but managed to borrow a thousand rubles from financier and patron of the Polish Theatre, Maurycy Spokorny. Szyfman ended up giving half of this sum to actress, Maria Przybyłko-Potocka, who had been left in straitened circumstances as a result of the closure of the theatre. Szyfman departed from Warsaw at the very beginning of August, having cut short a run of performances of Aristophanes's *Clouds* after only five performances, following its premiere on 25 July 1915. This date represents yet another marker in our attempt to establish some chronology for Markiewicz's activities and whereabouts during these years.

According to Szyfman's account, when he stepped off the train at Koziatywa, he was met by Markiewicz, dressed in traditional gentry attire and proudly displaying a gleaming horse trap that took them in some style along muddy lanes to his village of Różyn, which together with the village of Żywotówka and the surrounding countryside encompassed his family estate. In the company of his raconteur host and extended family who were visiting Markiewicz on holidays, Szyfman settled into what was an idyllic existence. Indeed, Markiewicz's world could not have been further removed from that of Szyfman's in Warsaw. Every day Kazimierz and his brother woke up at dawn and went hunting for birds, arriving back promptly at nine, when everyone sat down to a hearty breakfast of meats, fowl, fish, cheeses and garden vegetables. At regular intervals, the Markiewicz brothers would wash back their breakfast with large shots of vodka and gently poke fun at Szyfman for sipping tea and daintily nibbling his buttered sandwiches, cajoling him also for not having risen early to go shooting with them. Once breakfast was finished, everyone spent their day as they wished. Szyfman filled his days walking the surrounding fields and meadows, where he would inevitably find Kazimierz painting the landscape in an open meadow or in the shade of an overhanging tree.

Towards the end of August, Szyfman was informed that his papers no longer allowed him to stay in Różyn, and that he had to register in Kiev. Markiewicz left him in a comfortable hotel, but was forced to return home early as his brother had fallen ill. Kazimierz promised to return within a month with a portrait that he had made of Szyfman. However, the director left the city within a few days. Knowing he could rely on the support of friends in Moscow, Szyfman sought and gained a travel pass to Moscow, where he would run Moscow's Polish Theatre until the end of 1918.

The year 1916 seems to have been a happy year for Markiewicz if we are to believe an account by a distant cousin, which is held in the Lissadell House collection:

In those days, 1916, Casi, after recovering, was full of joy of life and wrote plays, painted pictures, drank like a fish, was loved by all men and women and known in all Uc [sic. k] raine as the best of pals and a regular sport. I was a schoolgirl, very much terrified by his rather wild reputation and although we were neighbours (about 50 miles) and related, our house being very convent-like, was never visited by Casi and I never did speak to him until 1919.[6]

Markiewicz's movements become sketchy at this point. However, sometime in 1917, he also wrote a pamphlet on Ireland as part of a series of missals published under the umbrella name of 'The Freedom and Brotherhood of Peoples', where he decried how England had killed industry and agriculture in Ireland, and 'left the masses of the people without schools and education and killed their native language'.[7]

Later that year, with his estate and the surrounding areas fast becoming a battleground for the White and Red armies, Markiewicz was forced to move to Kiev.[8] He was closely involved with Kiev's Polish Theatre for the 1918 season that lasted from August to December. Working closely with the theatre's artistic director, the proclaimed actress, Stanisława Wysocka, Markiewicz himself oversaw the staging of Synge's *The Playboy of the Western World* – which drew critical praise – and his own play *Wild Lilies*. At the end of 1918, like many of his neighbours and friends, Markiewicz chose to flee to Warsaw as a war-refugee, carrying all that was left to him in a suitcase. Markiewicz soon became part of a circle centred around Krzywoszewski's newspaper *Świat*, and he also attended the Thursday morning open-house hosted by theatre critic and crack marksman and hunter Władysław Rabski, and his wife, Zuzanna, a celebrated poet. The Rabskis had a spacious apartment in the Krasiński Palace on Krakowskie Przedmieście, and these large and exclusive gatherings were loud and rambunctious affairs, which hosted not only Warsaw's aging bohemian set of the Young Poland era, but also a hardy group of hunting enthusiasts. Needless to say, it was a society that Markiewicz found easy entry into. He was free with his own accounts from his several previous lives, and soon earned the epithet 'Zagłoba in a monocle', which alluded to Sienkiewicz's cunning and resourceful Odysseus-like character, Jan Zagłoba, of *Trylogia* [*The Trilogy*] (1884–1888).

However, Markiewicz was just about as impoverished as every other writer and journalist trying to eke out a living in the city. His first earnings would come from royalties for *Marta is Getting Married*, such as they were. The play was first performed in Warsaw's Variety Theatre, and then shortly after in Kraków's Teatr Bagatela [Bagatelle Theatre], as a support feature for Fijałkowski's *Pan Poseł* [*The Parliamentarian*] (1919). As Fijałkowski recalled, for quite some time Markiewicz had lived solely on the paltry proceeds from the play.[9] Once again, Markiewicz chose Ukraine as the backdrop for his play, with its mix of opulent landowners and peasantry living alongside one another, sharing both living space and customs. Even though the manuscript has been lost to posterity, fortunately an account of the play was provided by one of the foremost theatre critics of the day, Emil Breiter.[10]

For reasons painfully obvious, the play would have great resonance in the Ireland of today, as it was principally an exploration of the conspiracy of silence that domestic abuse fosters. Had it achieved notoriety and been supported by valiant critics, it may have come to be seen as an accusatory work in the tradition of Shaw's *Mrs Warren's Profession* and Margarete Böhme's *The Diary of a Lost Girl* (1905). But the play *Marta is Getting Married* was not destined to make any measurable cultural impact.

Markiewicz's play tells the story of a father who rents out his daughter, Marta, to his brother once a year; and this practice is continued for all of nine years. The daughter only manages to extract herself from this arrangement when she meets a young suitor. Marta confesses all to her paramour and in so doing threatens her own future happiness. She then risks her happiness further by choosing to confront her mother with the truth. This confrontation is played out in the third act and like Shaw's *Mrs Warren's Profession* it serves principally to explore the protracted nature of the outrage itself. In this instance, what is worked through in the exchange is that silent complicity within a family allows such abuse to continue unchecked. However, Marta will pull back from revealing the truth to her mother, even though it is hinted strongly that her mother had in fact known of the arrangement and chosen to remain silent.

In his review, Breiter was less appalled at the weightiness of the subject than concerned with the artistic qualities of the play. He understood that Markiewicz was attempting to achieve a naturalism, which, in accordance with the convention, presented a deeply shocking issue from an objective perspective. However, the critic also reminded the dramatist that an intended construct should not take a story beyond the bounds of plausibility. For Breiter, it was the believability of the plot and not the heinous misdeed, which stretched credulity. Indeed, he marvelled at the idea of Markiewicz banking on the fact that his play would *'épater les bourgeois'*, when in fact it had been clear on the night of the premiere that those of his class had felt sullied by the insinuation that this sort of abuse was commonplace. Markiewicz, Breiter so suggested, could claim a prize for having conceived the nadir of unpleasant situations. Perhaps the most damning criticism of the play was his contention that when its characters began to think, they stopped living. And this was because Markiewicz only understood 'the biological side of life',[11] a comment by which much could be inferred.

When Szyfman returned from his self-imposed exile, he looked to Shaw to relaunch the theatre, premiering both *Fanny's First Play* (1911) and *Major Barbara. Fanny's First Play* had first been staged in Warsaw's Little Theatre at the end of 1911, although it did not have anything like the kind of success that it had enjoyed in England and America. With theatrical penury still fresh in his mind, Szyfman hoped that he would dramatically improve on the play's first outing. However, the production proved to be only a qualified success. The technical challenge of 'a theatre within a theatre' had flummoxed the play's fledgling director Aleksander Zelwerowicz, who had chosen to place a framed stage at the back of the stage, which ended up forcing actors performing within the frame to carry the distance to the audience by speaking at the top of their voices throughout. For the next production of Shaw, the directorial reins were handed over to Markiewicz, who could claim some direct knowledge of the industrialized landscape of Britain's cities. Like *Fanny's First Play*, *Major Barbara* was a revived piece, having also been first premiered in Warsaw's Little Theatre a decade earlier. Markiewicz had at his disposal a new translation by the little-known Zygmunt Wołowski, who according to critic Stanisław Pieńkowski had managed to accentuate the play's Overman discourse.[12] This production distinguished itself principally by the stage backdrop, which depicted an English industrial landscape, albeit Pieńkowski thought it had needed the accompaniment of acoustics in order to impart the noise of an industrial city. Even though Markiewicz acquitted himself admirably with this production, he was not part of the core group of directors that Szyfman called upon regularly, and Kazimierz was unable to secure another directorial commission. Indeed, it is clear that at this time Markiewicz's career in the theatre had foundered, and even a staging of *The Memory of the Dead* failed to reverse his flagging fortunes. The fact that he could only secure for his play a small theatre in the district of Praga, indicates the extent to which his star had faded. Plays staged in these periphery theatres were not reviewed in the press. But having said that, the play did earn the briefest of mentions from Krzywoszewski in what was an overview article on Warsaw's recent theatrical productions, where Markiewicz's friend hailed the play as one of the high points of the season.[13] The final nail in Markiewicz's theatrical coffin came with Rabski's review[14] of *Nawrócenie łotra* [*The Conversion of the Rogue*], which premiered in Warsaw's Teatr Komedia [Comedy Theatre] on 15 November 1922. Rabski, who had been something of a mentor to Markiewicz, stated that some months previously he had unequivocally told Markiewicz, who had presented him with the completed manuscript, that the play could in no way be considered as a work of literature. Markiewicz had not taken this well, and Rabski surmised that they must have ended up speaking at cross-purposes. Having seen the play on stage, the critic could not hide his displeasure with the fact that Markiewicz had not taken on board any of his corrections or suggestions, and was flabbergasted that the theatre had agreed to produce the play, assuming that the decision to stage *The Conversion of the Rogue* could only have come about because the theatre management had considered the play as fresh material from a Polish dramatist. For Rabski and his fellow theatrical aficionados, however, the time for hailing Markiewicz as a promising playwright had long passed. Whatever of the continuing strength of his friendships, Markiewicz found himself out of the loop.

The Play That Was Never Staged

The only voice speaking in favour of Irish drama immediately after the war was Adolf Nowaczyński, who in 1918 wrote a book of collected essays entitled *Szkice literackie* [*Literary Sketches*], which, aside from a chapter entitled 'Teatr irlandzki' ['Irish Theatre'],[15] also featured a treatise on subjects that indicated his wide range of literary interests, such as the reception of Balzac, Shakespeare, Czech literature and the Belgian Bible. With respect to his chapter on Irish theatre, Nowaczyński reworked the speech he had delivered prior to the *Playboy* premiere and spoke of the extent to which Irish theatre had helped the Irish nation reclaim its Celtic identity. However, Nowaczyński made recourse to hyperbole and stereotype once again when he contended that Irish drama had managed to transform a drunken and mendacious people, depraved to the core, to a nation transfixed by Ireland's mythical heroes of old and their deeds. What is more, Nowaczyński, who seems to have been oblivious to the unfolding turmoil in Ireland, praised the engagement of writers of the revival who were of the people and for the people, a fact that had instilled in them an instinctive nationalistic outlook. Principally, Nowaczyński looked to reassert that the Irish Literary Revival had remained an informative chapter for Poland, and that Ireland was the 'Poland of the Western Worlds' wherein peasant culture had come to reflect both the paralysis of a nation and conversely its own cultural salvation, whereby the cult of rural simplicity and backwardness, shrouded in Yeatsian mysticism, had attempted to save the soul of the Irish nation. Additionally, drawing on the recountings of Markiewicz, who had first-hand knowledge and dealings with such writers, Nowaczyński sought to celebrate the flourishing of Irish drama, exemplified by its increasing number of exponents such as Lennox Robinson, Padraic Colum and George A. Birmingham, all of whom, to paraphrase Nowaczyński, had taken the lead from Synge and had tackled uncomfortable realities in order to reform, build and reshape; to praise not what had gone before, but to envision a future where things are better. That said, Nowaczyński described Ireland's rural people in terms that stripped them of any describable positive characteristics. Indeed, such were the depths to which he considered the Irish nation to have fallen that he compared the current batch of Irish dramatists to Saint George fighting a serpent that wrought engulfing chaos. This is yet another example of Nowaczyński's heavy-handed and prejudicial treatment of his subject. In fact, few writers have ever wielded such unpleasant epithets against the very culture that they feigned to advocate on behalf of.

From among his selection of writers, Nowaczyński was most taken with Birmingham, and in particular his satirical play *General John Regan* (1913). Nowaczyński's principal interest in the play stemmed from the fact that its performance in Westport had provoked a riot, and that his own play *Nowe Ateny* [*The New Athens*] (1913) had also met with hostile protestations from Warsaw theatregoers when it was staged in the Polish Theatre.

But aside from shared catcalls, Nowaczyński's play had little in common with Birmingham's, albeit the underlying themes could be construed to share similar traits. Nowaczyński's play, whose shenanigans and intrigues evoke the theatre of *commedia d'ell arte,* looked to show that the aspirations for a unified Polish nation was all talk and kerfuffle, and that political or electioneering speeches, which recalled Poland's fallen heroes, did the sacrifices of the same heroes a great injustice by usurping a noble cause for questionable ends. Also like Birmingham's *General John Regan*, Nowaczyński's *The New Athens* is an almost entirely forgotten play.

George A. Birmingham was the pen-name of Belfast born Canon James Owen Hannay, who was rector of Westport between 1892 and 1913.[16] Hannay was a vocal advocate of Home Rule and was very much a part of the movement of cultural nationalism sweeping across Ireland at the time. Hannay, or rather, Birmingham, came to literary prominence in 1911, when, following rejections by the Abbey and London's Haymarket Theatre, the play *Eleanor's Enterprise* was staged with critical success by the Independent Company. It may even have been directed by Kazimierz Markiewicz himself.

Birmingham's plays were rural Irish comedies and he drew inspiration for his characters from many of his local Westport neighbours, portrayed as common Irish types, including the Politician, the Squireen, the Publican and so on. But relations soured beyond repair when Birmingham caricatured the local priest in his play, *The Seething Pot* (1906). Such was the strength of the offense, the priest penned a number of articles unveiling the playwright's identity, whereas other local priests made life for the canon so unpleasant that he ended up leaving Westport. Despite the unpleasantness fresh in his mind, Hannay would not be dissuaded from his favoured subject matter, and he set to writing *General John Regan*, a play that took inspiration from a story related to him by AE Russell, wherein some years previously a journalist in France had hoodwinked unsuspecting local politicians into campaigning to erect a statue to a fictional leader, with embarrassing consequences for the politicians and locals when the hoax was revealed. This premise informs the plot of *General John Regan*. An American by the name of Horace Billings arrives in the town of Ballymoy in search of 'the deliverer of Bolivia', General John Regan. In reality, this recalled Bernardo O'Higgins, the Supreme Dictator of Chile between 1817 and 1823, whose father, Ambrosio O'Higgins, Viceroy of Peru, was born in Ballinary in County Sligo.

Even though the locals in the play have but a glimmering memory of this great Irish statesman, they are delighted that someone has come along and jogged their collective memory. Dr Lucius O'Grady, a scheming character who frequently appears in other plays by Birmingham, sees an opportunity to not only erect a statue but to exact largesse from the Lord Lieutenant. However, in accordance with protocol, the Lord Lieutenant must be greeted with a rendition of 'Rule Britannia', a ceremonial stipulation that is met with a stern refusal on the part of the local nationalists. Fortunately, no one in the village has ever heard 'Rule Britannia' being played before, and so Lucius is able to teach the villagers the melody as 'The War March of King Malachi the Brave'. The town also begins to take part in the ruse as they nominate a servant girl, Mary Ellen, to be the general's niece, and great debate and scheming ensues as to the way in which she should be turned out for the arrival of the Lord Lieutenant. The third act mocks the lavishness and triviality of the events that Lord Lieutenants and Viceroys attended throughout the length and breadth of the Empire, and the very notion that such acts of largesse could quell nationalist spirit. The mockery falls upon all parties to the event as the town stages a pageant in which the general's niece is attended upon by a group of fairies, which also satirizes Irish nationalism. This is in spite of the fact that the play is replete with Home Rule politics, where the governance of Ireland by the ruling British is decried as being the cause of the Irish nation's ills.

With its genial dialogue, delivered by winning heaps of stage Irishness, the play proved irresistible to audiences in London, where it first premiered on 8 January 1913 at the Apollo Theatre, and then in New York, where the play opened at the Hudson Theatre on 12 November of the same year. The critics, in turn, praised the fact that the play had clothed 'a satirical plot with the loving kindness of pure comedy', whereas one New York critic described *General John Regan* as "easily the cleverest as well as the wittiest play which has come across the water in many a long year"'.[17] So great was the anticipation when the play came to Ireland that two separate productions toured Ireland concurrently, with one focusing on Belfast, Cork and Dublin before traveling back across the Irish Sea to London, and the other taking in the midlands before moving on to Galway and then Westport, where the townspeople were determined to give it a hostile reception, knowing in advance that they would be looking at caricatures of themselves.

The action was pre-planned, but the protestors must have decided that they would not act until appropriate offense emanated from the stage. A suitable moment presented itself when the priest, frazzled by the preparations, is advised to step into the backroom to enjoy a quiet tipple. That proved to be the tipping point, as many of the youths rushed the stage and ripped the collar from the cowering actor playing the priest. The collar was later burnt in the town square. The rioters grew in number and broke the windows of the theatre, the box office and the hotel accommodating the theatre company. The riot was only quelled when the parish priest arrived and appealed for order. Twenty rioters were arrested, but they were all subsequently found not guilty, with the court adjudging that the offense taken had been entirely justifiable.

Recounting this riot, Nowaczyński wistfully bemoaned the fact that his play had not been met with the same rambunctious reception, cognizant he was, no doubt, of the fact that a decent theatre riot will always earn for a play a certain notoriety. And so, Nowaczyński praised the Mayo rioters for having shown more courage and sense of purpose in thrashing the theatre and attacking the actors than those in the Polish Theatre, who on the night of the premiere of his own play had been content to make catcalls and feign exaggerated yawning. Of course, Nowaczyński was not the only one with an opinion on what had transpired. Szyfman defended the production, but said that the quality of the play had undermined the company's Herculean efforts to stage it:

> The New Athens was badly received by the critics. It was not a question of the acting or the political or social viewpoints. The play contained too many construction mistakes and tactless commonalities [...].[18]

Perhaps what sealed Nowaczyński's fate in terms of future cooperation with the Polish Theatre was that Szyfman found him to be a poor collaborator, and like Markiewicz, he was sidelined in favour of the emerging lights of Warsaw's theatrical and literary world:

> Nowaczyński was not one of those writers who was able to accept either professional or friendly advice, particularly after great theatrical successes in both Kraków and Warsaw. In this regard he was the opposite to Włodzimierz Perzyński, and in later years – Jarosław Iwaszkiewicz.[19]

Indeed, it was Szyfman's favourable opinion of Jarosław Iwaszkiewicz and his fellow Picador poets – who later went by the name of Scamander – which may have been a strong factor in persuading Szyfman to distance himself professionally from both Nowaczyński and Markiewicz, as we shall discuss presently.

A Changing of the Guard

In order to get a sense of the literary mood of the early inter-war years and what subsequently followed, it is important to understand the phenomenon of the Picador poets, who comprised principally Julian Tuwim, Jan Lechoń, Antoni Słonimski, Jarosław Iwaszkiewicz and Kazimierz Wierzyński, all of whom were in their early twenties when they launched or joined in November 1918 a poetry café called Under the Picador. This proved to be an enterprise that captured the elation of the time following the German retreat from the city. The café was opened for evening performances that saw the poets recite their poetry and perform satirical sketches.

On Sunday 10 November 1918, at 5.00 am, Marshal Piłsudski entered the city, having been released from his imprisonment in Magdeburg. News of his release electrified the city.

At 10.00 am, crowds gathered after mass outside his house on Moniuszko Street. For the rest of the month, Warsaw's streets were teeming with expectation and prone to outbreaks of violence.[20] Such a climate determined the ambience of the café, which was a model of sobriety and decorum amidst the surrounding chaos.

From its very inception, Under the Picador both symbolized and exemplified the many emotions that accompanied Poland's first months of independence, and its participants were the first to proclaim a new democratic life for both the people and the nation's artistic outlook. The Picadors crystallized these changes occurring within the country by altering, albeit temporarily, the relationship between the public and the poet. Whilst the location of the café supported the Picadors' notion of 'poetry on the street', it is questionable whether it enjoyed patronage by the masses and it remained, in all likelihood, a gathering place for Warsaw's intelligentsia and student body.

The Picadors perceived themselves as playing a patriotic part in the rebuilding of Poland. Initially, their foremost concern was to present Poland's fortuitous circumstances as a 'fresh start' for the nation, and with this aim in mind they drew a literary parallel with the utopian motifs of Russian contemporary poets, most notably the Acmeists. The Picadors also underscored their link with Poland's Romantic tradition by way of articulating the aspirations – albeit unspecified and hazy – of a resurgent nation. Their futurist, nation-building agenda, tied to a reinterpretation of Polish Romanticism and drawing on urban motifs, also confined all talk of peasant literature to the past. And given that much of Irish literature was associated with a bygone era, then much like the generation of Young Poland, Irish drama must have been perceived as uninformative to the new age.

In keeping with the declared aim of defending Polish art and literature from cheap and compromising standards, the Picadors, on 21 December 1918, set out to make an impression on Warsaw's theatrical world, an action described by Iwaszkiewicz as an effort at solidarity; one, he said, that ended in victory.[21] The subject of their protest was the repertoire of Szyfman's Polish Theatre.

Szyfman had launched the season with a promise that high art would grace the theatre's boards. The first three productions had lived up to Szyfman's promise but box-office earnings had also been poor. And so, in search of a wider public, Szyfman chose to stage *Pani Chorążyna [Madam Chorążyna]* (1918), a drawing-room comedy that had been penned by Stefan Krzywoszewski. The Picadors perceived the staging of this drawing-room play as a threat to the standards of the theatre's repertoire and resolved to stage a demonstration on the night of the play's premiere.[22] The implications of their protest must have extended in Szyfman's mind to the entirety of Krzywoszewski's circle. Szyfman later recorded that he had not needed much persuading in this regard, as he had already been ill-disposed towards Krzywoszewski's plays.[23]

During the first two acts of the play, Słonimski and Iwaszkiewicz clapped and made inappropriate noises. The dénouement came when Jan Lechoń walked up onto the stage, taking the speechless actress, Maria Przybyłko-Potocka, completely by surprise, and presented her with a bouquet of flowers. Following this, Lechoń turned to the audience and proceeded to read out a prepared letter of protest. Lechoń never had an opportunity to finish reading out his letter. The audience, mistaking this protest for a communist demonstration, leapt from their seats and ran to the exits. Mieczysław Grydzewski, sitting in the gallery, flung copies of Lechoń's speech down into the theatre-pit. The police duly arrived and marched the poets down to the police station, but were satisfied to only take down the details of the incident.[24]

Szyfman quickly forgave the Picadors for their misadventures, and both parties soon realized that there could be plenty of scope for collaboration at many levels, including the editing and translation of manuscripts, as well as the penning of plays. One anecdotal fragment that alludes to this 'changing of the guard' is provided in a diary account by Iwaszkiewicz, who paints a vivid picture of how the previous generation of literati was regarded by the ascendant generation:

> I didn't like Kasprowicz. He came to Warsaw from time to time and sat in the Astoria at the 'great altar', that is, at the table of Kornel Makuszyński. Often Kazimierz Dunin-Markiewicz was there, sometimes Stefan Żeromski, sometimes Karol Szymanowski, throwing bored looks in our direction – and of course Kornel with his wife, Emma. We 'Scamanders' always bowed to them shyly from afar.[25]

This generational stand-off must have adversely affected Nowaczyński's advocacy of Irish drama in the eyes of the then more influential younger generation of writers and their associates. And though Nowaczyński's final essay on Irish drama did make a direct appeal to the directors of Poland's theatres, commissions of Irish plays proved stubbornly elusive. Perhaps Nowaczyński could himself have translated and promoted a select number of Irish plays, but ultimately, like Markiewicz, he must have realized that the championing of Irish drama in Poland had become a lost cause. It seems that during the inter-war years Nowaczyński had many other causes to fight for. It is only unfortunate that many of these same causes often involved the writing of ultra-nationalistic missives replete with anti-Semitic invectives. Indeed, it is because of his rabid anti-Semitism that today Nowaczyński's literary reputation lies in tatters. However, having made mention of what lay in the future for Nowaczyński, we may say that his advocacy of Irish culture up to 1918 was both highly significant and deserving of recognition.

The Sorrow of Sainthood

During the inter-war years Szyfman looked to place the activities of the Polish Theatre at the heart of the city's cultural life. Warsaw, in turn, became the centre of cultural activity, with many writers, artists and theatrical technicians choosing to settle in what was now the reborn nation's capital city. Principally, Szyfman's philosophy was that plays should not be performed as ensemble pieces but should instead look to accentuate a central performance.

This notion also applied to stage decoration, lighting and the music, all of which were placed at the service of individual roles. And perhaps nothing exemplified this approach better than the 1924-production of Shaw's *Saint Joan*. There had been rumours for months prior to the production that Szyfman had been planning to stage a blasphemous piece. But following the play's first performance, one critic was happy to report that it had in fact paid great tribute to the iconic martyr who had only recently attained sainthood.[26]

Saint Joan had had its premiere in New York in December of 1923, and the lukewarm reception it received from critics gave no indication that within a few short decades it would be universally hailed as a theatrical masterpiece.[27] First performed in the Garrick Theatre, the problems preceding the play have entered theatre lore and included the fact that the cast had been rehearsing from an unrevised script and were insisting that the six-act play (with epilogue) be trimmed. When news reached Shaw of these difficulties, he sent off an intemperate and now infamous missive: 'Begin at eight or run later trains ...'.[28] That said, the first night went well and full galleries were happily noted for the subsequent performances.

Shaw had spent ten years writing this play, which centres around the trial and death of Joan of Arc, and which looked to reclaim the simple peasant girl back from the centuries of layered and devotional recounting. For his play, Shaw had drawn freely on the contemporaneous transcription of the trial, and come to the conclusion that although Joan was innocent of all wrongdoing, this did not mean that the Inquisition had been wrong in its decision to sentence her to death by burning at the stake. This was because, according to Shaw, Joan had been tried and convicted in accordance with the laws of the epoch.

In the epilogue, intended to 'shew the canonized Joan as well as the incinerated one', the spectral Bishop of Warwick explains to Joan that she was a victim of political expediency, but this painfully honest assessment is made contemporaneous by the strong inference that a Joan of our times would as likely as not meet a similar fate. Essentially, the purpose of the epilogue emphasizes the loneliness of Saint Joan in life, at her death, and in her saintly state.

Following the New York run, the play opened in London in the April of 1924. Shaw was happy to note that the play is 'going like mad',[29] and that the controversial epilogue had been accepted by critics, who understood that its function was to explore the struggle of religious inspirations against established religions and patriotic and political imperatives. By the time the play had ended its run in London, Shaw had had time to reflect on it and the potential for its direction. In the end Shaw was convinced that they had trumped the American production.[30]

Saint Joan opened in Szyfman's Polish Theatre on 3 December 1924, and was directed by Aleksander Zelwerowicz, who had had little previous experience aside from his already-mentioned unsuccessful effort at directing *Fanny's First Play*. His task was made all the more daunting by the fact that he would be playing the part of the Duke de la Tremoille.

In spite of the fact that Shaw wrote *Saint Joan* in an old dialect akin to the formality and phraseology of fourteenth-century English, Sobieniowski as translator made a decision to render his translation in sixteenth-century Polish, basing his work principally on the Renaissance poet Mikołaj Rej (1505–1569), who was one of the first Polish writers to feature vernacular in his work. Sobieiowski's decision in this regard did not please a number of reviewers of the play, who felt that the language of *Saint Joan* was closer to the modern English idiom than that of Rej's to modern Polish. Emil Breiter, for instance, felt that Sobieniowski's chosen archaisms had rendered much of the dialogue incomprehensible to the ear, and he suggested that when the play was published, Sobieniowski should replace the archaisms with contemporary equivalents.[31]

Sobieniowski's translatorial decision in this regard would rankle decades after. In 1956 on the occasion of the centenary of Shaw's birth, Bohdan Korzeniewski offered a scathing assessment of Sobieniowski's contribution to the legacy of Shaw in Poland in a post-script to an article entitled 'Shaw dzisiaj u nas' ['Shaw Today with Us'].[32]

Describing his criticism of Sobieniowski as unpleasant but necessary, Korzeniewski stated that generations of Polish theatregoers had been under the illusion that they enjoyed an intimacy with Shaw unmet elsewhere when in fact the contrary had been true; and that Shaw's intelligence, precision, playfulness had been expunged by Sobieniowski; and that none of the characteristics of the playwright's style had been rendered. But Korzeniewski reserved the fullness of his ire for Sobieniowski's translation of *Saint Joan*, which he described as having introduced a dialect 'unknown to our beautiful Polish language'.[33]

Unquestionably, the high point of the production was the performance of Maria Malicka in the role of Joan. Few thought that Szyfman had made the right choice in casting the wide-eyed actress, famed for her delicate beauty and acclaimed for recent turns as a romantic heroine. But to the surprise of all and sundry, Malicka donned the heroic mantle of the Maid and gave one of the great performances of the era. As critic Jakub Appenszlak noted, '… she has managed to carry the burden. Shaw would be happy with this portrait of a noble, naïve young girl, with eyes so terribly beautiful during moments of exaltation.'[34] Other members of the cast were also lavished with praise, and it was generally felt that this play had been a landmark event, foregrounding the notion of the theatre as a forum for harnessing intellectual debate. But the fact that the play spoke of the violent reaction on the part of the state or the status quo to the emergence of individualism may have achieved a greater resonance a few short years later when Poland found itself once more in the throes of internal conflict.

Soap Boxes and Big Cheeses

Shaw's *The Apple Cart* (1928) has had its fair share of detractors over the years. But from today's perspective, and given what we know was stirring throughout Europe at the time, few would say that Shaw did not have his finger on the pulse of the age, whether they agreed with, or even understood, the sentiments that the Irish dramatist was looking to express, or not. Indeed, for theatrical audiences watching the play in its premiere year of 1929, *The Apple Cart* must have confirmed what many suspected: that something was seriously amiss in the practice of European politics. Democracy in Europe was failing and leaving a vacuum that was being filled by dictatorial regimes. In Poland democracy had already failed. For in May 1926, after three years of a right-wing government, and impatient with what he felt to be the fractious and factional nature of Polish governance, Marshal Józef Piłsudski came out of retirement and staged a military *coup d'état*. He then set about establishing an authoritarian regime called 'sanacja', a term from the Latin word 'sanare', meaning 'to make wholesome'. Given his leadership role in the regaining of Polish independence and in the later repelling of a Red Bolshevik army in 1920 – famously hailed as the Miracle on the Vistula [Cud nad Wisłą] – for the most part Marshal Piłsudski and his military government enjoyed popular support in Poland. As for Shaw, there is much to suggest that he knew that when the play had its world premiere in Warsaw it would effectively endorse the quasi-monarchical nature of the 'sanacja' regime. That said, given Shaw's long-held view on eugenics, first popularly formulated in *Man and Superman* (1903), it is hard to imagine that he did not approve of Piłsudski strong-arm actions.

In *The Apple Cart* Shaw argued for selective breeding as a way of reversing national decline, by creating a class of capable voters. The political system would then be replenished by the nation's best and brightest. In order to achieve this goal, Shaw was prepared to accept pre-eminent representatives from all the classes. But underpinning this was a radical reconstruction of social values in order to attain a meritocracy of the Superman. Somewhat paradoxically, Shaw conceived this process in order to prevent the rise of dictatorships, but he must surely have considered that a transitional iron-hand rule would have to play some role. Certainly, this transitional arrangement was being tested and tried by Piłsudski, who, in the wake of the military takeover, delivered a famous speech to the members of the Sejm and Senate, wherein he spelt out the new arrangements. The speech may not have perfectly matched the theme of *The Apple Cart*, but it certainly indicates that Piłsudski and Shaw could best justify autocracy by taking pot shots at the travesties of democracy:

> The main reason for the current situation in Poland is poverty and weakness both internally and externally. Thefts have occurred and have gone unpunished. In Poland the interests of the individual and the party hold sway, and also impunity for all excesses and crimes. I have declared war on scoundrels, murderers and thieves, and in this fight I shall not yield. The Sejm and the Senate have an excess of privileges and if they had their way, would acquire more rights. The parliament should rest. Give the rulers the possibility of being responsible for their actions. Let the President create a government, but free of party pressure. That is his right.[35]

Perhaps to keep the censors at bay, Shaw placed the action of *The Apple Cart* in a monarchist Britain in a 'neutral' era sixty years into the future, where only seven per cent of the voting population has the vote. In the play, the rather Wildean-aphoristic King Magnus must contend with the machinations of the popularly elected Prime Minister, Proteus, who plans to strip the monarch of his constitutional powers. Though Magnus holds no truck with such a suggestion, it is the reasoning and manner which he employs to defend his position that highlights the accomplishments of Magnus over the elected company he must face down. And it is precisely in the cabinet's inadequate dealings with the king that Shaw looks to ask the question: how is it that this rag-tag bunch of vested interests, vainglorious ambition and questionable background end up in such positions of power? And so, when compared to the performance of the king, Shaw feels that his 'Apple-Cart' politicians are not up to the task. Though Shaw had a great deal more to say in his 'Preface' beyond a precursory explanation of the plot, he was not at all effusive about what he considered to be the importance of his new play:

> Not being as pampered and powerful as an operatic prima donna, and depending as he does not on some commercially valuable talent but on his conformity to the popular ideal of dignity and perfect breeding, he has to be trained, and to train himself, to accept good manners as an indispensable condition of his intercourse with his subjects, and to leave to the less highly placed such indulgences as tempers, tantrums, bullyings, sneerings, swearings, kickings: in short, the commoner violences and intemperances of authority. His ministers have much laxer standards. It is open to them, if it will save their time, to get their own way by making scenes, flying into calculated rages, and substituting vulgar abuse for argument. [...] I intend to tell Mr MacDonald when he returns from Geneva that he must refuse to take any young man into his Cabinet who hasn't seen *The Apple Cart* at least six times. It is intended as a salutary lesson, as I feel it is a state of things into which we could drift.[36]

Gauging from the general excitement and fanfare being flagged by the press, Shaw's decision to stage the world premiere of *The Apple Cart* on 14 June 1929 sent Warsaw's political and cultural elite into a tizzy. There was also a brief period of press speculation that Shaw was going to make the journey to Warsaw for the play's opening.[37] However, Shaw soon threw cold water on such hopes, informing Szyfman by letter that he would not be travelling to Poland on the grounds of poor health. Instead, he empowered his representative, Florian Sobieniowski, to fulfil all the various media and diplomatic obligations. By this time Sobieniowski had had more than fifteen years involvement in the staging of Shaw's plays and was adept at whipping up pre-premiere publicity. However, in the interviews prior to *The Apple Cart* premiere Sobieniowski often chose to speak more of his recent English translation of Wyspiański's *The Wedding* and its planned performances in the United States than Shaw's play.

The publicity campaign cranked into gear in early May with a series of separate press interviews with author and translator. However, it is clear that Sobieniowski and Shaw were more intent on talking up the premiere as an event in itself than speculating on any possible overlap between Poland's suspended parliament and the democratic system being lampooned in Shaw's new play. For this they often made recourse to the tried and trusted defence of 'art for art's sake':

> George Bernard Shaw drew attention to the fact that the political meaning of the play is appropriate to Poland and not just any country at this given moment in time. [...]

The play is supposed to be difficult to stage in the light of its seeming simplicity; it has a universal application. The translator assures us that the Warsaw staging of the play will be remembered as a work of art, and not as political propaganda.[38]

In an interview entitled 'A Cart with Apples and the Polish Atmosphere', Shaw jokingly suggested to his unrevealed interviewer that his translator had bullied him into first staging the play in Warsaw, or at least had been insistent on the point. But Shaw also considered in retrospect that perhaps the atmosphere of Poland best suited the first performance of the play,[39] a comment that rang as resounding praise of the current Polish political system.

Knowing that so many great names from the world of culture and politics would be present at the premiere performance, Szyfman must have felt a great deal of pressure to deliver the goods. Added to his stresses and strains was the knowledge that Piłsudski was also due to attend. And in many ways Szyfman's determination to make the play a success can be gauged by the extent of his editorial excisions of the translated manuscript.

Given the nature of the play and its subject matter, Sobieniowski's talents were never going to be allowed to shine. Only the idiomatic register of the ministers provided something of a blank canvas for the interpretation of buffoonery. The shortcomings of Sobieniowski's work were duly picked up on by Antoni Słonimski, who thought that the translator had produced a stilted and artificial piece.[40] Although in fairness to Sobieniowski, Słonimski did not know the extent to which the translated manuscript had been subjected to excisions.

Whilst admiring the spectacle of the play, Lorentowicz did wonder whether English theatre audiences, and more specifically, 'the intelligent citizen of London' would enjoy better the various allusions to their social and political world: 'By the nature of things, a Polish theatregoer will not experience the same emotions.'[41] However, there is in fact very little of England to be found in the play, and one contemporary British critic even went so far as to describe the country of The Apple Cart as the 'suits and trappings of Nonsense Land'.[42] Indeed, Lorentowicz soon contradicted his own assertion by stating that Polish audiences would readily connote the play with events closer to home; and it was, in fact, the ease by which this play made such a cultural transposition that had contributed to its success. Lorentowicz also speculated that the play was perhaps not a theatrical work. But he could not quite put his finger on what was amiss with the play, and almost straight away abandoned such musings and proceeded to a summary of the plot. But Jakub Appenszlak also felt the need to fish about for terminology in an attempt to classify the play, and he came up with the following assertion: 'It is the most original, eloquent, and stylistically distinguished, theatricalized political brochure that could ever be imagined.'[43]

The question that everyone wanted to ask that night was whether Piłsudski had thought highly of the play. And the president found a way of expressing his approval of the play by making recourse to some staged choreography. In the interval between the first and second act, Szyfman came out from behind the stage and joined Piłsudski, who was seated in the centre of the front row. Following a brief exchange of niceties, Piłsudski gave a short speech that praised the play's propagandistic value. The president then retook his seat before curtain call and honoured all present by graciously watching the play to the very end.[44]

This link between Shaw's king and the Polish president would turn out to be a continued selling-point of the play, as it provoked endless speculation as to whether Magnus and Piłsudski were one and the same. It was even suggested in the English newspapers that Piłsudski had commissioned Shaw to write the play. This was an accusation that goaded Shaw into making a formal statement to the British press, which was printed in *The Star* on 30 September 1929:

> I cannot claim the privilege of personal acquaintance with Marshal Piłsudski. I never dreamt of using him, or any other living person, as a model, though every living ruler in the world will find a melancholy resemblance between his predicament and that of King Magnus. I cannot avoid the suggestion that I have been paid by him, because it has already been made, and will probably be repeated *mutatis mutandis* in every country where the play is produced. Finally, as to the alleged more enthusiastic reception of *The Apple Cart* in Poland than in London, all I can say is that the reception in London has reached its box-office limit, and that Polish enthusiasm, however frenzied, can go no further from the author's point of view. Naturally, I am glad to learn that King Magnus's Crown fits the heads of all the rulers and that his subjects in all lands vie with one another in appreciation of my picture of their political situation. That is all I need say at present.

Afterwards, in a letter to Szyfman, Shaw dismissed such speculation as trivial and naïve, but he also added that 'the longer they speak about *The Apple Cart* then all the better for us, whether they write nonsense or not'.[45] But for all the speculation and sniping surrounding his role, we may imagine that Piłsudski was not displeased by either the play or its subsequent international perception. Shaw had sanctioned his 'reign'. What is more, Shaw was seemingly saying that Piłsudski's benevolence should be taken on trust.

Following the play's great success in Warsaw, Sobieniowski travelled to Malvern in England to take part as an honoured guest in a two-week long festival to celebrate the dramatic achievements of Shaw. He must have felt jubilant by what had transpired in Warsaw. However, such jubilation was not to last. It turned out that Shaw's German translator, Trebitsch, was incandescent with rage, contending that Shaw had given the Berlin Deutsches Theatre assurances that *The Apple Cart* would have its premiere in Berlin. But Sobieniowski was sure that he was on safe ground. He had checked with Shaw weeks before the Warsaw premiere as to the writer's commitments, and had received a letter back from Shaw, so stating, 'contradict all this nonsense flatly'.[46] But Shaw's German translator was not to be appeased. Indeed, as Shaw recounted to Szyfman in a letter dated 18 October 1929, Sobieniowski was fortunate to have left Malvern before the arrival of the German translator, as Trebitsch had been intent on settling a score with his Polish counterpart, and blood could have been the asking price.

Horzyca and the Morality of Mrs Warren

It was perhaps fitting that Lwów, the city that had seen off *Mrs Warren's Profession*, should play a part in its revival. The production was directed by Wilam Horzyca and came at the end of his turbulent tenure as director of Lwów's Municipal Theatre. In 1924, Horzyca had co-founded with Leon Schiller the Warsaw Theatre of W. Bogusławski, where he was content to work as a low-profile literary director and sounding board for Schiller. Both men believed in a literary theatre wherein a drama's words were understood as possessing a poetic magic that acted on intuition and the imagination, and that, in turn, proposed a Monumental theatre that would harness the grandiose visions and ideals of Poland's Romantic tradition.[47] In 1931, when Schiller lost his position as director of Lwów's Municipal Theatre due to his left-wing sympathies, Horzyca promptly re-employed Schiller and his team.[48] This arrangement also suited Horzyca, as he did not have to direct plays himself and could focus on formulating the theatre's artistic direction. However, six years after his appointment, and with his tenure coming to an acrimonious end following a protracted run of unsuccessful productions, Horzyca chose to take the directorial helm for Shaw's *The Dark Lady of the Sonnets* (1910), which was immediately followed by *Mrs Warren's Profession*. Working on these two plays led Horzyca to write about the staging of Shaw in the programmes for all of Horzyca's future productions of *Mrs Warren's Profession*.[49] For Horzyca, in so far as Shaw's characters think and act within the parameters of a given problem or idea, *Mrs Warren's Profession* depersonalizes the characters in order to serve a higher purpose. In this respect the director saw a link with morality plays, with Crofts, for example, as the embodiment of Vice, becoming for Horzyca a more authentic figure within the confines of the play's reality. What is more, for Horzyca, Shaw had found a way of turning the world on its head by mixing congenial speech with weighty sermonizing, an approach which amounted to selling truths that, in turn, became part of public discourse.[50]

The play had its first performance on 17 April 1937 in Lwów's Teatr Wielki [Great Theatre], and enjoyed a run of thirteen performances. One perspicacious review featured in *Gazeta Lwowska*[51] declared that *Mrs Warren's Profession* was different from many of Shaw's other plays because it proposed heavy moralizing without the distraction of pleasant goings-on and beautiful ladies, and could only offer the distressing tragedy of a young girl who suffers the kind of earth-shattering shock that few could come to terms with. However, this opinion was clearly formed by the fact that the actress playing Vivie had become more and more visibly upset as the play's action unfolded, and ultimately had been reduced to a nervous wreck by the time the curtain was brought down on the evening. That being said, the critic was left most affected by Mrs Warren's cries of the heart: 'we feel that from the stage there speaks a profound authority on the human soul'.[52]

If Horzyca had wished to put his seal on his time in Lwów with an artistic and commercial success, he had clearly managed to achieve his aim. Moreover, the success of the play may also have persuaded sceptics on the board of the National Theatre of Warsaw to offer him the position of Artistic Director, although many were surprised at his appointment. Indeed, an editorial in the newspaper *Dziennik Narodowy* [*The National Daily*] wondered how it was that someone who had made such a mess of things in a provincial theatre could have been gifted with a position of such national prominence.[53]

The Curtain Falls on Geneva

When Shaw visited the League of Nations in September 1928, which was headquartered in Geneva, he was impressed by the sea of international delegates who were endeavouring, often in indifferent French, to forge paths of internationalism. And whilst sceptical of the League's ambition to prevent war, and already convinced of the failure of democracy in Europe, Shaw did see that the social program of the League of Nations, which was carried out under the auspices of the International Labour Organisation, accorded with the ideals of his own Fabian gradualism, such as a determination to strengthen economic ties, improve working conditions and combat disease and famine. Shaw understood that if these transformative missions could be achieved within the context of political realities, then the righting of social injustice could force up 'the moral standards of the Big powers'.[54]

Shaw began writing his play *Geneva* in 1936 at a time when the League of Nations had been discredited by its failure to prevent satisfactorily, respond to, or resolve the Japanese invasion of Chinese Manchuria, the Italian invasion of Abyssinia and the German reoccupation of the Rhineland. And whilst he had lost what little faith he had had in the institution, Shaw remained most intrigued by the cultural arm of the League, which was the International Institute for Cultural Cooperation. The institute was chaired by Gilbert Murray, a celebrated classicist and long-term collaborator of the Irish playwright. Aided by a roomful of secretaries ready to type and duplicate, Gilbert spent much of his tenure writing a study on the comedies of Aristophanes, which he dedicated to Shaw. Matters turned full circle when Shaw chose to set the opening of what he described as a contemporary Greek comedy in the same Institute for Cultural Cooperation, on the third floor of a 'tumbled-down old house of rats'.[55]

Here a series of visitors arrive and present their demands to the normally underworked secretary Bergonia Brown. One aggrieved plaintiff, for example, is a German Jew who complains about anti-Semitism in his country, whereas another plaintiff is an elderly English bishop who is angered by the fact that his footman has converted to communism. Bergonia ends up forwarding these complaints to the International Court at the Hague, and such an unprecedented initiative sets in train a series of events that leads to three European dictators – all of whom are strongly caricatured – being arraigned for having destroyed the liberty of Europe. During this trial, which takes place in the third act, each of these troublemakers gives unchallenged accounts of their actions. Hitler dressed in Wagnerian garb and going by the name of Herr Battler argues that he has saved Germany from a loss of face; Mussolini goes by the name of Bombardone and, attired as a helmeted Roman

Emperor, maintains that war harnesses courage. Finally, General Franco is represented by General Flanco de Fortinbras, who extols the virtues of governance by gentlemen.

This problematic third act was meant to represent a response to external events, but Shaw would choose to make many rewrites, as unfolding contemporary events began to outrun those being presented in the play. The play's genial quips and satirical commentary delivered much that audiences could delight in. However, popular reception would remain at odds with the critical readings of the play, which were perhaps more attuned to *Geneva's* darker portents. Indeed, the rapturous reception given to the play when it was staged for the first time at the Malvern Theatre Festival, which took place on 1 August 1938, greatly dismayed Alan Dent, a theatre critic for the *Spectator*:

> The Malvern audience only needs a little more intelligence to make it all that a festival audience ought to be. The opening play, Mr Shaw's long-awaited *Geneva* called on that intelligence and found it lacking. Over and over again, it let out indiscriminate whoops of laughter at things which Mr Shaw obviously meant for serious statements. The shrug with which this political exposition concludes is a genuinely despairing one, and the sallies which lead up to this are food only for thoughtful laughter, if laugh we must at the exposure of our plight.[56]

Given Germany's absorption of Czechoslovakia four months earlier in March 1939, Arnold Szyfman's decision to stage *Geneva* was audacious and provocative, particularly when we consider that Poland was in the immediate sense directly exposed to the very plight that Alan Dent had intimated. But Szyfman must have been determined that the tradition of accepting new plays by Shaw would not be interrupted by crisis. Shaw himself does not seem to have been particularly bothered by the potential risks that the play posed for Szyfman and his company. Indicative of Shaw's nonchalance in this regard is an undated letter that he wrote to Sobieniowski, which accompanied an amended manuscript of *Geneva*.[57] In the same letter Shaw made no enquiry as to the atmosphere or conditions in Poland, or indeed any related matter. Instead, he simply wrote that the cuts he had made to the play would make it possible to 'finish in a little over three hours', and concluded with a Shavian transition to monetary matters: 'Any edition of the play in which your translation is used is subject to your copyright and to mine. Any illustration would introduce the same copyright.'

The day after *Geneva's* Warsaw premiere, which took place on 25 July 1939, Szyfman was called into the Ministry for Internal Affairs and questioned at length on the merits of continuing to perform the play. Szyfman only managed to dissuade the Ministry from closing down the production by arguing that such a move would give the wrong signal to both Poland's western allies and its German adversaries. His stance was very much in keeping with a widely held view at the time that Polish artists should confront the perils of the moment. However, not all were of this opinion. Antoni Słonimski, in his 'Weekly Chronicle' for *Wiadomości Literackie* [*Literary News*] felt the need to respond to the impatient calls of the gazette *Polska Zbrojna* [*Armed Poland*] for Polish artists to rally to the defence of the nation.[58] However, Słonimski, whilst understanding the imperatives of an artistic 'call to arms', explained that art needs the perspective of time, and that such invectives were best directed at journalists, whose vocation would test their utilitarian ideals to the limits in the weeks and months ahead. Słonimski could just as easily have chosen to select cabaret artists to fulfil this patriotic role, as recent months had seen several revues choosing to send up the likes of Hitler and his henchmen. The most famous example of this was the Panopticum cabaret performed in the recently opened Ali Baba Theatre, which boasted sketches parodying Hitler, Mussolini and Chamberlain. The Hitler character was taken on by Ludwik Sempoliński, who had gone to great lengths to incorporate traits of Charlie Chaplin's tramp into his impersonation of the Fuhrer. The revue opened in July 1939 to packed houses, but soon German agents attended and sometime after the German Embassy lodged a direct complaint with the Polish Ministry for Internal Affairs, which subsequently bowed to this pressure and agreed to the sending of a Polish-German delegation to observe a performance. The commission instantly decided that Hitler had to be removed from the sketches and be replaced by Joseph Goebbels. Sempoliński recalled that the most disappointed enthusiasts of the revue were Jewish people, many of whom did not speak Polish, but who had enjoyed the visual spectacle and the caricaturing of the very man who had brought such uncertainty to their future.[59]

Like the cabaret *Panopticum, Geneva* enjoyed success in Warsaw for many of the same reasons, even though critics were mostly of the opinion that the play was an artistic failure. Generally they felt that it was hopelessly out of kilter with the present course of events, and that the actors playing the dictators had been so caught up in the seriousness of the arguments being presented that they had forgotten entirely about their comedic timing. This criticism was aimed in particular at Józef Węgrzyn, who played the role of Battler not as a contemporary Hitler, but as a more youthful Hitler, who was merely aping the gestures of Mussolini.[60]

Geneva played for forty-one nights, and its run would only be interrupted by the bombardment of Warsaw. Those who attended the final performances must have been laughing through gritted teeth as the country mobilized for an imminent invasion. Szyfman was advised to leave Warsaw immediately on account of his being Jewish, and also for the fact that his staging of *Geneva* would almost certainly lead to his arrest.[61] Józef Węgrzyn also had cause to regret his involvement with the production, for not only had his performance been almost universally panned, but following the invasion, he was arrested by the Gestapo for having lampooned the Fuhrer, and placed in Pawiak prison. Like Węgrzyn, Sempoliński was hunted by the Gestapo for having committed the same crime, and the actor was forced to go into hiding and remain so for the duration of the war. Whatever the motivations Szyfman had had for staging *Geneva*, he would have cause for considering its legacy. One thing is clear, however: *Geneva* provided Warsaw theatregoers with an opportunity to laugh at the absurdity of European politics one last time, before a cruel reality presented itself and changed their lives immeasurably and most horrifically.

When *Geneva* closed in London and went on tour around Britain, the country was at war. By this time, the play featured a joke that made mention of Battler's invasion of 'Ruritania', meaning Poland. As Stanley Weintraub writes: 'It was less than funny',[62] and indeed the thoughtless nature of the rewrite indicates the detached attitude that Shaw seemingly had for a country that had been blindly loyal towards his work to the very end.

Notes

1 Kornel Makuszyński, *Kurier Warszawski*, 198 (1935). See also Patrick Quigley, *The Polish Irishman. The Life and Times of Count Casimir Markiewicz*, 163–164.

2 Kornel Makuszyński, *Kurier Warszawski*, 198 (1935).

3 Arnold Szyfman, *Labyrint teatru*, 209.

4 Arnold Szyfman, *Labyrint teatru*, 210.

5 Arnold Szyfman, *Labyrint teatru*, 214.

6 See Lissadell Estate website: http://www.constancemarkievicz.ie/1917-1927.php. Accessed 12 April 2013.

7 See Eoin MacWhite, 'A Russian Pamphlet on Ireland by Count Markievicz', *Irish University Review*, I (1) (Autumn, 1970), 98–110.

8 Arnold Szyfman, *Labyrint teatru* [*The Theatre Labyrinth*], 220.

9 Mieczysław Fijałkowski, *Uśmiechy lat minionych*, 261.

10 Emil Breiter, 'Teatr Rozmaitości, *Marta* Markiewicza', *Gazeta Polska* (4 March 1918), 3.

11 '...rozumiał tylko biologiczną stronę życia.' *Gazeta Polska* (4 March 1918), 3.

12 Stanisław Pieńkowski, 'Teatr Polski. *Major Barbara*, komedya w 3 aktach Bernarda Shawa', *Gazeta Warszawska*, 299 (1919), 5.

13 Stefan Krzywoszewski, 'Z teatrów warszawskich', *Świat*, 40–48 (1919), 13.

14 Władysław Rabski, *Teatr po wojnie. Premiery warszawskie 1918–1924* (Warszawa: Wydawnictwo: Biblioteka Dzieł Wyborowych, 1925), 162–164.

15 See Adolf Nowaczyński, *Szkice literackie* (Poznań: Nakładem Spółki Wydawniczej Ostoja, 1918), 59–70.

16 See Joan Fitzpatrick Dean, 'The Riot in Westport, George A. Birmingham at Home', *New Hibernia Review*, 5 (4) (Winter, 2001), 9–21.

17 Joan Fitzpatrick Dean, 'The Riot in Westport, George A. Birmingham at Home', *New Hibernia Review* 5 (4) (Winter, 2001), 9–21. *New Hibernia Review*, 5 (4) (Winter, 2001), 12.

18 '*Nowe Ateny* zostały przez krytkę przyjęte niedobrze. Nie wchodziły tu w grę ani względy polityczne, ani społeczne. Sztuka miała zbyt wiele błędów konstrukcyjnych i pospolitych nietaktów.' Arnold Szyfman, *Labyrint teatru* [*The Theatre Labyrinth*] (Warszawa: Wydawnictwo Artystyczne i Filmowe, 1964), 139.

19 'Nowaczyński nie należał bowiem do pisarzy umiejących skorzystać z najbardziej nawet fachowej i przyjacielskiej rady, zwłaszcza po ostatnich wielkich sukcesach teatralnych, tak w Krakowie, jak i w Warszawie. W tym względzie był przeciwieństwem Włodzimierza Perzyńskiego, w późniejszych zaś latach – Jarosława Iwaszkiewicza.' Arnold Szyfman, *Labyrint teatru* [*The Theatre Labyrinth*] (Warszawa: Wydawnictwo Artystyczne i Filmowe, 1964), 132.

20   In some areas of the city a number of Germans were still holding out and shots could be heard for several months. See Kazimierz Wierzyński, 'Dziennik poety', *Tygodnik Powszechny*, 42 (1983), 7.

21   'Grupa nasza już w grudniu 1918 roku wytrzymała próbę solidarności, z której wyszła zwycięsko.' Jarosław Iwaszkiewicz, *Książka moich wspomnień* (Kraków: Wydawnictwo Literackie, 1957), 173.

22   Jarosław Iwaszkiewicz, *Książka moich wspomnień* (Kraków: Wydawnictwo Literackie, 1957), 173–175. See also a letter from Mieczysław Grydzewski to Iwaszkiewicz dated 10 October 1957. 'Ani ty, ani Leszek, ani Antoni nie gwizdaliście: oklaskiwaliście głupie miejsca. Witkowski i Świdwiński nie sekundowali, przeciwnie: sztuka się im podobała, może dlatego, że od lat nie byli w teatrze i nie reagowali. Nie byliśmy przetrzymywani kilku godzin w kryminale, spisano protokół, to wszystko.' ['Neither you nor Leszek nor Antoni whistled: you clapped in stupid places. Witkowski and Świdwiński didn't back you up. The opposite in fact: they liked the play: maybe they didn't react because they hadn't been to the theatre for years. We weren't kept in custody for long. They filled in a report and that was all.']. Ed. Malgorzata Bojanowska, *Mieczysław Grydzewski LISTY 1922–1967 Jarosław Iwaszkiewicz* (Warsaw: Czytelnik, 1997), 116.

23   '… ani Schiller, ani ja nie byliśmy zwolennikami twórczości teatralnej Krzywoszewskiego.' ['Neither Schiller nor I were enthusiasts of Krzywoszewski's theatrical works.']. Arnold Szyfman, *Labyrint teatru* [*The Theatre Labyrinth*] (Warszawa: Wydawnictwo Artystyczne i Filmowe, 1964), 273.

24   Jarosław Iwaszkiewicz, *Książka moich wspomnień* (Kraków: Wydawnictwo Literackie, 1957), 175.

25   'Samego Kasprowicza nie lubiłem. Przyjeżdżał czasem do Warszawy i siedział w "Astorii" przy wielkim ołtarzu, to znaczy przy stoliku Kornela Makuszyńskiego. Był tam Kazimierz Dunin-Markiewicz, czasem Stefan Żeromski, czasem, Karol Szymanowski, zerkający znudzonym wzrokiem w naszą stronę – no oczywiście Kornel z żoną, Emmą. My "skamandryci" kłanialiśmy się nieśmiało z daleka.' Jarosław Iwaszkiewicz, *Marginalia* (Warszawa: Interim, 1993), 12.

26   *Gazeta Poranna 2 Grosze* (6 December 1924).

27   See Alice Griffen, 'The New York Critics and "Saint Joan"', *Bulletin* (*Shaw Society of America*) 7 (January 1950), 10–15.

28   See Brian Tyson, *The Story of Shaw's St. Joan* (Quebec: The McGill-Queens University Press, 1982), 87.

29   Cited in Brian Tyson, *The Story of Shaw's St. Joan*, 95.

30   Brian Tyson, *The Story of Shaw's St. Joan*, 98.

31   See Emil Breiter, 'Teatr Polski, "Święta Joanna" Bernarda Shaw', *Świat* (13 December 1924). However, no less than a month later Władysław Zawistowski had the occasion to hail to publication of the play with publishers Wacław Czarski i S-ka, and he hailed Sobieniowski's archaic translation. So clearly opinions amongst critics had been divided. See also Witold Zawistowski, 'Święta Joanna', *Kurjer Polski* (19 January 1925), 3.

32   Bohdan Korzeniewski, 'Shaw dzisiaj u nas', *Pamiętnik Teatralny*, 1 (1956), 247–259.

33   '… dialekt dotąd nieznany pięknej mowie polskiej.' Bohdan Korzeniewski, *Pamiętnik Teatralny*, 1 (1956), 256.

in a form that is both unexpected and surprising. Only in this way may he sell truths which retain some sort of permanence.'] Wilam Horzyca, *Teatr*, 2 (1952), 223.

51 Article signed 'zastępca' ['replacement' / 'deputising'], '*Profesja pani Warren*', *Gazeta Lwowska*, 88 (1937), 3.

52 'czujemy, że ze sceny przemawia głęboki znawca duszy ludzkiej', *Gazeta Lwowska*, 88 (1937).

53 See Lidia Kuchtówna, *Pamiętnik Teatralny*, 2–4 (150–152) (1989), 225.

54 See Michael Holroyd, *Bernard Shaw*, 719.

55 Cited in Michael Holroyd, *Bernard Shaw*, 720.

56 See Alan Dent, 'Notice', *Spectator*, 161 (5 August 1938), 232. Cited in *Shaw: The Critical Heritage* (London/New York: Routledge, 1976), 357–358.

57 Extracts of the letter were cited in: From Our Special Correspondent, 'Poland's Long Connexion With Shaw's Plays', *The Times* (31 December 1956).

58 See Antoni Słonimski, 'Kronika Tygodniowa', *Wiadomości Literackie*, 31 (1939), 5.

59 See Ludwik Sempoliński, *Wielcy mistrzowie małych scen* (Warszawa: Czytelnik, 1968), 529. Cited in Tomasz Mościcki's *Teatry Warszawy 1939: kronika* (Warszawa: Bellona 2009), 256–257.

60 See for example, Irena Krzywicka, '*Genewa*', *Robotnik*, 212 (1939), 4; and Antoni Słonimski, '*Genewa* w Teatrze Polskim', *Wiadomości Literackie*, 33 (1939), 5.

61 See Arnold Szyfman, *Moja wojenna tułaczka* (Warszawa: Wydawnictwo Ministerstwa Obrony Narodowej, 1960), 14.

62 See Stanley Weintraub, 'GBS and the Despots', *The Times Literary Supplement* (22 August 2011). Available at: http://www.the-tls.co.uk/tls/public/article707002.ece. Accessed 14 July 2014.

Chapter 3

Walking on Eggshells: Irish Drama in the Post-War Era (1945–1960)

Introduction: Post-war Social Realism and the Re-emergence of *Mrs Warren*

With the establishment of the Repertoire Commission and Advisory Committee in 1946, the stable continuance and integrity of Polish Theatre seemed assured, particularly given the presence on the commission of figures such as Arnold Szyfman and Leon Schiller, both of whom also had prominent roles in the newly formed Theatre Council.[1] In 1947 the Ministry for Culture and Art brought Poland's main theatres under governmental control, which ensured that professional theatre companies were well funded. But of course, this generosity came with a catch, wherein the government reserved the right to interfere in theatre repertoires and budgets.[2] Even more worryingly, by 1949 theatres had begun to be infiltrated by card-carrying Party technical staff and artisans looking to promote the cause of a proletariat theatre. Also that year, the Professional Association of Polish Writers launched a competition to encourage dramatists to produce social realist drama, and in the months that followed the best adjudged plays were distributed amongst Polish Theatre directors, who had to grit their teeth and stage them.[3] However, some theatres fared better than others under such inscrutable conditions. And one theatre that managed to retain a great deal of freedom in deciding upon its own repertoire was Warsaw's Teatr Współczesny [Contemporary Theatre], whose administrative director was Erwin Axer, a giant of post-war Polish Theatre. Axer blind-sided any potential Russification policies by positing the artistic aims of the theatre as those that entailed the staging of contemporary European drama that was socially engaged, and which would help people to overcome the difficulties that everyday life posed.[4] The theatre also placed its activities on a commercial footing, and chose to focus on a small repertoire, wherein plays were expected to run for several months. An unusual decision, however, was to stage the new production of *Mrs Warren's Profession*, which after the war had been taken up for performance by Leon Schiller, who had been made the artistic director of Łódź's Teatr Powszechny TUR [People's Theatre TUR]. The play, which had its premiere on 26 June 1947, was directed by Stanisław Daczyński, who also played the part of Praed. In celebration of the fact that Łódź had relaunched Shaw in post-war Poland, the pamphlet *Łódź Teatralna* [*Theatrical Łódź*] dedicated an entire issue to Shaw. This, in turn, included an overview article penned by Tadeusz Grzebieniowski entitled 'G.B. Shaw i jego sztuka' ['G.B. Shaw and his Play'], which, in mentioning *Mrs Warren's Profession*, emphasized Shaw's campaign against the 'crime of poverty'. Elsewhere in the pamphlet was G. K. Chesterton's 1909 essay entitled 'G. B. Shaw', which treated Shaw's determination to speak of 'useful attitudes', which certainly had a nation-(re)building aspiration that could not have been lost on people still moving about amongst the city's bombed-out ruins. The remaining pieces featured Shaw's eulogy of communist Russia, delivered in Malvern in 1929, where the dramatist had praised the Soviet Union as a great Fabian experiment. This extract was complemented by an article written by Russian critic Anatoly Vasilyevich Lunacharsky, who hailed the revolutionary power of Shaw, speculating that had Shaw lived in Shelley's time, he would have shared the poet's fate in being forced out of the country by England's bourgeoisie. Lunacharsky recalled meeting a Scottish socialist who had proclaimed that Shaw's extravagances in offending every sacred English ideal could be put down to the fact that he belonged to 'the lesser race of the Irish'. As we may deduce, much of what appeared in the pamphlet was so presented as to not give England an inch and hail the fact that Shaw's natural homes were Poland and the Soviet Union. In all, the play enjoyed a run of thirty-five performances and played to fourteen-thousand theatregoers, a figure that must have confirmed in no uncertain terms that Shaw would continue to have an enduring appeal in the new era.

Horzyca re-entered this story when he staged *Mrs Warren's Profession* in Poznań's Teatr Dramatyczny [Dramatic Theatre] in February 1950. The following year, he took the play to Warsaw's Contemporary Theatre, and it was this particular production, which had its premiere on 30 November 1951, that proved to be the high point of Horzyca's directorial career. For many the play was so provocative that it seemed like a new and exciting work that reflected on the tumultuous times of the here and now. It was also greeted as a celebration of the new political system in Poland that had done away with a capitalism that had allowed vice to 'cripple human life'. In turn, it seems that Horzyca had by this time managed to attune the play more to his vision of the drama as a morality play. For now the way in which Vivie absorbed and reacted to the series of revelations was shown as evidence of her own flawed nature. In other words, she had always been a victim of her own illusory existence, even though she was still perhaps not cognisant of this fact by the end of the play. However, this 'depersonalizing' of the cast was ultimately undermined by the powerhouse performance delivered by the acclaimed actress Irena Eichlerówna who played Mrs Warren.[5] Indeed, Horzyca must have been ruefully mindful of the fact that by allowing his star actress to outperform everyone else, he had contravened Shaw's rejection of perfect plays written around popular performers.

Understandably, reviewers were particularly intrigued by Vivie and were keen to discuss her character as a critique of the capitalist system. This question was taken up by Alfred Degal at the end of January, by which time the play had been playing for more than a month.[6] According to Degal, Mrs Warren was a negative character, whereas her profession was blameless, as it arose out of the inherent injustices built into the capitalist system. However, he saw Vivie as a positive character by virtue of the fact that she was forging her own life through the pursuit of honest work. Notwithstanding, the publication of a diametrically divergent opinion in the same newspaper a few days later, stating that Mrs Warren was positive and passionate and that Vivie was cold and self-centred, set in train a

34 '... bo wielki ciężar zdołała udźwignąć. Shaw byłby zadowolny z tego portretu szlachetnej, naiwnej dziewczyny, o oczach szczególnie pięknych w chwilach uniesienia.' Jakub Appensziak, 'Scena Polska', *Nasz Przegląd*, (5 December 1924), 3.

35 'Głównymi powodami obecnego stanu rzeczy w Polsce – to jest nędzy, słabizny wewnętrznej i zewnętrznej – były złodziejstwa, pozostające bezkarne. Ponad wszystkim w Polsce zapanował interes jednostki i partii, zapanowała bezkarność za wszelkie nadużycia i zbrodnie. Wydałem wojnę szujom, łajdakom, mordercom i złodziejom i w walce tej nie ulegnę. Sejm i senat mają nadmiar przywilejów i należałoby, aby ci, którzy powołani są do rządów, mieli więcej praw. Parlament winien odpocząć. Dajcie możność rządzącym odpowiadać za to, czego dokonają. Niech Prezydent tworzy rząd, ale bez nacisku partyj. To jest jego prawo.' [Speech delivered by Marshal Jófef Piłsudski to the Polish Sejm on 29 May 1926. Polish State Archives.]

36 George Bernard Shaw, *The Apple Cart* (London: Constable and Company Ltd, 1930), vi–vii.

37 Jan Lorentowicz, *Dwadzieścia lat teatru,* Vol. II, 187.

38 'George Bernard Shaw uczynił uwagę, że polityczny sens sztuki bardziej stosuje się do Polski, niż do jakiegokolwiek innego kraju w danym momencie. [...] Sztuka ma być trudna do przedstawienia wobec jej pozornej prostoty; ma zastosowanie uniwersalne. Tłumacz zapewnia, iż postara się aby przedstawienie warszawskie pamiętało, że to jest dzieło sztuki, a nie politycznej propogandy.' 'Stragan z jabłkami i atmosfera polska', *Przedświt*, 129 (1929). For similar comments, see also R. C., 'Wywiad z Polskim Tłumaczem Sztuki Shawa', *Scena Polska*, 10 (1929), 14–15.

39 'Stragan z jabłkami i atmosfera polska', *Express Poranny*, (22 May 1929).

40 Antoni Słonimski, '*Wielki Kram*', *Wiadomości Literackie*, 25 (1929), 4.

41 'Widz polski, z natury rzeczy, nie może doznać podobnego uczucia.' Jan Lorentowicz, *Dwadzieścia lat teatru,* Vol. II, 181.

42 See Ivor Brown, *Manchester Guardian* (August 1929), cited in Tom. F. Evans (ed.), *George Bernard Shaw. The Critical Heritage* (London and New York: Routledge, 1999), 316.

43 'Jest to raczej najbardziej oryginalna, wykwintna, i dystyngowana w stylu, uteatralizowana broszura polityczna jaką można sobie wyobrazić.' Jakub Appenszlak, 'Wielka satyra polityczna B.Shawa w Teatrze Polskim', *Nasz Przegląd*, 164 (1929), 9.

44 Jan Lorentowicz, *Dzień Polski* (18 June 1929), cited in Edward Krasiński, *Teatr Polski Arnolda Szyfmana 1913–1939* (Warszawa: Wydawnictwo Naukowe PWN, 1991), 221.

45 Florian Sobieniowski, 'Wspomnienia tłumacza', *Teatr*, 9–10 (1936), 18.

46 Loose-leaf letter. The Polish Theatre Museum of Warsaw.

47 See Wilam Horzyca, *Polski teatr monumentalny* (Wrocław: Wiedza i Kultura, 1994).

48 See Lidia Kuchtówna, 'Wilam Horzyca (1889–1959): kronika życia i działalności', *Pamiętnik Teatralny* 2–4 (150–152) (1989), 213–214. See also 'Dyrektor Horzyca obejmuje jutro Teatry Lwowskie: specjalny wywiad Słowa Polskiego', *Słowo Polskie*, 5 (1932), 2.

49 The article was also published in the monthly journal *Teatr*. See Wilam Horzyca, 'O *Profesji pani Warren*. Uwagi reżysera', *Teatr* 2 (1952), 222–223.

50 '... aby więc trafić do uszu słuchacza, musi treść tę ubrać w kształt możliwie najbardziej nieoczekiwany i zaskakujący. Tylko w ten sposób można sprzedać prawdy, które jeszcze nie przemijają.' ['... so in order to reach the ears of the listener he has to dress his message up

circular argument as to the rights and wrongs of the stances taken by mother and daughter. In realization of this, some critics concluded that this level of confusion and ambiguity was what Shaw had had in mind all the time, and that he was neither looking to deal solely with prostitution nor pull at heartstrings and ask theatregoers to take sides.

Aside from the commercial success that the play had enjoyed with its ultimate run of one hundred and forty-four performances, Horzyca was very gratified to learn from the theatre's manager, Erwin Axer, that Bertolt Brecht had attended the play and had been greatly impressed with Horzyca's interpretation of *Mrs Warren's Profession* as a morality play. Brecht told Axer that the production should be shown in Berlin, although he also quickly added that a new stage set design would have to be conceived, whilst also recommending that some members of the cast be replaced. Axer relayed these comments in their totality to Horzyca. From a joyful letter to his wife dated 'III 1952', it is easy to discern from Horzyca's gratification that such generous praise was a rarity in his world: 'Just look! It took Brecht to come from abroad for them to see that once again (my) Warren is not so nonsensical.'[7] Sadly, Horzyca was unable to bask in this success for long. Before the play had even completed its run, Horzyca began rehearsing Alexander Ostrovsky's *The Forest* (1871) for Warsaw's National Theatre. However, Horzyca's mystical interpretation did not sit well with the new managers of the theatre, Bohdan Korzeniewski and Marian Meller, who had been tasked with implementing the principles of social realism. Korzeniewski and Meller sat in on the rehearsals and offered suggestions that were little more than couched warnings. Horzyca tried to dismiss such interference and thought he could brazen things out. However, when Korzeniewski and Meller moved against him, no quarter was shown. Korzeniewski fired Horzyca just weeks before the opening of the play, and took over the directorial reins. To add insult to injury, Horzyca's name was removed from the poster.[8]

As a further post-scriptum to this episode, Horzyca was fortunate to be offered the directorship of Wrocław's Dramatic Theatre, a role that he occupied between the years 1952 and 1955. However, his determination to keep with his monumental style in defiance of social realism made him the constant target of attacks from those bent on bowing to the egregious demands of the genre. And even his decision to stage *Mrs Warren's* Profession could not rescue him from his travails. Initially reluctant to re-stage the play, he was swayed by the persuasions of Irena Eichlerówna, who wanted to revive the part of Mrs Warren. However, if she had put the Warsaw cast in the shade, she strode like a colossus on the stage in Wrocław. It was soon painfully obvious that compared to Eichlerówna, the cast was third rate. Equally bothersome was the casting of Vivie. Although the part had been given to Renata Fiałkowska, Horzyca had wished for the role to go to his assistant, Halina Dzieduszycka, whom he wanted to relaunch as an actress. Initially, Eichlerówna did not agree to such a change, but then Fiałkowska, who was heavily pregnant, began to show signs of her condition. Life truly encroached on art when the audience began to suspect that Frank had had his way with Vivie, and that the bump was part of the plot. And so it was agreed to release Fiałkowska and replace her with Horzyca's favoured protégée.[9]

Shelley Won't Save Us

At the time of his Polish premiere, Sean O'Casey was largely a forgotten figure of the English-speaking theatre, particularly in his adopted England. With the exception of his Dublin Trilogy, few of his plays had been staged since the late 1920s, and indeed when they were brought to the attention of playgoers, they received only one or two productions.[10] However, early in 1955, O'Casey regained some of his old notoriety with the staging of *The Bishop's Bonfire* (1955) in Dublin's Gaiety Theatre. Given the anticlerical bias of the play, treating as it did the ferocious chastity of the Irish, it is hardly surprising that the Irish bishops had cast advance pre-premiere aspersions on the production. Consequently, those playgoers that came to see the play were a mix of loyal Catholic provocateurs and genuine theatre enthusiasts.[11] The trouble that followed could almost be regarded as a commemorative, yet pallid re-enactment of the riot that had greeted the Abbey's staging of *The Plough and the Stars* in 1926. With the galleries filled to capacity, as many as seven-hundred hopefuls were left outside on the street. They were soon joined by riot police expecting trouble. However, just prior to curtain call, those who were seated in the front row left their seats and emerged from the theatre to tout their tickets, fearing that they would be the unwitting targets of eggs and rotten tomatoes. Though the performance of the play was greeted with hisses and applause in equal measure, no riot ensued. An unnamed international correspondent for *Time* suggested that a riot had not taken place because the play had not been worth rioting over. It was simply one of many plays in Dublin that got hissed at when it caused offense.[12] At least with the staging of *The Shadow of a Gunman* in Warsaw, which had its premiere on 20 July 1955, it can be said that O'Casey's work met with a kinder reception. It may indeed just be that Zygmunt Hübner together with Bronisław Pawlik, both completing their degrees in theatrical direction with The National Higher School of Theatre in Warsaw, decided to stage O'Casey's *The Shadow of a Gunman*, translated as *Cień bohatera* [*Shadow of a Hero*], because the Irish playwright had been the subject of a growing interest in the USSR.[13] The prospective directors, who were employed on the basis of an apprenticeship programme, may also have been convinced that the staging of the play would not attract the wrong sort of attention from the censors.[14]

And indeed, judging from the surviving translated manuscript held at the theatre in which it was staged, their text was left unmolested by any outside hand. Never having previously undertaken to translate anything of note, Hübner and Pawlik worked together on the translation of the play. Undoubtedly it was a task that would have counted in their favour when it came to an official academic assessment of their work. They also enjoyed help from literary scholar and Oscar Wilde enthusiast, Juliusz Żuławski, who not only translated the play's songs and poems, but also must have proved invaluable when it came to providing literary and textual advice. It would certainly explain how two young greenhorn graduates with a limited knowledge of Irish history and even less familiarity with Dublin inner-city speech managed to produce such an accurate translation. Some indication of the background research that went into the production is the play programme itself, which featured a glossary of terms relating to the Irish War of Independence – the Black and Tans were awarded a particularly salacious entry. Also included was an open letter from O'Casey to the German public, which may have coincided with the performance of the play in Berlin a few months previously. The letter was entitled 'The Task of the Dramatist', in it he mostly spoke about the reluctance of theatre directors to accept new material. Clearly O'Casey had been lamenting his own misfortunes.

The Shadow of a Gunman offers a coloured microcosm of slum-life in Dublin during the time of the Irish War of Independence. The hero of the piece, if we may say that, is poet Donal Davoren, who is holed up in his room writing poor poetry, 'Or when sweet Summer's ardent arms outspread', which could be said to closely resemble the escapist Symbolist poetry of the Young Poland era. Shields, his roommate and the official tenant, is deep in arrears with the landlord. Their place of dwelling, once a resplendent Georgian returning room, is now dirty and slovenly kept; and the only colour to be found in the room is a bunch of wild flowers that have been placed on the desk beside Davoren's typewriter. In spite of Davoren's poetic status, 'an aesthete, an intrusive element in the environment, hoping for a quiet room in which to write his poetry', he is accursed with an indolence and paralysis that James Joyce had ascribed to his Ireland.[15] Davoren's torpor contrasts sharply with his lofty Shelleyan decrees and allusions to Shelley's heroic and self-sacrificing Prometheus. Hardly surprisingly, Davoren is out of place in the slums, and this leads other tenants to believe that he is a gunman on the run. When in a flirtatious exchange, the pretty wide-eyed Minnie Powell suggests that he is precisely whom they all suspect him to be, Donal does nothing to deny any of it, so saying, 'a fellow gets used to it after a bit, till at last, a gunman throws a bomb as carelessly as a schoolboy throws a snowball'. This pantomime boast is repeated to the other tenants of the building, who are all greatly honoured to think that they are in the company of a fighting patriot. Feckless young Tommy Owens, who roars patriotic songs and thinks he has the inside track with Davoren, offers his services to the cause, and declares that he is not afraid to die for his country. Things take on an even more farcical turn when Mr Gallagher and Mrs Henderson present their resident gunman with a letter addressed to the Gentlemen of the Irish Republican Army, requesting of them that they sort out the noisy neighbours in the backroom, 'whose language is something abominable and shocking'. The second act will see the consequences of Davoren's mendacity play out and unravel.

In the first scene, Mulligan, an acquaintance of Shields, has left a parcel for Shields to mind whilst he is off on a clandestine trip to 'catch butterflies'. Though Shields knows of Mulligan's conspiratorial activities, he fails to disclose this to his roommate. And when the Black and Tans raid the house, Davoren finds out that Tommy Owens has been bragging to all and sundry in the pub of his acquaintance with a General in the IRA, adding that he knows where bombs are being hidden. Realizing that the auxiliaries will search the room, Davoren and Shields decide to open the bag and to their terror and consternation find that it is in fact filled with bombs. Minnie runs in and takes the bombs to her room, 'if they do itself they won't harm a girl. Goodbye …. Donal'. She is not stopped by Davoren or Shields.

The auxiliaries ransack the home and find the bombs in Minnie's room. She struggles as they arrest her and shouts 'Up the Republic'. Shields hears her heroic defiance but cannot have the auxiliaries take her away soon enough, so saying 'God grant she won't say anything. Are they gone, Mrs Grigson?' When the convoy taking Minnie away is ambushed, we hear that she was shot trying to escape. Davoren despairs, but in his desolation he can only make recourse to his favoured Shelleyan contention 'Pain, pain, pain for ever!'

Coming to the reception of the play, from the outset we may wonder about the divide between what the Polish playgoers thought had taken place during Ireland's War of Independence, amply presented in the theatre programme, containing as it did authentic historical pictures and an overview, and the buffoonery and cowardice on display in the play. But in saying this, mistrust and derision of the masses had been a common trope of modernist Polish inter-war literature. And the following lines of a poem by Julian Tuwim amply illustrate this notion: 'Straszne mieszkania. W strasznych mieszkaniach / Strasznie mieszkają straszni mieszczanie' ['Terrible living. In terrible flats / Terrible dwellers live terribly'].[16] However, it is clear that the play struck a personal chord with playgoers, who themselves had had to contend with the horrors of Nazi occupation not so long previously: 'we know everything only too well from occupied Warsaw'.[17] Of course, in O'Casey's play the British are the accused standing in the dock, a fact not lost on the critics, who saw little in the play to distinguish between the two occupations. Indeed, according to August Grodzicki, during the war, Warsaw had also had its share of farcical pseudo-conspirators.[18]

One critic with a unique take on the play was George Bidwell, who, whilst working for the British Council in post-war Warsaw, had fallen in love with a Polish woman and had thrown in his lot wholly with Poland.[19] Bidwell's review of the play for the magazine *Przegląd Kulturalny* [*The Cultural Review*] was straightforwardly entitled 'Sean O'Casey', and was one of his earliest pieces of journalism in his newly adopted country. This most likely came about from his frequent personal correspondence with O'Casey, which he also wrote about in the review. It is a review in which Bidwell's socialist leanings are amply in evidence. Bidwell saw the actions of the Black and Tans as being the result of all imperialist methods of occupation, whether they be German, French or British. And here he spoke of the play's current relevance, given the military operations being carried out in places such as Kenya, Malaysia, Cyprus and North Africa. Unsurprisingly, Bidwell omitted to mention the USSR's prolific post-war military conquests, nor indeed did he miss the opportunity to do some communist banner-waving:

For years he has understood one thing – together with Picasso, Joliot-Curie, Aragon, Éluard, Andersen, Nexø, and Dreiser – that communism means the greatest service for mankind, a life put to the fullest use.[20]

Whilst generally positive about the play, Bidwell, like the Polish reviewers, was left unimpressed by the central performance of Andrzej Łapicki, who, despite looking the part of a handsome Irish poet, gave what was widely seen as a lifeless performance. Stanisław

Zborowski blamed Łapicki's poor performance on the fact that the actor had pigeonholed himself as a performer of slapstick comedies and had therefore been incapable of understanding the delineations of comedy and human tragedy that were intertwined in the character of Davoren.[21] Instead, Łapicki had struck an overly sombre note that all but scuttled the first scene, although another critic, Konrad Eberhardt, blamed the failure of the first act on the general grotesqueness of the characters.[22] In contrast with his fellow reviewers, Eberhardt was particularly taken with Davoren as played by Łapicki, and indeed for him, the play simply confirmed the isolation of the poet in society, and here he posed the question: 'Who has the right to accuse him [the poet]?'[23]

However, Eberhardt did reserve criticism for the farcical melodrama that arose from Davoren and Shields finding bombs in the bag. Indeed, here the critic thought that O'Casey had done his play a great disservice. But in terms of the production itself, Eberhardt commended Axer for having groomed the next generation of theatrical directors. He also praised Hübner and Pawlik for the second act in particular, which through the use of lighting and other such theatrical devices to hand had overcome what he saw as the weaknesses inherent in the written play, and had ratcheted up a sense of impending doom.

By any standards, in terms of the length of its run and the critical interest that the play generated, Hübner and Pawlik must have exceeded all expectations. Curiously though, Pawlik did not pursue a career as a director, whereas for Hübner, this play marked the beginning of what would be a long and distinguished career.

Angst and Expectations

In 1956, Poland under the leadership of Władysław Gomułka managed to wrest meaningful autonomy from Moscow, and within a short space of time the country transformed from a minion to an independent state run along one-party socialist grounds, which, in turn, was henceforth free to carry out its affairs within the benign, but ever-watchful, sphere of Soviet influence. This landmark achievement is often referred to as the October Thaw or Revolution, and almost immediately Poland's cultural life began to look west – albeit for many the most important aspect of this political sea-change was that Party regalia disappeared from the streets, more music was played on the radio, and people's social and cultural life improved greatly.[24] What is more, there is much to suggest that there was also a thrust at this very time to embrace contemporary French literature as a way of hailing this perceived new beginning. One illustration of this can be gauged by the fact that Jarosław Iwaszkiewicz's literary journal *Twórczość* [*Creativity*] gave over its November issue to French contemporary literature, publishing a declaration that had been formulated by writers gathered in Warsaw's Pen Club on 23 October, and which read: 'After years of lies and hurt, a time of hope has come.'[25] This pronouncement was openly supported by Iwaszkiewicz, who boldly asserted the following, 'Yes, socialism, but our own socialism, yes, friendship with the Soviet Union, but on the basis of equality.'[26] As we shall see, in anticipating and then witnessing the spectacle of Beckett's tramps, angst and expectation would prove to be the strangest of bedfellows.

In that very same heady month of October, dramatist Adam Tarn produced the maiden issue of the journal *Dialog*, whose aim was to bring Western plays to Poland by first introducing them in translation. Three years previously, at the very end of 1953, Tarn had made his theatrical debut in Warsaw's Contemporary Theatre with his play *Zwykła Sprawa* [*An Ordinary Affair*]. The play was directed by Erwin Axer, who, in turn, was assisted by Jerzy Kreczmar, the future director of Beckett's *Waiting for Godot*. For the unproven dramatist, the experience of collaborating with directors, actors and set designers was a revelatory apprenticeship as Tarn came to understand how a text evolved from the page to a living truth that theatrical drama aspired to be:

> And then, seeing the arduous work of the director, entailing the precise positioning of the actors, listening to their discussions and his explanations, bringing this and that into a discussion – only then did I understand what stagecraft is all about. Precisely this! Collective work. Which, when translated into the language of the theatre means: the patience of the director + the patience of the author + the patience of the actor, and then set design.[27]

From the outset, *Dialog* determined to take a programmatic approach to the featured plays, in that they were never translations of translations, as Tarn felt this had too often been the case in Polish theatrical tradition. Furthermore, translators were also expected to provide an informative introduction to the play, which represented a significant enhancement in their literary profile. *Dialog* staff would rigorously check the standards of these translated plays, and soon acquired a skill for spotting recurring weaknesses and idiosyncrasies. However, the translators did not always appreciate critical feedback, and soon Tarn found that an unexpected aspect of his job was contending with the tirades of piqued contributors.[28]

Initially, Tarn set out the agenda of the early issues, and commensurately farmed out commissions to translators in waiting. In this he was ably helped by the fact that the circle of translators was so small that Tarn knew who was working on a particular project at any given time and could forward-plan issues accordingly. One figure whom he was particularly anxious to have attached to the new journal was Julian Rogoziński, who to this day counts as one of Poland's greatest exponents of French literature, and who at the time was certainly the most eligible person for the task of translating Beckett.

In the 1930s, Rogoziński studied Polish philology and Iberian studies at Warsaw University, and during this time he began translating writers such as Balzac and Apollinaire. Over the following twenty years, he dedicated himself to the translation of large swathes of the French literary canon. After the war, Rogoziński served as a diplomat in France and Belgium, but by the mid-1950s he had embarked on a new life in the provincial town of Kielce. Rogoziński marked this new phase by focusing on more recent works hailing from France, and principally the great triumvirate of Sartre, Camus and Beckett.

However, in spite of having secured the services of a top literary translator for an exciting dramatic piece, Tarn allowed Beckett's play to be published in extract form only, and the translation took up a paltry nine pages of the journal. This was either because the translation was incomplete at the time or because issues of space had not been settled upon. At any rate, Tarn later regretted not having published the play in its entirety, ruefully accepting that a historic opportunity had been missed. On the basis of this experience, Tarn determined that henceforth plays would never be published in fragmentary form. It was to be all or nothing: 'As for extracts, well, they never again featured in our journal.'[29]

Rogoziński's introduction to the play for *Dialog*, unremarkably entitled 'Od tłumacza' ['From the Translator'], compared the inertia and hopelessness of Estragon and Vladimir to the fates of the dramatic characters as conceived by Sartre, although Rogoziński pointed to the fact that unlike Sartre or Kafka, Beckett's characters were unable to push back or move on. He also confidently stated that Godot was indeed God: 'Godot – to zapewne Bóg' ['Godot – is surely God], a widely held contention that Beckett had in fact dismissed earlier: 'if by Godot I had meant God I would [have] said God, and not Godot.'[30] However, Rogoziński argued that the Biblical allusions tipped the scales in favour of Godot being, in fact, God. His other argument, clearly more tenuous, if not a touch bizarre, was that Beckett was Irish and that Ireland was the Island of Saints, whereas in the camp of the sinners stood the giant figure of Jonathan Swift. Here Rogoziński may have been alluding to Swift's grotesque work, *A Modest Proposal* (1729), which critics have acknowledged as having been an informative piece for Beckett's writing of *Watt* (1953).[31]

In the run-up to the performance of *Waiting for Godot*, critics expressed their consternation at the way in which writers like Beckett had conceived of Man as being unable to speak up for himself, and further still, they decried Beckett's inability to give life some moral framework. However, though they also regarded the play as a declaration of the end of Western capitalism, there was some establishment nervousness that the play would somehow destabilize the kind of social harmony that Poland's socialist experiment had supposedly achieved – or more pointedly, that it was somehow an allusion to the perceived hopelessness of the individual living under communism.[32]

One critic who defended the play was card-carrying, party-faithful theatre critic Jan Alfred Szczepański, who wrote for the *Trybuna Ludu* [*The People's Tribune*]. Szczepański penned a defence of *Waiting for Godot* when it was three months into its run.[33] His article is particularly interesting as it sheds some light on censorial decision-making in Poland. Indeed, on the basis of the critic's account, it seems that the process was a great deal more transparent and democratic than many today would suppose. Szczepański had sat on a commission just prior to the premiere of *Waiting for Godot*, which had gathered to gauge the appropriateness of a batch of recent Western-European films due for a general cinema release. During the course of the meeting, one delegate took a bellicose stance against what was a seemingly inoffensive Italian film. He was promptly challenged by other participants to explain the reasons for his objections, to which he responded with a hatful of platitudes, the choicest of which was, 'you can harm people who are kept going on milk, if you suddenly give them goose or turkey'.[34] However, this stance was dismissed out of hand, the film was given its release, and Szczepański happily reported that cinemagoers were not suffering any problems with indigestion. In spite of the fact that in this instance cool heads won the day, Szczepański bemoaned the fact that his like-minded peers constantly had to counter arguments that Polish audiences were not mature enough to cope with the corrupting influences of Western culture. However, as Szczepański claimed, this anti-intellectual stance cut little ice with many leading cultural figures who were looking to present Beckett within the context of wider European literary and cultural traditions, of which Poland constituted an essential piece of the mosaic. Indeed, in as much as Beckett had brought the absurd to the Kierkegaardean outlook, so the critic argued, the Irish dramatist also fit in with the Polish traditions of existential angst that had had their beginnings in the era of Young Poland and that saw its pre-war literary acme in the 1930s with avant-garde writers such as Bruno Schulz, Witold Gombrowicz and Stanisław Ignacy Witkiewicz, who had merged existential musings with grotesque motifs.[35] Indeed, elsewhere from among the ranks of critics discussing Beckett, it was noted that Gombrowicz had declared in his personal writing that existentialism was an unavoidable characteristic of the human condition, and that it could not simply be brushed aside. In fact, it was necessary to confront existentialism and emerge victorious:

> If Polish Catholicism or Polish Marxism fence themselves off through their foolish disregard, they will become a backstreet, a tenement yard, a backwater. It isn't possible to step over existentialism, you must contend with it.[36]

We may imagine that this debate on expectancy must have been raging about Kreczmar as he assiduously prepared *Godot* for performance. However, for Kreczmar, the play could not be so easily pigeonholed. When asked by Swiss writer Walter Weideli, if Poland was waiting for its Godot, Kreczmar said unhesitatingly that it was, or more pointedly, that the Polish people were. However, the director prefaced this with the oxymoronic notion that waiting protects from death.[37] For the director, this was the cathartic revelation that the play offered. What was more, for Kreczmar, Beckett, in pointing to the absurdity of life, was not doing so as an end in itself, but to expose the absurdity of the judgements and values upon which people built their lives. Following that line of thought, it made no sense to look for a rationale to anything, but to simply accept existence without the anticipation of understanding. Here Kreczmar proposed Pascal's agnostic wager as a reasonably acceptable position to adopt.[38] Looking to encapsulate what he felt about Beckett from a textual and philosophical perspective, Kreczmar stated that the dramatist was a minimalist dealing with big things, who commensurately had revealed a condition that was not worth taking much trouble over.[39] However, he chose to believe that people's subjective hopes would always leave a chink of light, signifying hope. This hope brought the director to the conclusion that ultimately it is better to live than to end up swinging by the neck at the end of a rope tied to the leafless branch of a withered tree.

Kreczmar remained principally wedded to the notion of Godot as a meta-theatrical event, which was neither a proscriptive nor didactic piece, and which was therefore open to a subjective interpretation of the human condition. To this end, the director interpreted the play as a circus spectacle, wherein Vladimir and Gogo were made up as clowns and not tramps, and in keeping with their roles they would trip over the props in order to negate the illusion of reality. Indeed, Konrad Eberhardt, who had seen the Paris production, approved of Kreczmar's costume changes, having preferred also the delivery of the Polish actors to that of the French cast, who, according to the critic, had spoken as if they had had stones in their mouths.[40] Eberhardt, in turn, favoured the Warsaw production as it proposed characters with different individual styles, and what is more important from the perspective of the play's ambition to represent a human drama, he felt that the actors had managed to arouse some semblance of sympathy for their predicament. Gogo, for example, had evoked the persona of a provincial theatrical director or actor who had fallen on hard times and was wondering when the next job would come along. Didi, in turn, had called to mind a fallen intellectual who was grappling with forgotten facts and impaired deductive skills. Pozzo's journey from Paris to Warsaw saw him transform from a brutal landlord to a burlesque English overlord, wearing red women's trousers and replete with homosexual overtures. Lucky, in his Polish incarnation as played by Adam Mularczyk, was not the ghostly and trembling figure of the Paris production, but rather a stone-faced peasant resigned to his lot in life:

> What we have here is a circus: one clown cannot pull his shoe off, the other is helping him, both end up falling down, one clown gives the other a kick, they don't hear one another, they scream, they mispronounce words, they chase one another, they trip up, they invent games, and they even juggle with bowler hats.[41]

It seems also that like a Laurel and Hardy movie, the clownish gags filled the silences and made the time pass in a more pleasant fashion. However, for Eberhardt, if anything tipped the scales in favour of the Paris production it was the fact that the Polish production was almost too pleasant an affair. This he put down to the translation, which, in his opinion, had been too smooth and had failed to impart the coarseness of the original.

On the night of the premiere, which took place on 25 January 1957, and for the following two weeks, audiences who attended the play were subjected to what was frequently described as a disorienting experience. Indeed, the initial reception almost mirrored that of the scenes in Paris and elsewhere, in that the reaction of the audience almost became a secondary event, with people turning heads and sharing bemused looks.[42] Frequently people left after the first act, unable to take or give time to the starkness of what was being proposed. However, beyond the plain fact that the play had upset some patrons, critic Karolina Beylin, writing for *Express Wieczorny* [*The Evening Express*], thought the spectacle had potentially launched a generation of young people with notions about themselves.[43] Apparently, Beylin was particularly appalled when she heard a young couple enthusiastically praise the play aloud as they were shuffling to the exit. Beylin couldn't figure how this same couple could have come to such a favourable judgement, facetiously suggesting that the poster should have come with a health warning for people suffering from nerves or who could come down with a bout of existential angst. We are all, the critic maintained, waiting for a Godot, but that did not mean that people wished to be necessarily reminded of that fact. Sometimes denial or ignorance were better ways of proceeding in life. It has to be said, though, that Beylin did in fact review the play favourably.

Undeniably, the overall critical reception of the play was exceptionally positive, with many reviewers proclaiming that Kreczmar had surpassed the Paris production. Indeed, many commented on the fact that the play seemed to grow in popularity as its run continued, with many theatregoers choosing to attend a second and third time in order to listen more carefully to the English humour. As Stefan Treugutt wrote: 'A humour-filled atmosphere amongst the audience, some giggle all the time. Perhaps it is going to do well?'[44] Furthermore, it was generally accepted that the actors greatly improved on their performances as time went on, and that they began to explore better the play's comedic potential.[45] Having said that, there were rumblings in some quarters that it was difficult to see how the play could contribute to the development of theatrical values other than reaffirming that the grotesque was ensconced as a staple of Poland's avant-garde outlook.[46] Indeed, one critic wondered if other theatres should not consider performing the play in a more stark and realistic way, his general thesis being that the play still left plenty of room for experimentation: 'Generally speaking, all experiments with this play can be exciting – both for artists and for spectators'.[47] Beckett would not have approved of the sentiment.

Ask the Cockerel

In the winter of 1956–1957 Zygmunt Hübner received a stipend from the International Theatre Institute funded by UNESCO, which allowed him to travel to Paris, London and Rome. This trip opened his eyes to a less self-reflective theatre, and when offered the position of artistic director of the Teatr Wybrzeże [Coastal Theatre] of Gdańsk, Hübner accepted and set about revolutionizing its repertoire by introducing contemporary European and American plays. In doing so, he transformed the theatre into one of the leading dramatic centres in Poland. Indeed, under Hübner, Andrzej Wajda made his directorial debut, staging Michael Gazzo's *A Hatful of Rain* (1957) in 1959. Hübner himself directed William Saroyan's *The Time of Your Life* (1939), Jean Paul Sartre's *La Putain respecteuse* (1946) and *Morts sans sépulture* (1946). In 1957 Hübner put on the world premiere of Witkacy's *Szewcy* [*The Cobblers*] (1933), which through the form of cabaret attacked the tyranny of authoritarian rule. Despite having won the support of local censors, it was shut down by a censor who had deliberately travelled from Warsaw to see the play.[48] On completing his tenure with the Coastal Theatre, there followed a period of years during which Hübner was affiliated with a number of theatres in Warsaw. And Hübner marked the beginning of these freelancing years by staging O'Casey's *Cock-a-Doodle Dandy* for Warsaw's Polish Theatre. The play had its premiere on 26 October 1960.

Written in 1949 and first staged by an amateur dramatic company in Newcastle on Tyne in 1950, *Cock-a-Doodle Dandy* was slow to find its way in the world. In 1958 the play was performed in New York's Carnegie Hall and a year later at the Edinburgh Festival. But like other late works of O'Casey, it failed to make the kind of mark on the era that it perhaps should have.

Cock-a-Doodle Dandy almost defies summary. The setting is the village of Nyadnanave, a name which puns the Gaelic Nest of Saints with Nest of Knaves. The themes of the play have, as O'Casey contended, a factual basis in the Ireland of the 1940s and 1950s, which means that the wild festivity of the play is also accompanied by various accounts of personal tragedy.[49] An enchanted Cockerel is running loose in this world and is responsible for what is thought to be a series of supernatural events, such as the transformation of a whiskey bottle and the creation of a hole in a hat. The Cockerel also inspires the local girls to enter into an ecstatic dance – a dance that is violently brought to an end by the despotic Father Domineer, who later in the play demands the destruction of a copy of Joyce's (1922), a book that is symbolic of the boundlessness of the Cockerel's appetites. Though the Cockerel is a positive life-force and leads the fight for freedom from superstition and clerical repression, ultimately many of the young people are hounded out of the village. They can only hope to find a place 'where life resembles life more than it does here'. A separate thread of the play involves Julia, who is terminally ill and wheelchair-bound, and who sets off to Lourdes in the hope of a miracle at the end of scene one. She is given a great send-off with much pomp and ceremony, but she returns at the end of the play only to see her sister Lorna leaving Nyadnanave forever. Julia will have to remain in the village with her destitute father, who in vain has sacrificed everything to secure a 'glorious miracle' for his daughter.

In Poland, *Cock-a-Doodle Dandy* was first featured in *Dialog* in the May edition of 1959, and was accompanied by an overview article on O'Casey's life and works. O'Casey's play was translated by Cecylia Wojewoda, who at the time was closely involved in overseeing the republication of Polish translations of Shaw and Wilde. Wojewoda gave the play the title of *Kukuryku* [*Cock-a-Doodle-Do*], but the play, which premiered in the small Chamber Hall of the Polish Theatre on 25 October 1960, was changed to *Kogut zawinił* [*The Cockerel is to Blame*], a change that perhaps led critics to believe that Hübner had introduced many modifications to the translation. Indeed, one reviewer made good use of the irony that the new Polish title afforded with the wordplay 'zawinił raczej tłumacz' ['the translator is to blame'].[50] Here the critic suggested that the play should have been freely adapted, and lamented the passing of poet and cabaret wit, Konstanty Ildefons Gałczyński, as he would have been the ideal candidate to make something of its melancholic buffoonery. Of course, however appealing this notion may have been, Wojewoda's task for *Dialog* had been to provide a close literary translation of the original play. And in this respect, she had succeeded. Whether this translation had needed to be reworked again for the purposes of performance is another question.

In terms of the translation itself, Wojewoda dealt very well with the poetic speech of the play. What is more, she also trawled through Polish pejorative terms for addressing women, made necessary by their variety and frequency in the original. Indeed, never perhaps had Polish Theatre witnessed the casting of such aspersions on the fairer sex. For the most part, the reviewers refrained from commenting upon Wojewoda's translation, though generally they agreed with one another that Hübner had been too reverential in respect of the manuscript. Bogdan Wojdowski, writing for the journal *Współczesność* [*Contemporaneity*], had no doubt that the play had posed many challenges, particularly given its plebeian humour and peasant-like sarcasm, but at the same time he felt that Hübner had taken a very heavy-handed approach to the material, 'he got lost in the realistic literalness', and particularly to the stage gestures and costumes.[51] Wojdowski also had much to say about one change that irritated him greatly, and it was that the mention of Joyce's *Ulysses* (1922) had been changed for Camus' *The Rebel* (1951). This substitution is not to be found in the theatre manuscript and so this was either the director's idea or the actor involved had simply improvised the lines on the stage. These supposed changes were brought to light by Stefan Polanica,[52] normally a mild-mannered reviewer, who considered the play an affront to Polish Theatre, and who felt that all parties involved in bringing the play to the stage had demeaned themselves and tarnished their careers. Polanica had particularly harsh words for Hübner, whom he thought had trivialized the work, although the reviewer was by no means defending the integrity of the play itself.

Polanica was convinced that the company had been playing to the gallery on an improvisatory basis, and that Hübner had been trying to squeeze as much laughter out of the final scene as possible. And so, contrary to what transpires in the original, Julia's return from Lourdes is also greeted by a marching fire-brigade band. Polanica found this scene highly distasteful, and asked what it was about a dying girl bereft of hope that was so funny. What precisely was Hübner celebrating? he asked, 'it's all so funny, don't you think?'[53]

Roman Szydłowski had attended the Warsaw premiere of *The Shadow of a Gunman* and regarded O'Casey as deserving of a special place in Polish Theatre, particularly given the Irish writer's commitment to freedom and social reform. But writing for the *Trybuna Ludu*, Szydłowski blamed the actors for the failure of *Cock-a-Doodle Dandy*.[54] This opinion was also voiced by Andrzej Jarecki, who thought that both the theatre and its troupe of actors had been too swept up by the grandiosity of their lofty surrounds: 'More life and less ceremonial regard for the theatre ....'[55]

Many of the reviewers even wondered why Hübner had put on such a play when he could have chosen from a number of O'Casey's earlier and better dramas. Indeed, Grzegorz Sinko, future translator of Brendan Behan's *The Quare Fellow*, thought that the entire exercise of staging *Cock-a-Doodle Dandy* in Poland had been a futile one, arguing that the play could not be imparted in any language other than its Anglo-Irish dialect.[56]

The specific failures of the play in performance were enumerated by Elżbieta Wysińska[57] who felt compelled to defend O'Casey against what she regarded as an ill-considered interpretation of the play. The principal problem, she contended, was that Hübner had decided to be vague about the setting in order to move the action away from rural Ireland so as to reflect more closely life in the Polish countryside. However, Wysińska wondered why the director had chosen to be so unsubtle about his associations. Even though she accepted that it was important to note that local tyrants are to be found throughout the world, Wysińska contended that this observation brought no added depth to the play itself. Instead, Wysińska felt that Hübner should have retained a confidence in his Irish setting and trusted that the audience would have been quick to conjure up their own analogies, which would almost certainly have had minds wandering to religious practice in the Polish countryside with its attendant traditions and superstitions. It was the naïvety of the characters encapsulated by their perception of the fantastic or demonic events taking place in their midst that provided potential for the production to have been made a more visual spectacle. But Hübner had relegated these fantastic elements to hearsay and minor gestures, and in doing so had done away with a great deal of potential for laughter and amusement. In order to illustrate this point, Wysińska stated that the reason the actors playing Michael and Mahon had not shown any fear when witnessing fantastical events was that there had been nothing in the visual sense to be frightened about. For example, in the culminating scene featuring a fight with the Cockerel, where slates had fallen from the roof of Michael's home, within the interior of the house a red light began to flicker against tin foil. Such cheap effects were in the estimation of the critic unworthy of the theatre and the play itself. Other aspects of the performance grated, such as the uncertainty of the actors who really had no sense of what the play was about, or who had been unable to arrive at convincing characterizations. In addition to this, many of the scenes that should have been lively affairs were interrupted by painfully long pauses, which Wysińska thought had come about because the bemused actors had needed occasions to regroup and find their bearings.[58] Ultimately, Wysińska concluded that the play had warranted a pacier tempo with more emphasis placed on the gags and humorous exchanges.

Wysińska ended her piece by saying that both O'Casey and Wojewoda required words in their defence, as poorly staged plays were often blamed on both playwright and translator. Whereas, in this instance Hübner, as director, had failed to capture the middle ground between realism and fantasy. What is more, he had made colourless and drab what should have been a bright and cheerful spectacle. And finally, the director simply should have given a better account of himself. The Cockerel had deserved better:

> If the Cockerel had been a fairground clay figure and the entire story a naïve tale, based on folklore poetics, *Cock-a-Doodle Dandy* would have been a unified piece in terms of theatre.[59]

Certainly, Hübner had been aware of the difficulties that a play like *Cock-a-Doodle Dandy* posed. Indeed, in the foreword to the play's theatre programme, Hübner had written of the need to find a dramatic form of interpretation that would accentuate the play's symbolic elements. But this, we may conclude, is precisely what the director had failed to do.

Hübner did not return to O'Casey following this production, but he still retained an interest in Irish literature and drama, although there would follow a ten-year hiatus. Despite the fact that *Cock-a-Doodle Dandy* was never staged again in Poland, Cecylia Wojewoda evidently retained her admiration for the playwright, providing translations of *Red Roses for Me* (1961) and *Bedtime Story* (1969). Surprisingly, *The Shadow of a Gunman* was also never re-staged in Poland, and generally Polish productions of Sean O'Casey's plays remain a rarity. Undeniably, we cannot avoid the speculation that the debacle involving a cockerel strutting across a national stage in defiance of a tyrannical parish priest dealt a mortal blow to the reputation of the Irish playwright in Poland. We may even contend that Poland would have been receptive to the plays of Sean O'Casey for decades to come had *Cock-a-Doodle Dandy* either been presented differently ... or never staged at all.

Notes

1   See Stanisław Marczak-Oborski, *Teatr polski w latach 1918–1965. Teatry dramatyczne* (Warszawa: Wydawnictwo Naukowe PWN, 1985), 200–204.

2   Elżbieta Wysińska, 'Teatry dramatyczne powojennego pięćdziesięciolecia.' In: M. Fik (ed) *Teatr. Widowisko* (Warszawa: Instytut Kultury, 2000), 60.

3   Stanisław Marczak-Oborski, *Teatr polski w latach 1918–1965*, 232–234.

4   Zygmunt Hübner and Jerzy Rakowiecki, *Rozmowy o teatrze* (Warszawa: Wiedza Powszechna, 1955), 187.

5   Roman Szydłowski, 'Profesja burżuazyjnego wyzyskiwacza', *Trybuna Ludu*, 352 (1951).

6   See Alfred Degal, 'Filozofia pani Warren', *Nowa Kultura* 4 (1952), 8.

7   'Popatrz się! Trzeba było aż Brechta z zagranicy, by zobaczyli, iż znowu Warren (moja), to nie taki nonsens.' Cited in Lidia Kuchtówna, *Pamiętnik Teatralny* 2–4 (150–152) (1989), 260.

8   See Wojciech Dudzik, *Wilama Horzycy: dramat niespełnienia: lata 1948–1959* (Warszawa: Uniwersytet Warszawski, Katedra Kultury Polskiej, 1990), 141.

9   See Irena Bołtuć, 'Z wrocławskich wspomnień', *Pamiętnik Teatralny*, 2–4 (150–152) (1989), 359–367.

10 See Heinz Kosok, *O'Casey the Dramatist*. Trans. Joseph T. Swan (Irish Literary Studies 19) (Gerrards Cross: Collin Smythe, 1985), 360.

11 Heinz Kosok, *O'Casey the Dramatist*, 259.

12 Unsigned, 'The Theatre: New Play in Dublin', *Time* (14 March 1955). Available at: http://content.time.com/time/magazine/article/0,9171,807100,00.html. Accessed 12 August 2011.

13 See Heinz Kosok, *O'Casey the Dramatist*, 350.

14 See Robert Looby, 'Looking for the Censor in the Works of Sean O'Casey (and Others) in Polish Translation', *Translation and Literature*, 17 (1) (2008), 47–64.

15 See Bernard Benstock, 'Sean O'Casey and/or James Joyce.' In: D. Krause and R. G. Lowery (eds), *Sean O'Casey. Centenary Essays* (Irish Literary Studies) (Gerrards Cross: Collin Smythe, 1980), 41–66.

16 Julian Tuwim, 'Mieszkańcy', *Biblia cygańska* (Warszawa: J. Mortkowicz, 1933).

17 'wszystko to znamy aż nadto dobrze z okupacyjnej Warszawy.' Roman Szydłowski, 'Bohaterowie i Tchórze', *Trybuna Ludu*, 269 (1955), 8.

18 August Grodzicki, 'Jak u nas za okupacji' ['Recalling our Lives Under Occupation'], *Życie Warszawy*, 232 (1955).

19 George Bidwell, 'Sean O' Casey', *Przegląd Kulturalny*, 41 (1955), 2.

20 George Bidwell, *Przegląd Kulturalny*, 41 (1955). 'Przed laty zrozumiał jasno – razem z Picasso, Joliot, Curie, Aragonem, Eluardem, Andersenem, Nexø, i Dreiserem – że komunizm oznacza najpełniejszą służbę dla ludzkości, najpełniejsze wykorzystanie życia.'

21 Stanisław Zborowski, 'Poeta i jego klęska', *Dziś i Jutro*, 39 (1955), 6.

22 'Dramat o klęsce poety', Konrad Eberhardt, *Teatr*, 44 (1955), 17.

23 'Kto ma prawo go oskarżac?' Konrad Eberhardt, *Teatr*, 44 (1955), 17.

24 Antoni Libera, *W cieniu Godota* (Warszawa: Wydawnictwo Znak, 2009), 9.

25 'Po latach kłamstw i krzywd, nastaje czas nadziei.' Cited in Tadeusz Drewnowski, *Literatura Polska 1944–1989. Próba scalenia. Obiegi – wzorce – style* (Kraków: Universitas, 2004), 324.

26 'Tak socjalizm, ale nasz własny socjalizm, tak, przyjaźń ze Związkiem Radzieckim, ale na zasadzie równości.' Cited in Tadeusz Drewnowski, *Literatura Polska 1944–1989*, 324.

27 'I wtedy, widząc mozolną pracę reżysera nad właściwym ustawieniem aktorów, przysłuchując się ich dyskusji i jego wyjaśnieniom, sam wnosząc to i owo do dyskusji – wtedy dopiero zrozumiałem, co to jest warsztat sceniczny. Właśnie! Praca kolektywna. Co przełożone na język teatru znaczy: cierpliwość reżysera + cierpliwość autora + cierpliwość aktora, oraz dekoracje.' Adam Tarn, 'Lekcja Warsztatu Scenicznego', *Teatr*, 1 (1951), 65.

28 Danuta Żmij-Zielińska, 'Z młodości *Dialogu*', *Dialog*, 2 (2009), 164–165.

29 'Co zaś do fragmentów, nigdy się więcej w naszym piśmie nie powtórzyły.' *Dialog*, 2 (2009), 165.

30 James Knowlson, *Damned to Fame. The Life of Samuel Beckett* (London: Bloomsbury, 1996), 412.

31 See John Fletcher, 'Samuel Beckett et Jonathan Swift: vers une étude comparée', *Littératures X: Annales publiées par la Faculté des Lettres de Toulouse*, 11 (1962).

32 See Dorota Wyżyńska, 'Godot w garnizonie [Godot in a Garrison]', *Gazeta Stołeczna*, 216 (2001), 4.

33 Jan Alfred Szczepański, 'Na przykładzie: *Czekając na Godota*', *Trybuna Ludu*, 103 (14 April 1957), 6.

34 '… ludziom tak długo trzymanym na mleczku, może zaszkodzić nagle podana gęś lub indyczka.' Jan Alfred Szczepański, *Trybuna Ludu*, 103 (14 April 1957), 6.

35 Tadeusz Drewnowski, *Literatura Polska 1944–1989*, 216–219.

36 'Jeśli polski katolicyzm czy też polski marksizm odgrodzą się od tego niemądrym lekceważeniem, staną się zaułkiem, podwórkiem, prowincją. Egzystencjalizmu nie można przeskoczyć, trzeba go przezwyciężyć.' Zbigniew Dolecki, 'Godot czeka najdłużej', *Kierunki*, 8 (24 February 1957), 3.

37 Jerzy Kreczmar, *Stare nieprzestarzałe* (Warszawa: Państwowy Instytut Wydawniczy, 1989), 356.

38 Jerzy Kreczmar, *Stare nieprzestarzałe*, 371–372.

39 Jerzy Kreczmar, *Stare nieprzestarzałe*, 372–373.

40 Konrad Eberhardt, 'Dramat o ludzkiej bezradności', *Sygnały*, 9 (1957), 2.

41 'Tu zaś cyrk: jeden błazen nie może ściągnąć buta, drugi mu pomaga, obydwaj się przewracają, błazen błaznowi daje kopsa, nie słyszą się nawzajem, wrzeszczą, przekręcają słowa, gonią się, podstawiają sobie nogi, wymyślają zabawy, nawet żonglują melonikami.' Andrzej Kijowski, 'Koszmar czasu', *Teatr*, 7 (1 April 1957), 11–12.

42 Stefan Treugutt, 'Godot', *Przegląd Kuturalny*, 27 (1957), 6.

43 Karolina Beylin, 'Czekając na Godota', *Express Wieczorny*, (25 January 1957), 6.

44 Stefan Treugutt, 'Godot', *Przegląd Kulturalny*, 27 (1957), 6.

45 Jeremi Czuliński, 'Francuska Awangarda', *Żołnierz Wolności*, 35 (1957).

46 Kazimierz Koźniewski, 'Godot w Warszawie', *Przekrój*, 622 (1957), 6.

47 'W ogóle wszelkie eksperymenty z tą sztuką mogą być pasjonujące – dla artystów i dla widzów.' Kazimierz Koźniewski, *Przekrój*, 622 (1957).

48 See Zygmunt Hübner, *Theatre and Politics* (Illinois: Northwestern University Press, 1988), 52; see also Grażyna Antoniewicz, 'Termos z herbatą, czyli bomba', *Dziennik Bałtycki*, 57 (2008), 25.

49 Heinz Kosok, *O'Casey the Dramatist*, 242.

50 Zofia Karczewska-Markiewicz, 'Kukuryku', *Życie Warszawy*, 258 (1960). Available at: http://www.zygmunthubner.pl/22_Sean_OCASEY_-_Kogut_zawinil_1960. Accessed 14 April 2011.

51 'zagubił się w realistycznej dosłowności....' Bogdan Wojdowski, 'Rzecz dzieje się w Nyadnanawe', *Współczesność*, 2 (1960), 10.

52 Stefan Polanica, 'Czy tylko *Kogut zawini?*' *Słowo Powszechne*, 260 (1960), 4. Polanica gave the example of the First Rough Fellow describing to Father Domineer how both he and the villagers had dragged Loreen and Sailor Mahan out of a car for engaging in an extra-marital dalliance:

> 1st Rough Fellow: Th' people pelted him back to his home an' proper wife, Father, an' he's there now, in bed, an' sorry for what he thried to do.
>
> [Ludzie zaciągnęli go z powrotem do domu, do prawowitej żony, ojcze. Leży teraz w łóżku i żałuje, że chciał brzydko postąpić.]
>
> However, what the reviewer heard from the stage was entirely different and not to his liking.
>
> [Ludzie zaciągnęli go z powrotem do domu, do prawowitej żony. Leży teraz i czyni z nią w łóżku akt skruchy.]
>
> The people dragged him back to his rightful wife. Now he's lying on the bed with her and is doing an act of contrition. [A play on 'compunction']

53 'jakie to wszystko dowcipne, prawda?' Stefan Polanica, *Słowo Powszechne*, 260 (1960).

54 Roman Szydłowski, 'Kogut z podciętymi skrzydłami', *Trybuna Ludu*, 300 (1960), 6.

55 'Więcej żywności i mniej ceremonialnego stosunku do teatru.' Andrzej Jarecki, 'Sztuka dla wsi', *Sztandar Młodych*, 259 (1960), 2.

56 Grzegorz Sinko, 'Kłopoty i Niespodzianki', *Nowa Kultura*, 46 (1960), 3.

57   Elżbieta Wysińska, 'Konfrontacja: w obronie Seana O'Casey', *Dialog*, 12 (1960), 134–137.

58   'Bezradność aktorów była przyczyną żenujących pauz, które nie wiadomo dlaczego pojawiały się nagle w ruchliwych scenach.' Elżbieta Wysińska, *Dialog*, 12 (1960), 137.

59   'Gdyby ten kogut był jarmaczną, glinianą figurką, a całość naiwną opowieścią, opartą na ludowej poetyce – *Kukuryku* okazałoby się prawdopodobnie utworem jednolitym pod względem teatralnym.' Elżbieta Wysińska, *Dialog*, 12 (1960), 137.

1.

2.

3.

4.

5.

6.

7.

Chapter 4

Towards the Modern Era (1960-1979)

Introduction: Finding Space

Kazimierz Braun subtitled his book *A History of Modern Polish Theatre* as 'Spheres of Captivity and Freedom', but reserved the most chilling epithet for his chapter on the years 1960–1980, so describing them as 'The Twenty Captive Years'.[1] And indeed, following the building of the Berlin Wall, and with the Cold War having reached fever pitch, the Polish government set about restricting unwanted political and cultural expression. Many writers were arrested during this period, particularly in the wake of a letter by Antoni Słonimski, signed by thirty-three writers and academics, which called for the alleviation of censorship and the securing of paper supplies for literary journals.[2] But in spite of the widespread unrest and discontent at the degenerating social conditions within the country, theatre saw a flourishing period, with repertoires vibrantly harnessing both traditional and internationalist outlooks. What is more, the prevailing harshness of everyday life spawned an avant-garde theatre in Poland that attempted to express the obliqueness of reality within new spatial settings. One of the leading lights of this new movement was Tadeusz Kantor, who began his career in the mid-1950s with a visual theatre called 'happenings', which took the action beyond the stage and honed a highly choreographed spontaneity to the movements of the cast. Built principally around the absurdist plays of Witkacy, these 'happenings' toured abroad to great acclaim and earned Poland the reputation of being a home to experimental theatre.[3] However, experimental theatre was not confined to the theatre proper, but also to private houses and churches, which secured a measure of autonomy for the performance. An iconic figure for this freedom in captivity was poet and dramatist Miron Białoszewski, who created an alternative world of art, including theatrical performances within his own apartment in the Warsaw district of Ochota. His writings were highly idiosyncratic but the poem 'Ballada o zejściu do sklepu' ['The Ballad of Going Down to the Shop'], written in 1956, illustrates a capacity to find exaltation in the ordinary experience of the day. In terms of the Polish theatrical production of James Joyce's *Ulysses*, a discussion of which follows, the poem indicates the extent to which Polish audiences understood that there was more to the drabness of life than meets the eye:

Ballada o zejściu do sklepu	The Ballad of Going Down to the Shop
Najpierw zszedłem na ulicę schodami, ach, wyobraźcie sobie, schodami.	First I went down to the street by the stairwell steps, oh can you just picture it, by the stairwell steps!
Potem znajomi nieznajomych mnie mijali, a ja ich. Żałujcie, żeście nie widzieli, jak ludzie chodzą, żałujcie!	And later the friends of strangers passed me by, and I them. What a great pity you didn't see how people were walking, What a great pity!
Wstąpiłem do zupełnego sklepu; paliły się lampy ze szkła, widziałem kogoś – kto usiadł, i co słyszałem? … co słyszałem? szum toreb i ludzkie mówienie.	I stepped into the entire shop; the glass lamps were lit, I saw someone – who took a seat, and what did I hear?… what did I hear? the rustle of bags and people's talk.
No naprawdę naprawdę wróciłem.	I'm telling you, it's true, it's true. I had returned.

Dead Men Sending Their Regards

Maciej Słomczyński's theatrical adaptation of James Joyce's *Ulysses* had its premiere on 14 February 1970 in the city of Gdańsk. This marked the culmination of what had been a period of intense interest in Joyce following the publication of Słomczyński's translation of the novel *Ulysses* in the early months of 1969. Even though as many as forty thousand copies had been printed, the book sold out within a matter of days, which was an accomplishment curiously considered by a number of critics to have been symptomatic of a snobbery prevalent in certain quarters of Polish society.[4] Whatever people's motivations were, Słomczyński's translation soon began to trade on the open market for three times the retail price. In celebration of this unabated interest, and in order to publicize *Ulysses* the theatrical spectacle, the night before its premiere the Gdańsk student theatrical society ZAK held an auction and invited bids for a copy of Słomczyński's translation. The room was filled to capacity and the asking price was set at 101 zlotys. This reserve was soon exceeded, and the book eventually went on to fetch 1700 zlotys. It was bought by a certain Artur Bartoldi, an economist, who resided in the neighbouring seaside town of Sopot.[5] The success of this auction would prove auspicious for the upcoming production. Like copies of the book, such was the demand that tickets for the spectacle proved almost impossible to come by.[6]

The excitement that greeted Słomczyński's translation of *Ulysses* could arguably be put down to the fact that there was a wide perception that Joyce had made his arrival in Poland decades later than he should have, or at least that his works had come in drips and drabs, with his most celebrated work having arrived last. However, over the preceding decades Poland had, in fact, played host to a Joycean tradition of sorts. The story of this tradition could be said to have begun with Jarosław Iwaszkiewicz, a writer who has already made several appearances in our account. Fluent in French and in thrall to Rimbaud, Wilde and the Russian Acmeists, Iwaszkiewicz made his literary debut in 1919 with a poetry collection entitled *Oktostychy* [*Octostichs*], which also happened to be both thematically and formally in places similar to Joyce's *Chamber Music* (1907). As a later affirmation of this close identification, Iwaszkiewicz also translated in the mid-1920s several poems from *Chamber Music*, such as 'Gentle Lady', 'Sleep Now', 'Lean Out', and 'Rain has Fallen'. However, these translations remained unpublished until 1949, when composer, Karol Szymanowski, put them to music.[7] What is more, Iwaszkiewicz met, or rather sat at a neighbouring table to Joyce at the 1925 P.E.N. Club gathering in Paris. Whilst in Paris, Iwaszkiewicz also befriended French literary critic Valery Larbaud, who had penned a celebrated early review of *Ulysses*, and the Polish poet would later write a short note on *Ulysses* for the Polish press based on Larbaud's review.[8]

A Portrait of the Artist as a Young Man (1916) was published in Poland in 1931, and failed to generate a great deal of critical interest. It was the only novel of Joyce to be published in Poland during the inter-war period. Its translator, Zygmunt Allan, remains a mysterious figure about whom almost nothing is known, and it has even been suggested that the translator's name could have been a pseudonym. Nevertheless, Allan's translation was remarkably idiomatic, albeit it failed in places to account for stylistic differences within the text, which meant that many literary allusions to Dante, Milton and others were lost. It was anticipated that with the arrival of *A Portrait of the Artist as a Young Man,* a translation of *Ulysses* would soon follow, but this expectation proved to be a false hope. That said, the influence of *Ulysses* began to be seen with the ascendancy of the avant-garde in the Poland of the 1930s, particularly supported by a clutch of lengthy articles in *Wiadomości Literackie*, which offered literary conspectuses of Joyce's achievements. One article of note was penned by Jerzy Stempowski, who set out to explain the Freudian backdrop to *Ulysses*.[9]

In Polish prose the farcical and grotesque aspect of the works of Bruno Schulz and Witold Gombrowicz were greatly beholden to *Ulysses*. In 1934, Gombrowicz attempted to read *Ulysses* in French despite having a mediocre knowledge of the language. The writer pronounced it the most interesting book he had read that year and *Ulysses* almost certainly informed the writing of his landmark novel, *Ferdydurke* (1938), which Gombrowicz had begun writing in 1935.[10] Like other avant-garde writers of this time, Gombrowicz's literary indebtedness to Joyce expressed itself in the explicit treatment of sex and bodily functions, and the exploration of states of mind as understood within the context of Freudian psychology. As Gombrowicz wrote: 'But perhaps my work came from imitating master works? From an inability to create normal work? From dreams? From complexes?'[11] What is more, narrative and stream of consciousness in Gombrowicz's works were interwoven with snippets of inter-textuality, the focus being less on the external world and more character interaction and experience. Gombrowicz perhaps expressed his generation's debt to Joyce best when he declared that the Irish writer had raised the bar for Polish writers. Aside from Allan's translation, however, little of Joyce was translated in the 1930s. The only other significant contribution was Józef Czechowicz's translation of a fragment of the 'Calypso' episode, published in the journal *Pion*,[12] which was an organ of the Żagary literary group, based in Vilnius, and which today is principally synonymous with its association with Czesław Miłosz.

Iwaszkiewicz reappears in the story of Joyce after World War II. Aside from his publication of the aforementioned poems, he may also have played an early role in facilitating the translation of *Ulysses*. As intermittent head of the Polish Writers' Association, Iwaszkiewicz was a fêted figure in the literary world of Poland's post-war era, and in 1955, having edited and cooperated with numerous literary journals, he was awarded the helm of Warsaw-based literary journal *Twórczość*. And it was in the pages of this journal that Słomczyński published the first chapter of *Ulysses*, in 1958.[13]

Like Joyce's Leopold Bloom, Słomczyński had always been something of an outsider. He was the progeny of an extra-marital romance between Merian C. Cooper, an American squadron ace serving in the Kościuszko squadron and Marjorie Słomczyńska (née Crosbie), a British diplomat married at the time to Aleksander Słomczyński. Based in Warsaw, Marjorie chose not to accompany her swashbuckling lover back to America, and her husband gave his surname to his stepson.[14] Barely out of short trousers, he took part in conspiratorial activities against the occupying Germans. In April 1944, Słomczyński was captured and imprisoned in Pawiak prison in Warsaw. Miraculously, he managed to escape and, in the aftermath of the failed Warsaw Uprising – which he did not take part in – made it as far as France, where he enlisted in the advancing American army and distinguished himself as a military translator.[15] After the war, he was determined to try his hand at a literary career. He also published a number of ballads and poetic trifles in a number of newspapers at this time, which were critically well received, and in addition tapped out three war novels in quick succession, which earned him membership of the Polish Writers' Association.[16] He then chose to live in Kraków and for a time resided in a writers' residence. However, his parentage and service in the American army soon attracted the wrong kind of attention.[17] The hammer fell when he was denounced by Adam Włodek, the then husband of Wisława Szymborska.[18] Needing to distance himself from a city filled with Party-faithful bohemia, and desperate to extract himself from the clutches of the secret police who were 'working him' as an informer, in 1953 Słomczyński moved to Gdańsk where his wife, Lidia Zamkow, had received the position of Artistic Director with the Coastal Theatre. During this time, he licked his wounds by writing a cathartic, anti-authoritarian novel entitled *Cassiopeia*, which unsurprisingly remained in a concealed drawer until 1957 following the political thaw. Słomczyński then embarked on a career as a literary translator, which was supplemented by the writing of crime novels under the pen-name Joe Alex. The earnings from these books gave Słomczyński something approaching the financial security that allowed him to work on his translation of *Ulysses*.[19] Precisely the circumstances of how he opened his literary account with *Twórczość* is uncertain, but it is legitimate to speculate that Iwaszkiewicz commissioned Słomczyński with the task. Publication in *Twórczość* was certainly an auspicious opportunity for the translator, but Słomczyński's rendition of chapter one of *Ulysses* would only mark the beginning of what came to be an epic translation in progress. It was an undertaking that engaged him for the following decade. Following his *Ulysses* debut in *Twórczość*, Słomczyński published completed chapters in various literary journals in the period between 1958 and 1968, and the translator generally accompanied these translations with scholarly introductions wherein he proclaimed the accessibility of Joyce. A flavour of his nonchalance can be seen in this pronouncement: 'I never found *Ulysses* to be a difficult book, "Oxen of the Sea" and "Sirens" gave me some headache, but the Polish language is very rich and has great elasticity. Once you get used to *Ulysses* there is nothing mysterious or enigmatic about it.'[20] Słomczyński offered this same sentiment to his own Polish readership when he asserted in the introduction to the 'Circe' episode in *Dialog*[21] that *Ulysses* was neither enigmatic nor difficult, and that it only required of readers that they concentrate on the material so as to be able to cope with the constructional traps that the author had set. Indeed it was the publication of the 'Circe' episode that perhaps first suggested to Polish readers the possibility of staging *Ulysses* in some theatrical form, whereas the inevitable close identification with Joyce must have fed into Słomczyński's own creative ambitions. And he was surely justified in wanting to maximize the earning potential of a project that he had invested so much of his time in. Once he had made the decision to adapt the novel, Słomczyński studied the texts of both Marjorie Barkentin's adaptation *Ulysses in Nighttown* (1958), which had been an off-Broadway hit, and Alan McClelland's *Bloomsday* (1958). Słomczyński, however, decided to venture beyond 'Circe' and prepare an adaptation that would convey what he described in the theatre programme as 'demonstrating Joyce's mind with the help of living people',[22] which was another way of saying that he had wanted to provide a flavour of the novel's characters and the unfolding day. In the same article, Słomczyński further stated that his goal had been to create a communicative piece, whereby *Ulysses* as theatre would help readers to achieve a fuller understanding of the novel, and also claim an autonomous space as a dramatic form:

> No less so, because the entire mechanism of this play is my own property and the fruits of my imaginings and creativity. I allowed myself to put my name to the work – as based on James Joyce's novel, only so as to avoid any misunderstanding. Any other approach would have represented a disservice to the author of *Ulysses*.[23]

In order to bring his idea to the stage, Słomczyński sought out the collaboration of Zygmunt Hübner. The project came along at a good time for Hübner as in the run-up to working on the production he had been at a loose end, having resigned his directorship of the Stary

Teatr [Old Theatre] in Warsaw in the wake of attacks from the Party following his staging of Ernest Bryll's *Kurdesz* [*Kurdesh*] (1969).[24]

His directorship of *Ulysses* would represent a defiant beginning to what was a second period of freelancing years, during which time Hübner was forced to work as a director for hire. The precise division of artistic input is unclear, but between adaptor and director the two men conceived their two-hour spectacle as a 'lyrical drama of human loneliness'.[25] The only set decoration in the background were nets entangling old clothes and rags, which several critics rather fancifully felt had evoked Dublin's grey skyline.[26] (Clearly no one hung washing out to dry in Gdańsk.)

In all, the play had two acts. In the opening scene the entire cast stood on a dimly lit stage and then retreated backwards into the darkness, leaving Bloom in the kitchen frying kidneys for Molly. Then there was Buck Mulligan shaving in Martello Tower, followed by Mulligan's condemnation of Stephen for not kneeling and praying by the bed of his dying mother. From this moment onwards, the first act featured a rapid and seamless change of scenes, taking Bloom through his day in the city from his home to the street, cemetery, bar, strand, natal clinic and finally the brothel. Importantly, the play was principally based around the fragments of Molly Bloom, who remained present in bed on the stage throughout the play, wherein her monologue both intertwined and informed the play as it proceeded. Patrick Dignam, whose coffin remained on the stage throughout, also framed the play, and together the presence of bed and coffin were intended to symbolize the circle of life and death. Molly's shifts of character were generally subtle, in that a slight change of garment or a change of voice was enough to denote the presence of a new character. It was on this principle of seamless character changes that the premise of the play was based, and also facilitated the secondary characters who remained fixtures in the background. The following extract from the English synopsis of Słomczyński's manuscript prepared by Daniel C. Gerould and Zbigniew Lewicki[27] illustrates the frenetic nature of these transformations. Although equally so, we can appreciate how the dramaturg linked various strands whilst striving for thematic coherence. Here is Act II, Scene II:

> Molly is in bed again. She says that it is Leopold's fault that she has not been faithful to him; men and women regard love differently. Then she thinks of Mina Purefoy who is in the hospital giving birth to another child. At this moment Molly starts to moan and writhe on the bed. We are in the hospital, and Molly has become Mina. Two nurses come to the bed. Bloom, who has just come in stands by the bed, joins them in bed utilizing the introductory portions of the Oxen of the Sun episode.

Joycean scholar, Egon Naganowski, contributed a piece for the theatre programme, declaring that the play illustrated how characters in *Ulysses* merge in the ether of the subconscious in accordance with Jung's theory of collective consciousness.[28] However, as Naganowski pointed out, many of the internal monologues differed from one another by allusions to personal histories and interests, families, reminiscences and so forth. Gratifyingly for the production, theatregoers and reviewers were left dazzled by the scene changes, which saw, for example, a table and coat stand transforming into a pub bar. These sudden transformations were understood as reflecting the realities of the characters' internal and external worlds, and their perception of these worlds. For Elżbieta Wysińska this was best exemplified by the scene of Patrick Dignam's funeral, wherein the singular utterances of those in the procession, beginning with 'Some people believe we go on living in another body after death', combined to make one sentence.[29]

Both Hübner and Słomczyński won praise for having attempted to throw light upon whatever was remotely fathomable, whereas in general it was thought that Słomczyński had succeeded in inspiring the audience to actually read a book that so many people had gone to great lengths and expense to acquire, but had hitherto anecdotally been only content to have sitting proudly and conspicuously on their bookshelves. However, the afterlife of this production was short, which is surprising, given the play's success. Indeed, Hübner and Słomczyński had the wind taken out of their sails when they took the play to a Venice theatre festival a few months later, having anticipated the kind of rapturous reception that they had received in Gdańsk. But it seems that they had not given due consideration to their Italian audience, who had to view the play with headphones on whilst listening to a simultaneous translation. This was all the more unfortunate as Słomczyński had bombastically declared in a press conference prior to the performance that he had wanted to focus on what Joyce said and not how he said it. As a soundbite this declaration may have provided good copy for the journalists present, but Słomczyński must have anticipated that the play would be assessed in the light of such a remark, which was in any case far removed from the actuality of his experiment. And unsurprisingly, the chief criticism of the play was that Joyce's language had been completely done away with, whereas the frantic scene changes were adjudged to have been 'too numerous for the time allowed'.[30]

Lost in Night Town

The generous reception given to Słomczyński's *Ulysses* in Poland was due in part to the fact that the play had tapped into Poland's own more recent modernist dramatic traditions, and that it accorded with the visual and spatial explorations being pioneered by Kantor. Three years later, this enquiry after the theatrical space afforded by *Ulysses* was further examined in what could be described as a sequel production. The name of the play was *Bloomusalem* and its premiere was intended to inaugurate for Warsaw's Teatr Ateneum [Ateneum Theatre] a night-time season, conceived as a forum for the presentation of more risqué artistic ventures. The play began at 10 o'clock on the evening of 27 March 1974 and the entrance fee was an exorbitant 70 zlotys.

The director of the production was Jerzy Grzegorzewski, a graduate of Warsaw's State Drama School, who had come to prominence with his stage adaptations of Wyspiański's *The Wedding*, Jean Genet's *The Balcony* (1956), and Franz Kafka's *America* (1927). Grzegorzewski had first been made aware of the theatrical importance of Joyce when he read the 'Circe' episode in *Dialog* in 1964 and later had been as caught up as his contemporaries in the frenzy surrounding the publication of the 1969 *Ulysses* translation.[31] And it was the 'Circe' episode in Słomczyński's translation that Grzegorzewski made the focus of his play. However, Grzegorzewski proceeded with rehearsals without ever having made contact with Słomczyński, who may have been rightly concerned about the integrity of his work, especially given that it was in the hands of a young director not known for being reverential with texts. The matter was only settled when Słomczyński wrote to the director explaining his reservations about the potential staging of the episode. His protests would presumably also have absolved him of criticism should the production have been panned. An attempt to mend the broken bridge was also made by the Ateneum's artistic director, who printed a profuse apology to the translator in the journal *Życie Literackie* [*The Literary Life*] and elsewhere. He firstly begged pardon for not having sought permission to use the translation, and secondly for not affording Słomczyński the right to formally accept the manuscript.[32] However, for all of Słomczyński's bluster in this spat, one critic thought that the translator must have been happy with the unsought-after publicity.[33]

For the first act, the director famously drew a black canopy from the stage over the front nine rows so that the audience felt a part of this enclosed world. This ambition to include the audience in the theatrical reality would play out in the second act. This first act, however, depicted Bloom's hallucinations, where he set his wits against policemen, whores, family members and all those who judged him severely for his dissolute lifestyle. The scene ended with his coronation as King of Bloomusalem, and Bloom leading the ecstatic procession of characters offstage. Throughout the act, much of the emphasis had been placed on contemporary dance routines and the musical score composed by Stanisław Radwan, with the singing of Elżbieta Kępińska, playing Cissy Caffrey, winning special praise.[34] In keeping with the disorientating visual nature of grotesque theatre, the stage also had Bloom grappling with shopping trolleys.

The second half consisted of various episodes taking place simultaneously throughout the foyer and in the various nooks and crannies of the theatre. Here the audience found itself in Bella Cohen's brothel, with the appallingly garbed hostess holding court in the cloakroom sitting atop a grand piano and speaking through a giant seashell. During this act, the audience could wander through this phantasmagorical Nighttown mingling with the actors who recited snippets of text, which they repeated whenever a new clutch of onlookers approached. A singular challenge for the actors involved negotiating their way through the onlookers when it was their cue elsewhere.[35] But somehow this chaos and action converged in the finale when Leopold saved Stephen from himself. Stephen, who was in a slumber for most of the second act, suddenly burst into life, shouting 'Non serviam'. He then broke the chandelier, and seemed to be itching for a quarrel. Bloom rushed over to Dedalus, handed him a box of matches that he had dropped, and addressed him with the words: 'Don't smoke? […] You have nothing?'[36] Bloom then escorted his worse-for-wear spiritual son out of the brothel through a taunting drunken crowd – and the audience – towards the open main doors of the theatre. A car then drove through the exit with its headlights glaring and took them away into the night. The door then closed revealing a labyrinthine artwork on the back of the same door, which was intended to symbolize the 'climate of mystery which pervades all aspects of everyday reality'.[37] With this, the evening's entertainment was drawn to a close.

Whilst critic Marta Fik thought that Grzegorzewski had commendably explored what contemporary theatre can do with Joyce, for her the stylization had done little to demonstrate the vulgarity and atmosphere of the Nighttown episode.[38] Moreover, although Fik felt that the second act represented an interesting experiment in breaking up the action, the audience could only appreciate snippets of the larger work. In turn, the success of the second act depended on the audience taking the trouble to proactively meander from one isolated scene to the next. Here Fik remarked that many patrons had begun to simply talk amongst themselves, indicative, it followed, that art would always play second fiddle to trivia. In fact, several reviewers felt that Grzegorzewski had failed to anticipate the potential ambivalence of the audience. But placing this criticism to one side, the general sense was that the play had been a resounding artistic success, and in keeping with the originality of contemporary theatre. The production was all the more triumphant for the fact that many had predicted that the play would be a fiasco, particularly given that some dissenting voices had emerged from the cast and crew, exhausted by the lengthy duration of rehearsals. Indeed, in the opinion of reviewer Janusz Płoński, it was one of the most beautiful spectacles he had ever seen.[39] But nerves had been frayed, and at the end of the play's run, Grzegorzewski left the Ateneum Theatre under an acrimonious cloud. Notwithstanding, the play had left its mark, having proposed as it did new boundaries within which theatre may take spatial and real-time experimentation. Just as *Ulysses* had demanded a great deal from its Polish readers, *Bloomusalem* also proved to be a challenging experience for its audience, particularly as the spectacle proposed that they be as avant-garde as the proceedings purported to be.

Singing Regrettable Necessities

Had he lived, Brendan Behan would surely have had florid things to say about the fact that Poland as a home for his work had been something of a lost cause. Both of his completed plays *The Quare Fellow* (1954) and *The Hostage* (1958) were performed here much later than elsewhere. The theatre journal *Dialog* did in fact feature translations of Behan in the early 1960s, but stage adaptations did not follow straightaway. Some Polish critics did attempt to explain these delays, surmising that the air of scandal surrounding both Behan's plays and the infamous persona of the playwright meant that those with a deciding voice in Poland's theatrical world had opted to keep the Irishman under wraps for as long as possible. Ironically, by the time *The Quare Fellow* and *The Hostage* were given their theatre premieres in Poland, they were no longer the celebrated pieces that they had been some years previously. In fact, they were very much the plays of yesteryear, and consequently ended up playing short runs in small theatres. It is just possible, however, that Behan may have had a different career in Poland had it not been for the disastrous affair as represented by the Polish Theatre's staging of Sean O'Casey's *Cock-a-Doodle Dandy*.

Indeed, Grzegorz Sinko must have been mindful of his contention that O'Casey's dialects could not be rendered in Polish when he himself took on the challenge of translating Brendan Behan's *The Quare Fellow*, which was published in *Dialog* in the 1963 November issue. Sinko had spent time in London on an academic stipend in the years 1957–1958 and had been particularly inspired by the Angry Young Men generation of dramatists, an interest reflected in his article 'Stara i młoda Anglia' ['Old and Young England'].[40] However, breaking with tradition in *Dialog*, Sinko did not provide an introduction to his translation, and it is difficult to build an informed story around his endeavours. However, at the bottom of the first page Sinko wrote of the difficulty in translating Behan's prison jargon, and gave the title of *The Quare Fellow* as an example of the problems he had had to face, having found no colloquial term in Polish for someone awaiting execution. Consequently, he had only been able to come up with the straightforward Polish title of *Skazaniec* [*The Condemned Man*]. Being scholar first and foremost, Sinko listed a number of reference books that he had made recourse to whilst also acknowledging the advice given to him by Zbigniew Bożyczko, who was an author of works on penal law and prison life.

Sinko's translation was destined to anticipate, if not inspire, the play *Czapa czyli smierć na raty* [*The Hood, that is death on the Gallows*], written by Janusz Krasiński in 1966, featuring as it did two condemned men conversing in their prison cell awaiting execution by hanging for multiple murder. They try to delay their execution by admitting to the murders, which brings a temporary stay of execution by a further two months. All the while, the men hope against hope that something out of the ordinary will take place – a change in government, for instance – which may alter events in their favour. For the rest of the play, their remaining time is presented like the falling sands of an hour glass. However, soon they are joined by another condemned man, who is resigned to his fate. The manner in which events play out explores depths of the kind of despair where gallows' humour thrives. Even though Krasiński's play had been written after the appearance of *The Quare Fellow* in *Dialog*, *The Hood* premiered a year earlier. Consequently, critics adjudged Krasiński's play to have stolen a march on *The Quare Fellow*, not only in terms of timing, but also in having explored more directly the humanity of condemned men, as opposed to Behan's play, which looked to show the debasing effect that capital punishment had on society.

The Quare Fellow had its premiere in Warsaw's Teatr Ludowy [Folk Theatre] on 16 March 1967, which no longer exists today. However, somewhat ironically, it was situated on Puławska Street, close to Warsaw's main prison on Rakowiecka Street, where condemned men awaited their appointment with the gallows.

Set in Dublin's Mountjoy Prison, the play is filled with song and the conversations of prisoners and guards over the course of one day concerning principally the imminent execution of a man who is never seen. All that is known of him is that he has committed murder. One of the grimmest moments of the play, adding extra-textual and theatrical gloom, comes in the second act, as prisoners dig a grave in the courtyard. Behan himself understood the horror of capital punishment, so speaking on Irish television in February 1963, following the Minister for Justice's announcement that the death penalty for murder would be abolished but retained in principle for certain specific types of murder.

> Nobody who was ever inside before likes goin' the gallows. Because in various cases people have swung for … eh, half hour, or maybe an hour, and just left there in the pit. If they happen to be a Catholic, they slit the hoods so that the priest can anoint them. Well, I think the priest has the worst job of the lot.[41]

Over the decades, much has been made of the difficulty of staging Behan's play and in particular of the logistical nightmare posed by the fact that it has such a large cast. However, the director, Jan Bratkowski, chose to be as faithful as possible both to the text and to the visual spectacle as envisioned by the dramatist. Generally it was felt that the production had managed to illicit the starkness of the setting and merged it with the lyrical power of the dialogues.[42] However, the fidelity of the production did not please all critics, with some feeling that it had been hard to relate to the litany of characters who came across as dramatic archetypes and not real people. Critics also maintained that the play never got further than the minutiae of prison life in Ireland where an execution was due to take place.[43] Andrzej Jarecki, writing for *Sztandar Młodych* [*The Banner of the Youth*], commended the play for its humanity, wherein it was clear that judicial killing demeaned a society, even if the crime warranted such a punishment. Indeed, if disenfranchised prisoners saw the senselessness of the punishment, then so too should people who were in a position to exercise better judgement. However, Jarecki contended that the legal system was inherently unjust and argued that such injustices continued to thrive because society in its broadest sense had failed to arrive at a common humanity: 'Society is not just. The courts see nothing beyond the letter of the law, justice is blind and dark, prisons are inhuman – but everything works, and must work this way because man fails in life.'[44] In turn, Jarecki stated that in as much as the actors were onlookers of events, this somehow extended to the audience, who in the second act were swept up by the horror of the approaching execution. However, here Jarecki was not being totally complimentary, as he sensed that the audience had felt that time dragged in the play in a manner that must surely resemble the unendurable stretch of prison life itself, made ever more unbearable because of the dialogue relating to the death of Gaelic Ireland, which could have been happily dispensed with, particularly as it detracted from the central drama.

Jan Kłossowicz regarded the play as lacking intellectual rigour, but discerned also in it a passion for realism and human interest that had characterized the generation of Angry Young Men, and that had been markedly absent from Polish theatres.[45] Kłossowicz was also keen to praise Sinko for having displayed a 'commitment to human affairs'[46] and for having gone to such lengths to arrive at an appropriate register for the play. But as Jarecki also noted, prison lingo had changed in the intervening years, and for those in the audience familiar with such lingo, the play had come across as contrived.[47] And so it seems that there had been no pleasing everyone, least of all ex-prisoners in this instance, looking to return to the familiar world of their incarceration.

The Disappointment of Jingle Jangle

In 1966 Erwin Axer reflected on his working relationship with Polish theatre translators.[48] In principle, he sympathized with this group of unsung, poorly remunerated heroes. But his sympathy only extended so far. Indeed, Axer was more than willing to state publicly that he would like to see off the current batch of theatre translators associated with *Dialog*, branding them as mechanical specialists and fourth-rate writers, whose only qualifications were their knowledge of languages. And here Axer even questioned the manner in which this group of translators had acquired their second or third languages: apple picking in Germany, for instance. The reason for such a slanderous stance was that Axer felt that far too often both he and his fellow Polish directors were having to contend with slavishly precise translations that gave little appreciable thought to the actability of the translated manuscript. Axer compared this problem to the different approaches taken in France and England. In these countries, so the Polish director claimed, creativity extended to the process of translation. Consequently, it was inconceivable that a translator would not play a central visionary and insightful role in the adaptation of a foreign play.

> They understand very well that in drama, as supposedly in poetry, a strict translation is impossible. Literalness represents a betrayal of the author, and the beauty and sense of the whole either justifies or condemns the translator-adaptor.[49]

Given that the Polish translation of Behan's *The Hostage*, which featured in *Dialog* in the December edition of 1960, was rendered by a relatively inexperienced translator, it is entirely possible that Axer would have considered this enterprise as having fallen into this discredited category. Indeed, prior to her translation of *The Hostage*, Maria Skroczyńska had distinguished herself primarily by her 1957 translation of Sherpa Tenzing's *Man of Everest* [*Człowiek Everestu*], which featured a Polish introduction by alpinist Wawrzyniec Żuławski, the brother of Juliusz. This personal contact seems to have led to her working with Juliusz Żuławski on this translation of Behan's play. Żuławski translated the songs and presumably provided literary expertise and insight.

In spite of the fact that *The Hostage* was translated in 1960, the play would have to wait over a decade before it was given its Polish theatrical premiere. Eventually it was staged in the small Warsaw venue of the Dramatic Theatre, which had made its mark in post-war Poland by staging national and international drama. Once again, Hübner, who was filled with confidence following his recent successful theatrical adaptation of *Ulysses*, took the directorial reins. However, even though he chose to stage the play on the basis of the *Dialog* translation, Hübner did not consult with the translators on any eventual revisions or changes.[50] And as we shall see, this decision to 'go it alone' may have proven to be one of the singular factors that scuppered all chances of Hübner staging a successful production.

The Hostage is a zany and disturbing play, and the list of ascribable adjectives could run to paragraphs. Here politics, drama and endless cultural and historical Irish-specific one-liners pertaining to the Anglo-Irish conflict and the wretchedness of De Valera's post-war Ireland are thrown together in a farce that followed the tradition of Brecht's Berliner Ensemble. Indeed, Behan would contend that the play could seem artificial 'only to people who do not [know] music-hall, vaudeville'.[51] Adapted from Behan's Irish language play *An Giall*, the English version was first staged in Damer Hall in Dublin on 16 June 1958, and later developed over the course of a series of improvisatory theatre workshops under the guidance of Joan Littlewood at her London theatre of Stratford East, which was a process that augmented the original play by its inclusion of ballads and songs that Behan himself had written. This workshop adaptation was initially intended for a London audience and the text was deliberately left open-ended in parts so as to allow other adaptations to take a similarly improvisatory approach, and also to accommodate foreign directors who sought to mount eccentric productions for the particular needs of a local audience.[52]

Set in a Dublin 'brockel' run by Pat and his consort, Meg, this is a world that has seen better times. It is a home to waifs and strays, and most notably working girls aiming to please an array of goofy clientele. Pat was 'out in 1916' but fought against the Free State in the Civil War, and continued the fight when the conflict had ended. Tried in absentia in 1925, he has been holed up in the house ever since. There is also Monsewer, an Englishman, and something of an Erskine Childers figure, in that he is fully wedded to the cause of the six counties, and has become more Irish than the Irish themselves. He is often to be found playing the bagpipes and has immersed himself in the Gaelic language. In the house, good-humoured banter and squabbles are the order of the day, and everyone seems to live by the maxim 'live and let live'. Rent and his rebel memories are all that interest Pat, and given that the house has been 'a good hole [...] for many a decent man on the run', IRA 'fanatics', so described in the play, decide that Pat and Monsewer can hold prisoner a British private by the name of Leslie, who has been taken hostage in the unlikely hope that he can be traded for a young IRA man who is to be hung in a Belfast jail the following morning. If the hanging takes place, then the British soldier will be executed in an act of reprisal.

If we are to accept Hübner's view that the censors did not know what to make of Behan's persona,[53] and that this uncertainty extended to the play itself, as matters transpired, they were not alone in their holding of such opinions. Given that *The Hostage* had its Polish premiere on 19 December 1971, two years after the outbreak of what by then had come to be known as the Troubles, Polish critics and theatregoers had been expecting to find in the play some examination of a sectarian conflict that had earned worldwide infamy. Principally,

Polish critics expressed disappointment that both the setting of the play and the dialogue, not to mention the featured sing-a-longs, left them none the wiser as to the causes and course of the conflict. However, the main criticism was principally reserved for Hübner. In the main, theatre reviewers stated that he had remained too faithful to the translated text, with one critic Maciej Karpiński noting that the director had not sufficiently expressed his own approach to the matters in hand, or to the characters in the play.[54]

Contrariwise, Bohdan Drozdowski, writing for *Teatr*, thought it natural for Hübner to have wanted to remain as close to the text as possible, but felt that Hübner must have known well in advance of the opening night that he had taken on an unperformable play.[55] The reviewer also extended his sympathy to the actress, Ryszarda Hanin, playing Meg, whom he contended had been extremely embarrassed at having to deliver some of the play's racier lines. But in truth, the Polish Meg was spared utterances that would have caused a lot more embarrassment, with lines such as 'Well, she was a dirty little no good ...' excised entirely from the play. In turn, Drozdowski thought it ludicrous that Meg had had to sing of the murdered women and children of 1916 for the song only to be followed by the spectacle of Leslie and Teresa gaily dancing around the stage. The reviewer also rated pitiful the sight of young actors with a promising career ahead of them having to play transvestite prostitutes, although he did admit that Maciej Damięcki, playing Princess Grace, had sported an enviable figure: 'a shapely boy with his belly button on display can be as sexy as a dolled up shapely girl!'[56] Finally, in terms of what the critics had to say on the play, Jan Alfred Szczepański praised Hübner for having kept intact the songs that Żuławski had translated, but at the same time he thought that they should have been integrated better into the play as each and every song had come across as a 'stuck-on beard'.[57] To make matters worse, it seems that the songs were sung in a hysterical, over-the-top manner, and were consequently hard to make out. That said, one reviewer, Andrzej Hausbrandt, lay the blame squarely with the play, which he described as outdated and little more than a series of unseemly scenes in a bordello. Indeed, having exonerated the efforts of the cast, the critic could only bring himself to say that, 'It's not their fault [the cast's]. Judgement on *The Hostage* has been passed.'[58]

Hübner himself was disappointed by the adaptation. And it seems that for the director there had been a disconnect between what he had originally conceived and what he had produced: 'on seeing the first performance I felt something in the way of disappointment'.[59] Perhaps Hübner had also realized that he could have done more to make *The Hostage* current for Polish theatregoers, and that such a re-examination of the play may have involved a complete rewrite of both the play and its songs. But for such a task, a visionary-adaptor of the kind envisaged by Axer would have been needed. As things stood, Behan's play had aged and reflected little on a conflict far removed from the world of vaudeville. Indeed, it may just be said that the play had fallen victim in Poland to the very conflict that it was thought to have presaged. This production would not only mark the end of Hübner's adventures with modern Irish drama, but Behan's plays forever disappeared from the repertoires of Polish theatres.

Familiar Territory

Unquestionably, the reception of Behan's *The Hostage* spelt the end of Poland's increasingly tepid love affair with Irish drama. And the truth of this statement can be seen in the absence of Irish plays from the Polish stage for the entire 1970s and 1980s. What is more, this general neglect extended to much of Irish culture and current affairs, aside from intermittent reports about the Troubles, which left many Polish people thinking that the delight 'entire' island of Ireland was engulfed in a war of attrition between Protestants and Catholics.

By rights, Brian Friel should have made his Polish theatrical debut in this period of the early 1970s, but his plays were perhaps too suggestive of the social unrest gripping Poland, which had been sparked by wage decreases on the one hand and the price hikes of staple goods on the other. Convinced that a workers' revolution was underway, Prime Minister Władysław Gomułka and his political cohorts ordered a crackdown on protests. A bloodbath ensued as riot police shot at workers either striking or attempting to return to work. The crisis was only quelled when Gomułka was forced to resign and his successor, Edward Gierek, a self-proclaimed man of the people, took office and introduced policies that slashed food prices and stabilized wages. But even though an accommodation had been arrived at, the spirit of national protest, dormant for decades, had resurfaced, and would continue to fan the flames of discontent, culminating a few short years later in the emergence of the Solidarity movement.

The only play of Friel's to be performed in Poland in the 1970s was *Freedom of the City* (1973), which, set in Derry, relates the story of how three jovial protesters take shelter in the Mayor's office following the dispersal of a civil rights rally. Even though the protesters were only looking to find sanctuary, soldiers surrounding the building soon regard them as militant occupants. Comedy turns to tragedy when the protesters find that they are unable to explain their way out of the predicament. In 1975, the play was featured in *Dialog* in the February edition, and once again Maria Skroczyńska was the translator.[60] The play was then staged two years later on 4 June 1977 in Częstochowa, a town principally associated with Polish resistance during the Swedish invasions in the seventeenth century.

Directed by Ryszard Krzyszycha, who at the time was embarking on a career that would keep him with the same theatre for the next thirty years, the production clearly reminded theatregoers of the turmoil of recent years, although critic Jan Ławnikowski[61] chose circumspection when it came to pointing out the similarities between the unrest in Poland and that taking place in Northern Ireland: 'Ryszard Krzyszycha, with dramatic aplomb, has imparted the intentions of the Irish writer, so close to our own historical experience and sentiment.'[62] The critic praised both the values of the production and the play itself and also had warm words for the accompanying music, composed by Janusz Papaj, which must have contributed to creating an impression that the play had two conjoined national settings. Perhaps most importantly, Ławnikowski declared that the production represented a high watermark for Polish Theatre, showcasing as it had both high-quality acting and directorial ingenuity. But in spite of the play's success, it tellingly remained a once-off provincial production, and was never performed in Poland again.

It was not only political and social crises that may have impacted on the place of Irish drama in this era, but there was also a prevailing perception in Poland that Irish drama was going through a protracted phase of stagnation. As Andrzej Wróblewski wrote in February 1975: 'Ireland is in no need of theatre. Ireland itself is a great stage ….'[63] This general conviction was confirmed at the end of the decade in an editorial published in *Dialog*, simply entitled 'Teatr irlandzki – dzisiaj' ['Irish Theatre Today'],[64] which limited itself to relaying the irreverent observations of German critic, Jan Kaestner,[65] who had suggested that the best seat to have in an Irish theatre was in the buffet, which was a criticism of both the moribund repertoires of the Abbey and Gate theatres and the indifferent playwriting talent that was being championed. In particular, Kaestner was incredulous of the fact that new Irish plays – and here he singled out Tom Murphy's fantastical *The Morning After Optimism* (1971) – were often hailed as classics of their time in Dublin, only to end up being laughed off the stage when they were subsequently performed in continental Europe. Indeed, the critic pulled no punches when he contended that the parochial nature of modern Irish drama, and by extension its domestic critical reception, was proving injurious to the image of Irish culture abroad. Whatever the merits of such censure, this article must have been responsible in part for the fact that Polish theatres would choose to look askance at modern Irish-themed drama for many years to come.

Beckett Redrawn

From the time of the premiere of *Waiting for Godot* in Warsaw's Contemporary Theatre in 1957, interest in Beckett never waned, and many Polish theatrical exponents and practitioners, living in exceptionally difficult times, found a strong dialogic link between the Irish playwright's work and the ideological intensity of post-war Poland, where human existence grappled with a traumatic past and an uneasy acceptance of present circumstances. The earliest comparable Polish literary figure to Beckett was Sławomir Mrożek, whose play *Policja* [*The Police*] was staged to national acclaim in 1958 in Warsaw's Dramatic Theatre.[66] Given the controversial theme of the play, treating as it did how a state-security apparatus invented crimes in order to perpetuate its own activities, the fact that it was staged at all shows that the boundaries of censorial tolerance were often wider than one may generally supposed to have been the case. Similarly to the dénouement of Beckett's final play *What Where* (1982), in *The Police* all the political offenders are arrested so that by the end of the play there is no one left to prey upon. Mrożek is often regarded as the Polish representative of the Theatre of the Absurd, but the extent to which he drew on the satirical and surrealist traditions of inter-war Polish literature sets him apart from the more iconic representatives of the movement. That said, Mrożek was aware of the affiliation. Indeed, in his surrealist work of children's fiction entitled *Ucieczka na południe* [*Escape to the South*] (1961), which Mrożek himself illustrated, two brothers and their Ape companion arrive in a village where posters hail the imminent arrival of Godot, the mention of which attests to the iconic status of Beckett's play in Poland at the time.

Another early literary response to Beckett was provided in 1960 by poet and dramatist Tadeusz Różewicz. In his first play entitled *Kartoteka* [*The Card Index*], Różewicz featured a bed-ridden survivor of World War II, who wanders through the events of his life that are presented as scraps of information, emotions and sensations. The play also features a Chorus that invokes Beckett so as to encourage the passive hero 'to do something', although like Beckett's protagonists he is unable to do so.[67]

Throughout the 1960s, *Dialog* under the direction of Adam Tarn ensured that translations of Beckett's plays continued apace. But in 1968 Tarn fell foul of the Party to which he had faithfully belonged for his entire career and was forced to step down from his position as editor of *Dialog*. He was also invited to leave the country. But because of his nemetic associations, there was no possibility of him being allowed to settle in the United States, and the next option that presented itself was western Canada, which had a climate regarded as unfavourable to a now elderly man, who had for some time been beset by ill-health. On what was a journey of exile, Tarn stayed for a short time in Paris and met Beckett in a café where they shared stories of the hardships of their lives for several hours. During the course of this meeting, Beckett pleaded with Tarn to accept financial assistance, letters or manuscripts, anything in fact, that would ease the way ahead of him. Tarn managed to deflect Beckett's insistent generosity but was greatly buoyed by the gesture. However, Beckett was determined to do what he could and later wrote letters to wealthy patrons of the arts in Canada, asking that they 'look out for Adam Tarn, who was one of the world's special people.'[68] It is an insightful episode, because it points to the extent to which Beckett knew of his literary legacy in Poland, and the debt that he owed to his translators for their considerable efforts. Having said that, a few short years later, Beckett would be persuaded by a young Antoni Libera that his entire oeuvre in Polish translation needed reworking.

Antoni Libera's father, Zdzisław, an esteemed literary scholar, had been a close friend of Jerzy Kreczmar, and when he received two tickets for himself and his wife to see the premiere of *Godot* in 1957, they decided to smuggle their young son into the performance also. Sitting on one of his parents' laps, it was the first time that Antoni Libera had attended a theatrical performance. In what was a case of fancy taking flight, in later years Libera would feel that political conspiracies lay behind the failure on the part of *Dialog* to feature the play in its entirety. But for all Libera's initial suspicions, it was his reading of the old issues of *Dialog* that marked the beginning of a life that he defined as 'affinity from choice'.[69] What is more, Libera would retain a life-long conviction that his work on Beckett was a calling and a vocation, and it was perhaps this impassioned notion of his role that allowed him to look askance at the contribution of others prior to his own ascendancy, starting with the first production of Beckett. If proof of this were needed, when Roger Blin brought *Endgame* (1957) in 1970 to Warsaw's Teatr Powszechny [People's Theatre], Libera, who was at the time a student of Polish literature at the University of Warsaw, met the director backstage as part of a retinue of Beckett aficionados, and promptly told Blin that *Godot* in Poland had been understood as an exploration in disillusionment with the Marxist promise of a utopian world; which had never really been the case.[70]

In an article entitled 'Beckett and Poland', published in 1975, and delivered at a Beckettian international symposium in Ohio, Libera pleaded for a more responsible and consistent practice of translating Beckett into Polish. In particular he criticized uninformed attempts to provide 'instantaneous' translations of Beckett's works, which was a singular put-down of his predecessors that also hailed the dawn of a new era where Libera himself planned to occupy centre stage.[71] Soon after the publication of this article, Libera wrote to Beckett introducing and recounting his activities. Their relationship flourished after they met in Paris over coffee on 6 January 1978, a propitious date as it coincided with the twenty-fifth anniversary of the premiere of *Godot* in Paris, a nugget that Libera was anxious to share with Beckett:[72] 'I said to Beckett: "Do you remember that 25 years ago today it was the premiere of this play?" and he said, "So you remember it, too?". I said to him: "My connection with your work is very, very deep because while you were writing *Waiting for Godot* between October 1948 and January 1949, my mother was pregnant with me. So you created this play while my mother created me."[73]

Libera's intimacy with and reverence for Beckett was harnessed by his own considerable intellect, which gave him a certainty in interpretation that is unique to directors and translators of Beckett. Over time, Libera formed a credo that understood his role as the assistant of the playwright, who like a conductor must work with the score. This analogy also aligned with Libera's veneration for the musicality of Beckett's plays. Yet, even though Libera believes that to interpret a Beckett play is to doom the production to failure, he himself has often been criticized for having over-rendered Beckett's plays. As fellow Beckettian scholar and translator, Marek Kędzierski, comments:

> As a translator, Libera has set new standards of accuracy. It is good that the whole body of Beckett's work has been rendered by one person as it secures the unity of the writer's vocabulary and style. [...] Also, a careful comparison of originals and his translations shows the tendency on Libera's part to render Beckett's texts more comprehensible than they themselves are. This may or may not have to do with the fact that Libera assumes the role of both translator and commentator. And the passion of the exegete may be at conflict with the duty of the translator, the latter being to enable the reader to perceive the translated work in a semantic context as wide as that of the original.[74]

Kędzierski own standing in terms of Beckett's legacy in Poland is almost on a par with that of Libera, and like his counterpart, Kędzierski also established a close personal relationship with Beckett. On meeting Beckett for the first time in 1980 in Paris, Kędzierski suggested to the Irish writer that he direct *Endgame* in Kraków's Stary Teatr [Old Theatre], with which Kędzierski had a strong affiliation. Beckett politely refused, claiming that 'I am too old and I don't know Polish. But Walter [Asmus] will do it much better than I.'[75] But Beckett did take steps to encourage Asmus, his most trusted directorial collaborator in Germany, to take up the challenge. A year later, in September, Asmus arrived in Kraków and embarked on month-long rehearsals. Kędzierski would be Asmus's assistant director on the production, for which Kędzierski also provided a fresh Polish translation, inspired by the numerous suggestions that Beckett had offered.

Endgame had been slow to establish itself in Poland's theatrical repertoires, even though it had been performed in as early as 1958 by Kraków's avant-garde Theatre 38. Perhaps buoyed by the notoriety of the previously mentioned Blin production, Wrocław's National Theatre included the play in its 1971–1972 winter repertoire, which made recourse to the Rogożiński translation. Directed by Jerzy Krasowski, the production was notable for its stage design, which, in contrast to the play's traditionally closed setting, suggested an open space littered with objects. The production was bolstered by the star quality of the cast, most notably the actress chosen to play the role of Hamm, Maja Komorowska, who was the muse of film directors Andrzej Wajda and Krzysztof Zanussi during this era. The play was performed to record attendances and when it transferred to Kraków's Słowacki Theatre in October 1974 it enjoyed the same kind of success. One critic, Maciej Karpiński was particularly taken by the way in which the production had looked to show how one person 'when confronted by defeat, humiliation and paralysis requires the existence of another as a point of reference, or rather as a confirmation of the existence of the World'.[76]

Asmus's production of *Endgame* coincided with bi-centennial celebrations to mark the founding of Kraków's Old Theatre, and a small number of critics wondered why such a play had come to be chosen for what was widely regarded as a landmark event deserving of an appropriate showcase production. One local theatre reviewer, Włodzimierz Szturc, had particularly harsh words about both the decision to stage the play, and also reserved some unsparing words for both the play and the performance:

> It is a tedious production, with no clear line of interpretation, without a trace of directorial input, bereft of humour, which creates the tragic vision of a world which is always to be found in Beckett's plays. To make matters worse, it is played badly: *Endgame* has been turned into a radio play for stage.[77]

To some extent we may understand Szturc's standpoint, as given both the political fractiousness of the times and the international interest in the bi-centennial celebrations, which unduly focused on the impasse between the ruling Communist Party and the Solidarity movement, an opportunity had been missed to present a play that best represented Polish culture, or that could elucidate a political crisis which was beginning to intensify. Indeed, Asmus and Kędzierski could not have chosen a more intractable time to stage Beckett in Poland, and the fact that the performance almost coincided with the declaration of Martial Law, which took place a few short weeks after the play's premiere, has lent more historical weight to the production than would otherwise have been the case.

Food shortages had become an ever-pressing issue in the months and weeks preceding the premiere, and it was widely suspected that the Communist government, determined to restore its iron grip on rule, had been reducing the supplies of basic goods as a coercive response to the flourishing activities and growing popularity of the Solidarity movement.

Worse would follow in the months and years to come. But as Kędzierski recalls, when during the performance Clov had occasion to speak his refrain, 'There is no more', which translates into Polish as 'Nie ma', the audience responded with laughter, as this was often the curt response offered by shop assistants when something wasn't in stock.

Some weeks after the production ended, on 13 December 1981, Polish state television turned green with the presence of military journalists, and General Jaruzelski in his distinctive dark glasses declared Martial Law. Militia and soldiers poured onto the streets and Solidarity activists were arrested in their thousands.[78] Polish artists and cultural activists like Agnieszka Holland and Marek Kędzierski found themselves abroad at the time and had no immediate prospect of being allowed to return to Poland. Libera had in fact returned to Warsaw from abroad just prior to the declaration of Martial Law and Beckett was greatly concerned for his welfare. As a gesture of solidarity, Beckett sent royalties collected from his Polish productions to the families of imprisoned writers and also made strenuous enquiries into the possibility of helping Libera to leave Poland, but ultimately Libera would choose to remain.[79] An equally remarkable gesture was made by Walter Asmus, who organized a food truck in conjunction with the Cologne City Theatre on behalf of the actors and staff of Kraków's Old Theatre. He ended up co-driving the truck to Poland, passing countless checkpoints in the process.[80]

Unlike what took place in Czechoslovakia, Beckett productions in Poland during this era were perceived as more theatrical than political events and were positioned between Visual Art theatre, which had flourished in Poland during the 1970s, and the theatre of Kantor. The framing of a political response by Solidarity's cultural activists drew principally on either Poland's literary, historical or religious traditions. In 1982 Zygmunt Hübner, for example, chose to stage *Nederlaget* [*The Defeat*] (1937) by the Norwegian writer Nordahl Grieg (1902–1943), a play that was about the events of the Paris Commune. The play's similarities to the spirit of the time were not lost on one reviewer, Józef Szczawiński, writing for the Catholic newspaper *Słowo Powszechne* [*The Daily Word*], when he wrote: 'Great historical events uncover certain truths, which come to the fore in different eras where society must deal with similar issues, tensions and dramas.'[81] And indeed, Hübner had attempted to bring the events in the play closer to Polish audiences by featuring a patriotic ballad written by poet Władysław Broniewski, entitled *Komuna paryska* [*The Paris Commune*] (1929), which enjoined people to bear witness to revolutionary times. Interestingly, this production was also reviewed positively by critics writing for Party-associated newspapers, who chose to disregard its overt allegorical missives. That said, critic Marzena Wiśniewska writing for *Sztandar Młodych*, wondered how the acclaim that had greeted the production had not been matched by the number of seats sold, as the theatre had only been half-full on the evening she had attended the play. This same fact led Wiśniewska to speculate that audiences were not looking for analogies but 'would like to see a play that related to the "here and now".'[82] Ironically, this gauntlet had already been taken up by the Catholic Church, which would harness the kind of devotional resistance that set Solidarity apart from other dissident movements in the Eastern Bloc.

In the early to mid-1980s, the Polish Catholic Church was also the only functioning institution that could openly oppose communism and provide an inviolate space for an array of artistic events and gatherings to take place. Actors who had boycotted the mass media found that performances in churches afforded a unique cultural loophole for reconnecting with the public. One such theatrical event was a production of Ernest Bryll's *Wieczernik* [*The Upper Room*], which took place on 5 April 1985 in a church on Warsaw's Żytnia Street. The play was a traditional Easter-themed play, written in verse after the fashion of Wyspiański, which presents the apostles gathered in the Upper Room cowering in despair just before the arrival of a resurrected Jesus. Bryll wrote the play at the end of 1984, just one month after the death of Father Jerzy Popiełuszko, who had been brutally murdered by security police. In time the perpetrators were subsequently arrested, tried and sentenced to life-terms of imprisonment. Popiełuszko's own sermons in a Warsaw suburban church had been uncompromising in their criticism of the communist regime, and had had the power to raise congregations to states of religious exaltation, something that Bryll's play also attempted to do. Originally it had been intended that *The Upper Room* would be staged in the Ateneum Theatre, but the censor without explanation withdrew its license for performance and also halted the play's publication. It was at that point that Andrzej Wajda and a group of his associated actors intervened and made a decision to stage the play over Easter Weekend in a church that was still under construction. Its unplastered walls, scaffolding, columns, mixers and so on provided a magnificent backdrop for the performance. The stage was also lit with checkpoint lamps, which had come to be seen as symbols of oppression. This was just one aspect that made the play relate to Wiśniewska's 'here and now'. Another element was the decision to dress the apostles after the fashion of Polish workers, although Jesus would remain in his traditional white robes. Ernest Bryll poetically described on the inside flap of the front cover to the 1990 publication of the book: that the thousands of onlookers gathered in the church 'experienced with bated breath the bitter defeat of the Apostles, asked themselves the same questions, doubted with Thomas and searched for the same hope'.[83] This exalted position was for many in the Polish artistic and dissident world the dominant narrative and sentiment of the times, and it was mirrored in a collective letter from the play's director and cast, which was also published in the same book publication of the play:

> Each and every one of us who has been reared in the national culture knows that the relationship of art, and that includes theatre, with the Church is nothing new. It has always been so, and always will be, and we cannot imagine the cultural heritage of world civilization without this aspect of art which is derived from religious inspiration.[84]

Interestingly, as Solidarity began to achieve its goals in the late 1980s, Church theatre began to be seen as anachronistic. And it is perhaps because the reception of Beckett had not been so politicized that productions of his works had managed to become a part of the mythology of the Solidarity age whilst not being associated with its cultural ephemera. Indeed, in 1985 Libera was still working hard to establish Beckett's credentials with a mainstream audience. His production of *Krapp's Last Tape* (1958) for Warsaw's Teatr Studio [Studio Theatre] was shortlived, and received greater success when it was taken on an international tour. Indeed, the singular talking point to come out of the production was the fact that the actor, Tadeusz Łomnicki, playing Krapp had produced and eaten three bananas during each performance, leaving the audience aghast and wondering how the theatre had managed to get hold of bananas in a country that had not seen exotic fruit for years. But matters did not end there, as Gabriela Pewińska recalled: 'Even greater was the shock when Łomnicki threw an uneaten banana on the floor! The audience almost dropped dead. I think if someone had thrown a diamond into the bin, it would not have made so strong an impression.'[85]

One fascinating theatrical undertaking of Libera came in 1986, which coincided with the release of many Solidarity activists, some three years after the lifting of Martial Law. In Warsaw's Studio Theatre, Libera presented over the course of three evenings a selection of Beckett's plays in celebration of Beckett's eightieth birthday, such as *Not I* (1972), *Catastrophe* (1982) and *Krapp's Last Tape*. Critics were struck by the efforts to unpeal the secrets that lay behind the performance of these dramas and by Libera's search for form and expression. One reviewer remarked that it had taken an outsider like Libera to remind Polish theatre practitioners of the need to take an organic approach to the literary material so as to achieve an essential performance. The occasion may have been Beckett's birthday celebrations, but in Warsaw it was Libera who was being fêted. As Jacek Sieradzki wrote in his review of the cycle, Libera is: 'A perfectionist who works on the piece, and renders it perfectly in Polish; this perfectionism is a visible attribute of the Studio review. It commands respect coupled with melancholy: so rare is the phenomenon.'[86] But most importantly for Beckett and his Polish exponents, the Irish writer had become part of the cultural landscape in Poland, and was henceforth free 'to be received in a normal fashion.'[87] However, the normalizing processes of post-transformational Poland proved less welcoming to theatrical enterprises than many had hoped, and reduced state funding and market forces would stymie the dreams of a brighter tomorrow for many, at least in the short term. But disenchantment would not figure in Libera's plans for the oncoming era. He would remain as active as ever, a powerhouse of directorial and literary achievement, conversing calmly through Beckett with the age, and incapable of keeping silent.

Dancing to Indifference

Brian Friel returned to Polish theatres in 1993 with two major productions of his internationally acclaimed play *Dancing at Lughnasa* (1990). The play was first staged by Warsaw's People's Theatre as part of an Irish literary festival and could boast the fact that Judy Friel, the daughter of the playwright, had been asked to take the directorial reins. The participation of Judy Friel reflected the kind of Polish-Irish cultural exchange that had begun to flourish in the realms of Polish and Irish poetry in the early 1990s. Seamus Heaney was a significant literary figure in Poland during this time, and was himself an exponent of the poetry of Czesław Miłosz and Zbigniew Herbert. Also, an entire generation of Polish poets spearheaded by Piotr Sommer and Jerzy Jarniewicz centred around the Warsaw journal *Literatura na Świece* [*Literature in the World*], translated Irish poetry and forged strong friendships with its creators, which subsequently led to further literary initiatives that could be said to have extended to prose and drama.

Told in a lyrical language, *Dancing at Lughnasa* explores the disquietudes of characters who inhabit a shared domestic space where daily tedium is interrupted by a Marconi radio that bursts into life of its own accord whenever it has a lively tune to play for the heroines to dance to. The play is set in the village of Ballybeg in County Donegal in 1936 just prior to the Celtic harvest festival of Lughnasa, and tells the story of the five unmarried Mundy sisters and their brother Jack, who, frail in health, has returned home from the African missions after 25 years away. This is a family that is tetering over the precipice in terms of its acceptance in the community and because of the financial straits that they find themselves in. One sister, Rose, is mentally unbalanced, whereas another sister, Christina, has a young son named Michael out of wedlock, which in Ireland at the time could not just bring shame on a family but attract the interest of the authorities. Michael's adult persona stands on the stage throughout, only to occupy the foreground at certain times and comment on happenings as recollections of his childhood. If the presence of illegitimacy casts a pall over the family's standing in the community, Jack, suffering from the onset of senility, digs a deeper hole for his family by babbling public pronouncements in favour of pagan worship centred around the approaching Lughnasa festival. Such is the sense of community outrage that the eldest sister, Kate, who is herself mortified by Jack's comportment, is threatened with the loss of her teaching position in the local school. Whilst romance briefly blossoms for some and opportunity beckons for others, as Autumn approaches the consequences of penury will break all their hearts.

Because Friel had been largely an unknown figure in Poland prior to this event, some reviewers were not swayed by the playwright's reputation and questioned how such a traditional theme could have been perceived elsewhere as groundbreaking. That said, Jacek Wakar, reviewing the play for *Teatr*, described the performance of *Dancing at Lughnasa* as a play where the actresses had managed to find the essence of their characters and win the sympathy of the audience. What is more, the choreographed dances during which the sisters temporarily threw off the shackles of their lives were seen as having harnessed the poetic sensibilities of the play.[88] Judy Friel would also garner praise from several quarters for her use of pastel and golden lighting which had aimed at creating a dimly remembered dreamscape.

The only outright negative criticism of the play came from Jacek Sieradzki writing for *Dialog*, who seemed to have many concerns on his mind other than the play itself.[89] Sieradzki was not at all moved by the fiscal crisis that hovers above the play and he wondered how there was so much pent-up frustration to be found in a small village where aspirations should be more attuned to the limitations of one's circumstances. Here Sieradzki was alluding to the fact that the average monthly income in 1993 for a small farm holding in Poland barely exceeded 600 zlotys (approximately 100 British sterling); and so, whilst *Dancing at Lughnasa* lamented a time in Ireland of biting poverty and rural alienation, Sieradzki was more inclined to express sympathy for the unfortunate current actualities of Poland's rural populace. Although Sieradzki's philippic was an exception, recommendations from other reviewers came with caveats, particularly relating to the play's narrow appeal and its lengthiness.[90]

Another production of *Dancing at Lughnasa* would have its premiere in Kraków's Słowacki Theatre just three days before Christmas that same year. The accompanying theatre programme is particularly informative, as it contains the transcript of a conversation that the director, Bogdan Hussakowski, held with the play's translator, Małgorzata Semil, where she reflected on her own failure to bring Friel to notoriety in Poland, which by rights should have taken place decades earlier:

> I really do blame myself. In the 1960s Friel had achieved success in Dublin, London and New York with the play *Philadelphia, Here I Come*. On the basis of the reviews which I had seen, I felt that the play was too Irish to interest anyone, and I didn't take the trouble to get a hold of the work. And what a shame! Now after *Dancing*, I have read the play [*Philadelphia...*], and I regret not doing anything at the time to popularize the play in Poland, and publish it in *Dialog*. Now I intend to make amends.[91]

Friel would remain in Kraków for the next two significant premieres of his work. *Faith Healer* (1979) was staged in February 1996, and *Translations* (1980) in June 1999, and both were produced by the internationally acclaimed director Katarzyna Deszcz for the Old theatre. Deszcz had trained under Kantor in the 1980s and had become a part of the vanguard of Poland's Alternative theatre, which espoused the organic integration of all aspects of a theatrical performance, to include lighting, actors, music and text. Deszcz should have been the ideal dramaturge to make a mark with *Faith Healer* and bring great theoretical and practical experience to bear on the production. However, the play ended up perplexing and annoying audiences and critics in equal measure.

Faith Healer is a play that depends on the considerable talents of three actors to deliver four very lengthy monologues, which are conflicting versions of events that took place twenty-five years earlier. The actors must not only visibly crumble under the weight of their memories but also be gifted storytellers. *Faith Healer* tells the tale of charlatan Frank Hardy and his wife Gracie – who may also be his mistress depending on whom we believe – and their impresario manager, Teddy, who once travelled together in a bumpy van to small towns throughout the British Isles, where Frank on occasion managed to heal sceptical people, who were then pleasantly surprised with the results. The accounts converge on their return to Ballybeg, where people believe in Frank's ability, which throws his act off balance, and a series of tragic events ensue. Pain, distortions of the truth and thwarted hopes fill these conflicting accounts, and yet Andrzej Hudziak playing Frank and Lidia Duda playing Gracie could not take their performances beyond monotonous recitation. Only the actor Zbigniew Ruciński playing Teddy acquitted himself well in his role, having introduced gesticulations that matched his vaudevillian character. Delivered under differently coloured spotlights that shone from a silver tube placed over the stage, the intricacy of the monologues, and the fascination that they held, did not compensate for the lack of action in the play. Several reviewers found themselves jaded by this marathon of words, and considered closing their eyes so as to imagine that they were listening to a radio play. However, smoke that was intended to engulf the actors each time they completed their speech actually wafted into the seating area and began to sting people's eyes. One scornful description of the tedium and the smoke was provided by Magda Huzarska-Szumiec, whose annoyance ran deep:

> Because absolutely nothing was happening on stage, I closed my eyes and tried to surrender to the cadences of the words. I imagined that I was sitting on a soft armchair and not one of the hard chairs in the Modrzejewska room, sipping tea and listening to Polish radio theatre. But even that proved to be impossible as the billows of smoke wafting beyond the stage began to sting my eyes.

> - What can we do to stop the audience from falling asleep during the performance? – so must have thought certain creators of this production.
> - Well why don't we add some smoke – proposed one of the artists. And they filled the place with smoke![92]

The Old Theatre's production of *Translations* would goad Huzarska-Szumiec into writing an even more stridently critical review, which questioned the play's relevance to current times and the manner in which it had been staged.

Translations possesses several intriguing parallels with Polish history and the theatre of Young Poland, but it was seemingly such familiar echoes that prevented the play from being regarded as a novel spectacle. Set in a hedge school, a historical bastion of Catholic cultural resistance, the teacher Manus imparts through Irish a wide spectrum of learning to charges who have widely differing educational needs, whether it be correct pronunciation or advanced Latin and Greek. The central drama of the play focuses on the arrival of colonizing soldiers who wish to survey the area and standardize the local names. There follows much talk between opposing sides about what it means to be speaking, thinking and acting on either side of the cultural divide. Indeed, Yolland, the surveyor, will have the occasion to remark to his Irish assistant, Owen, on the Irish language, 'Even if I did speak Irish, I'd always be an outsider here.' Declan Kiberd has described the colonial process at work here, 'as the specific basis for all the politics which will ensue'[93] and ultimately the play suggests that the loss of Irish can only be understood as a process of decline that allows for its intermittent re-flourishing. The play, when it was first performed in Northern Ireland at the height of the Troubles, certainly prodded the societal and political fault-lines, and it remains as current today for the island of Ireland as when first staged all of thirty-five years ago. But in Kraków midway through 1999 it seems that *Translations*, cut adrift from the context in which it had been written, left audiences thinking that they were watching some quaint revival piece.

Huzarska-Szumiec's response to the play was incredulous, so stating that if *Translations* had been produced to remind theatregoers about incidents of historical resistance against Germanization in Galicia, then the producers should have adapted an episode from the annals of the Polish peasantry, which would have yielded forth all the stock characters to be found in Friel's play. Indeed, the sight of drunken Manus standing on a sacred stone and reciting a paean to Ireland between traditional refrains was all too much for Huzarska-Szumiec, who described this moment as the height of absurdity. Another unfortunate feature of the performance came with the romantic tryst between Yolland and Maire, where they rapturously listed local place names in their own tongue. The episode was seemingly accompanied by a loud-speaker that provided interpretations intended to bridge the linguistic gulf. Other criticisms followed, and plainly not since the staging of Sean O'Casey's *Cock-a-Doodle Dandy* had a reviewer taken so much trouble to express displeasure at the production of an Irish play; she concluded by asserting: 'with the decision to stage *Translations* I have ceased to understand the theatre's repertoire policy.'[94] Significantly, Huzarska-Szumiec was not alone in her criticism. Janusz Kowalczyk writing for the national newspaper *Rzeczpospolita* entitled his review 'Wymyślne chińskie tortury' ['Sophisticated Chinese Tortures'] from which we may infer the tenor of the assessment that followed.[95]

In spite of Katarzyna Deszcz's best efforts, the play *Translations*, with its remote injustices and questioning themes failed to connect with audiences. However, if the plays of O'Casey, Behan and Friel had suffered in Poland from being too Irish in their treatment of culturally local issues, Polish Theatre companies approaching the new millennium were determined to interpret the next generation of Irish dramatists as either European, or at least nation-neutral, which allowed them to absorb the plays into the national repertoire and as a consequence bring about a sea-change in how Irish drama was perceived.

Notes

1   See Kazimierz Braun, *A History of Polish Theater, 1939–1989: Spheres of Captivity and Freedom* (Westport: Greenwood Press, 1996).

2   See Joanna Kuciel-Frydryszak, Słonimski. *Heretyk na* ambonie (Warszawa: Fortuna i Fatum 2012), 249–256.

3   See Józef Chrobak and Justyna Michalik (eds), *Tadeusz Kantor i Artyści Teatru Cricot 2. Vol. 1 Dokumenty i materiały* (Kraków: Cricoteka, 2009).

4   Jadwiga Ćwiąkała, 'Joyce in Poland', *James Joyce Quarterly*, 9 (1971), 93. See also Zdzisław Wróbel, 'Gdański rekonesans. Teatr, do którego nie można dostać biletów', *Pomorze*, 21 (1970) Available at: http://www.zygmunthubner.pl/48_James_JOYCE_-_Ulisses_1970. Accessed April 20 2013; and Elżbieta Wysińska, 'Teatralny wstęp do Joyce'a', *Teatr*, 7 (1970), 19–20.

5   Roman Szydłowski, 'Ulisses w Teatrze Wybrzeże.' *Trybuna Ludu*, 72 (1970), p. 6.

6   Roman Szydłowski, *Trybuna Ludu*, 72 (1970), p. 6. See also Barbara Lasocka, 'Joyce'a przypowieść o człowieku', *Teatr*, 7 (1970), 17–19.

7   See Jadwiga Ćwiąkała, *James Joyce Quarterly*, 9 (1971), 93–98.

8   Jadwiga Ćwiąkała, *James Joyce Quarterly*, 9 (1971), 95. For an analysis of the literary parallels between Iwaszkiewicz and Joyce, see Jerzy Paszek, 'Iwaszkiewicz i Joyce (O dwóch próbach literackiej fugi)', *Twórczość*, 2 (1983), 82–91.

9 See Jerzy Stempowski, '*Ulisses* Joyce'a jako próba psychoanalizy stosowanej', *Wiadomości Literackie*, 6 (1932), 2.

10 See Jerzy Paszek, *Sztuka aluzji literackiej* (Katowice: Uniwersytet Śląski, 1984), 101; see also Thomas Anessi, 'The Impact of Joyce's *Ulysses* on Polish Literature Between the Wars.' In: Geert Lernout and Wim Van Mierlo (eds), *The Reception of James Joyce in Europe* (New York and London: Thoemmes Continuum, 2004), 230–235.

11 Witold Gombrowicz, *Ferdydurke* (2005), 67. Translated by E. Mosbacher.

12 Józef Czechowicz, 'Ranek', *Pion*, 8 (1938).

13 Maciej Słomczyński, *Twórczość*, 7–8 (1958), 40–56.

14 See Małgorzata Słomczyńska-Pierzchalska, *Nie mogłem być inny. Zagadka Macieja Słomczyńskiego* (Kraków: Wydawnictwo Literackie, 2003), 50–61.

15 Małgorzata Słomczyńska-Pierzchalska, *Nie mogłem być inny*, 118–129, 137–144.

16 Małgorzata Słomczyńska-Pierzchalska, *Nie mogłem być inny*, 176–180.

17 Małgorzata Słomczyńska-Pierzchalska, *Nie mogłem być inny*, 214–216.

18 See also Anna Bikont and Joanna Szczęsna, *Pamiątkowe rupiecie. Biografia Wisławy Szymborskiej* (Kraków: Znak, 2012), 100–102.

19 Małgorzata Słomczyńska-Pierzchalska, *Nie mogłem być inny*, 248–249.

20 Maciej Słomczyński, 'A Point of View', *James Joyce Quarterly*, 4/3 (1967), 237.

21 Maciej Słomczyński, 'Przedmowa', *Dialog*, 12 (1964), 21–22.

22 '… o zademonstrowaniu myśli Joyce'a przy pomocy żywych ludzi.' Maciej Słomczyński, '*Ulisses* na scenie' (Theatre Programme for *Ulysses*), *Teatr Wybrzeże* (1970), 6.

23 'Niemniej jednak, ponieważ cały mechanizm tej sztuki jest moją własnością i wynikiem moich rozmyślań, pozwoliłem ją sobie podpisać moim nazwiskiem – na podstawie powieści Jamesa Joyce'a – po prostu dlatego by uniknąć nieporuzumień; gdyż jakakolwiek inna moja postawa wydawałaby mi się nieprzywoitością wobec autora *Ulissesa*.' Maciej Słomczyński, *Teatr Wybrzeże* (1970), 6.

24 See Daniel Gerould (Foreword to) Zygmunt Hübner, *Theatre and Politics* (Illinois: Northwestern University Press, 1992), xi.

25 Zygmunt Hübner, *Theatre and Politics*, xi.

26 See Konrad Eberhardt, '*Ulisses* Hübnera', *Ekran*, 23 (1970), 15; see also Andrzej Wróblewski 'Dzień Powszedni Pana Bloom', *Panorama Północy*, 14 (1970), 12.

27 Daniel C. Gerould and Zbigniew Lewicki, '*Ulysses* in Gdańsk', *James Joyce Quarterly*, 9/1 (1971), 99–116.

28 Egon Naganowski, 'Odyseja XX wieku', *Ulysses* (Theatre Programme for Teatr Wybrzeże, Gdańsk), 8. Available at: http://www.zygmunthubner.pl/materialy/inne/597.pdf. Accessed 20 August 2013.

29 See Elżbieta Wysińska, 'Teatralny wstęp do Joyce'a', *Teatr*, 7 (1970), 19–20.

30 See Niny Rocco-Bergera, '*Ulysses* by Joyce in a Modern Performance at Palazzo Grassi in Venice', *James Joyce Quarterly*, 9 (1972), 397–399.

31 Elżbieta Morawiec and Lillian Vallee, 'The Theatre of Grzegorzewski: Between Theatre and Non-Being', *Performing Arts Journal*, 8/2 (1984), 75–88.

32 Janusz Warmiński, 'W sprawie *Ulissesa*. List otwarty do Macieja Słomczyńskiego', *Życie Literackie*, 11 (1974). Available at: http://www.e-teatr.pl/pl/artykuly/94145.html. Accessed 15 April 2013.

33   Lucjan Kydryński, 'Skandalik towarzyski. Co robić w Warszawie nocą', *Przekrój*, 1517 (1974). Available at: http://www.e-teatr.pl/pl/artykuly/47509.html. Accessed 20 April 2013.

34   Lucjan Kydryński, *Przekrój*, 1517 (1974), 23.

35   Ewa Bułhak, 'Zamysł ogólny', *Dialog*, 12 (1974), 117–118.

36   'Niech Pan już nie pali (…) Czy nie macie tu nic do jedzenia?' *Ulysses*, 457.

37   Theatre programme for *Nowe Bloomusalem* 1994. The Polish Theatre Museum of Warsaw. Call no. 263.

38   Marta Fik, '*Bloomusalem*', *Polityka*, 16 (1974), 10.

39   Janusz Płoński, 'W środku rzeczy', *ITD.*, 18 (1974), 17.

40   Grzegorz Sinko, 'Stara i młoda Anglia', *Dialog*, 4 (1961), 89–102.

41   Brendan Behan on Capital Punishment. http://www.rte.ie/archives/exhibitions/925-brendan-behan/139236-brendan-behan/.

42   Karolina Beylin, 'Trzy godziny w więzieniu', *Express wieczorny* (29 March 1967).

43   Jerzy Koenig, 'Behan po raz pierwszy', *Współczesność* (11 April 1967), 9.

44   'Społeczeństwo jest niesprawiedliwe, sądy nie widzą nic poza literą prawa, sprawiedliwość jest ślepa i ciemna, więzienia są nieludzkie – ale wszystko tak działa i musi działać dlatego, że człowiek nie zawsze zdaje w życiu egzaminy.' Andrzej Jarecki, '*Skazaniec*', *Sztandar Młodych*, 71 (1967), 3.

45   Jan Kłossowicz, 'Pierwszy z gniewnych', *Teatr*, 18 (1967), 268.

46   '… zaangażowania w ludzkie sprawy ….' Jan Kłossowicz, *Teatr*, 18 (1967), 268.

47   Andrzej Jarecki, *Sztandar Młodych*, 71 (1967), 3. Jarecki's criticism contrasted with the praise heaped upon Sinko's translation by Roman Szydłowski, 'Na szczególne uznanie zasługuje przekład Grzegorza Sinki, któremu udało sie znaleźć polskie opowiedniki bardzo trudnego, soczystego języka Behana, a nawet gwary więziennej, którą mówią jego bohaterowie.' 'Bunt, gniew i rozpacz', *Trybuna Ludu*, 79 (1967).

48   'Rozumieją przy tym doskonale, że w dramacie, podobnie jak w liryce, ścisły przekład jest rzeczą niemożliwą, dosłowność stanowi o zdradzie autora, a piękno i sens całości usprawiedliwia lub oskarża tłumacza-adaptatora.' Erwin Axer, *Sprawy teatralne* (Warszawa: Państwowy Instytut Wydawniczy, 1966), 132.

49   Erwin Axer, *Sprawy teatralne*, 132.

50   Maria Kosińska, 'Zakładnik z opóźnieniem', *Życie Warszawy*, 6 (1972). Available at: http://www.eteatr.pl/pl/artykuly/63539,druk.html. Accessed 12 April 2012.

51   See Sylvère Lotringer, 'The Thin Man: An Interview with Brendan Behan', *Field Day Review*, 1 (2005), 3–25.

52   Gordon M. Wickstrom, 'The Heroic Dimension in Brendan Behan's *The Hostage*', *Educational Theatre Journal*, 22/4 (1977), 402.

53   'Zygmunt Hübner powiedział.' (Interview with the magazine *Szpilki*). Available at: http://www.zygmunthubner.pl/51_Brendan_BEHAN_-_Zakladnik_1971. Accessed 15 April 2013.

54   Marcin Karpiński, 'Gorzkie komedie.' *Sztandar Młodych*, 3 (1971). Available at: http://www.zygmunthubner.pl/51_Brendan_BEHAN_-_Zakladnik_1971. Accessed 15 April 2012.

55   Bohdan Drozdowski, 'Salto Mortale', *Teatr*, 4 (1972), 9.

56   'zgrabny chłopak z nagim pępkiem może być również sexy jak podobnie odziana zgrabna dziewczyna!' Bohdan Drozdowski, *Teatr*, 4 (1972), 9.

57 '… przyklejona broda.' Jan Alfred Szczepański, 'Z dalekiego kraju', *Trybuna Ludu*, 13 (1972), 6.

58 'Nie ich to wina. Wyrok na "Zakładniku" został wykonany.' Andrzej Hausbrandt, 'Wyrok na Zakładniku', *Express Wieczorny* (6 January 1972), 6.

59 'Zygmunt Hübner powiedział.' '… po obejrzeniu już gotowego przedstawienia poczułem coś w rodzaju rozczarowania.' Available at http://www.zygmunthubner.pl/51_Brendan_BEHAN_-_Zakladnik_1971. Accessed 15 April 2013.

60 Brian Friel, *Obywatelstwo honorowe*, Dialog, 2 (1975), 59–94. Trans. Maria Skroczyńska.

61 Jan Ławnikowski, 'W Irlandii Briana Friela', *Życie Częstochowy*, 134 (1977), 8.

62 'Częstochowska premiera potraktowana przez Ryszarda Krzyszycha z wyjątkowym inscenizacyjnym rozmachem przekazała trafnie intencje irlandzkiego pisarza, tak bliskie zresztą naszym polskim historycznym doświadczeniom i odczuciom.' Jan Ławnikowski, *Życie Częstochowy* 134 (1977).

63 Andrzej Wróblewski, 'W Irlandii teatr właściwie jest niepotrzebny. Irlandia sama jest wielką sceną.' 'Irlandczycy zawsze wymyślą coś, żeby sie bić', *Dialog*, 2 (1975), 103.

64 'Teatr irlandzki – Dzisiaj', *Dialog*, 3 (1979), 173–176.

65 See Jan Kaestner, 'Der beste Platz ist an der Theke. Irisches Theater – zwischen der Last der Tradition und der Lust am Spiel.' *Theatre heute*, 11 (1978), 47–49.

66 See Antoni Winch, 'Mrożek robi sceny', *Dialog*, 2 (2012), 150–163.

67 See Halina Filipowicz, 'Tadeusz Różewicz's *The Card Index*: A New Beginning for Polish Drama', *Modern Drama*, 27/3 (1984), 395–408.

68 See Deirdre Bair, *Samuel Beckett: A Biography* (New York: Touchstone 1990), 576.

69 Antoni Libera, *Godot i jego cień* (Kraków: Wydawnictwo Znak, 2009), 81.

70 Antoni Libera, *Godot i jego cień*, 81.

71 Antoni Libera, 'Beckett i Polska', *Literatura na Świecie*, 49 (1975), 246–251.

72 See Antoni Libera, *Godot i jego cień*, 371–389.

73 Antoni Libera (Interview), 'Assistant to the Playwright', *Irish Times* (15 April 1999).

74 Marek Kędzierski, 'Samuel Beckett and Poland.' In: Mark Nixon and Matthew Feldman (eds), *The International Reception of Samuel Beckett* (London: The Continuum International Publishing Group, 2009), 179.

75 See Marek Kędzierski, *The International Reception of Samuel Beckett*, 176.

76 '… pozwala dostrzec […] człowiekowi, nawet w najgłębszej klęsce, w poniżeniu, w bezradności – potrzebny jest drugi człowiek, jako punkt odniesienia, jako potwierdzenie istnienia Świata.' Maciej Karpiński, 'Z duchem czasu', *Sztandar Młodych*, 287 (1974), 5.

77 'To nużące przedstawienie, pozbawione jakiejś klarownej linii interpretacyjnej, bez śladu warsztatu reżyserskiego, wypłukane z humoru, który zawsze współtworzy tragiczną wizję świata w dramatach Becketta, jest zagrane źle: "Końcówka" zamieniła się w słuchowisko radiowe na deskach teatru.' Włodzimierz Szturc, '*Końcówka* Becketta', *Echo Krakowa*, 208 (1981), 2.

78 See Kazimierz Braun, *A History of Polish Theater, 1939–1989*, 99.

79 See James Knowlson, *Damned to Fame*, 96.

80 Maja Komorowska also connects *Endgame* with the story of Martial Law as the actress spearheaded an organization that brought parcels to actors and theatre workers who had been imprisoned in the crackdown.

81 Józef Szczawiński, 'Na barykadach Paryża', *Słowo Powszechne*, 49 (1982), 4.

82 Marzena Wiśniewska, 'Anatomia Upadku', *Sztandar Młodych*, 70 (1982), 9.

83 'Widownia stłoczona w nieprawdopodobnych warunkach, przeważnie na stojąco, w czapkach i paltach, przeżywała bez tchu gorycz klęski apostołów, zadając sobie te same pytania, wątpiąc z Tomaszem, szukając tej samej nadziei.' Ernest Bryll, *Wieczernik* (Warszawa: Instytut Wydawniczy Pax, 1990), inside jacket.

84 'Każdy z nas, wychowany na kulturze narodowej, wie, że związek sztuki, w tym także teatru, z Kościołem nie jest niczym nowym. Tak działo się i dzieje, i nie sposób wyobrazić sobie kulturalnego dziedzictwa cywilizacji bez tego nurtu sztuki.' Ernest Bryll, *Wieczernik*, 75.

85 Gabriela Pewińska, 'Spadkobiercy kawy', *Polska Dziennik Bałtycki*, 286 (2011), 4.

86 Jacek Sieradzki, 'Beckett: zagęszczanie materii', *Polityka*, 34 (1985), 9.

87 Marek Kedzierski, *The International Reception of Samuel Beckett*, 187.

88 Jacek Wakar, 'Taniec jest życiem', *Teatr*, 7/8 (1993), 29.

89 Jacek Sieradzki, 'Tańcząc w Ballybeg', *Dialog*, 9 (1993), 117–125.

90 See Ewa Zielińska, 'Świat kobiet', *Kurier Polski*, 86 (1993), 3.

91 'Na podstawie recenzji wiedziałam, że jest to sztuka interesująca, ale wydała mi się zbyt irlandzka, by mogła tu kogokolwiek zainteresować i nie zadałam sobie trudu, żeby do niej sięgnąć. A szkoda. Teraz, *Tańczancych* ... przeczytałam ją i żałuję. że nic nie zrobiłam wtedy, żeby ją u nas spopularyzować, wydrukować w *Dialogu*. Zamierzam teraz ten błąd naprawić.' Theatre Programme. 'Uwagi o tekście: Małgorzata Semil – tłumacz i Bogdan Hussakowski – reżyser', (1993), 2.

92 'Ponieważ na scenie kompletnie nic się nie dzieje, zamykam oczy i usiłuję poddać się rytmowi słów. Wyobrażam sobie, że siedzę w miękkim fotelu, a nie na twardym krześle w sali im. H. Modrzejewskiej, piję herbatę i słucham teatru polskiego radia. Jednak nawet to nie jest możliwe, gdyż spojówki drażnią unoszące się nad sceną kłęby dymu.

   - Co by zrobić, żeby publiczność nie zasnęła już na samym wstępie - zastanawiali się pewnie twórcy przedstawienia.
   - Proszę państwa, dajmy trochę dymu - wpadł na odkrywczy pomysł któryś z artystów.' Magda Huzarska-Szumiec. 'Entliczek pentliczek', *Gazeta Krakowska,* 110 (1996). A similar experience informed the choice of title for another review, which was entitled 'The Hypnagogic Faithhealer'. See Marek Mikos, 'Usypiający uzdrowiciel', *Gazeta w Krakowie*, 54 (1996). Available at: http://www.e-teatr.pl/pl/artykuly/162460.html. Accessed 14 August 2015.

93 Declan Kiberd, *Inventing Ireland* (Harvard: Harvard University Press, 1997), 616.

94 '... wystawienie *Przekładów* spowodowało, że już zupełnie przestałam rozumieć politykę repertuarową tej sceny.' Magda Huzarska-Szumiec, 'Wóz Drzymały na irlandzkich łąkach', *Gazeta Krakowska*, 143 (1999), 4. Available at: http://www.e-teatr.pl/pl/artykuly/162463. html. Accessed 15 August 2015. The title of the review in translation: 'Drzymała's Caravan on Irish Meadows', refers to the story of Michał Drzymała (1857–1937), a Polish peasant from the Poznań region who circumvented German anti-Polish building regulations by moving his wheeled home every day.

95 Janusz Kowalczyk, 'Wymyślne chińskie tortury', *Rzeczpospolita*, 146 (1999), Supplement A, 11.

Epilogue

The Millennial Surge

In the late 1990s, emergent voices in Irish drama, such as Martin McDonagh, Conor McPherson, Mark O'Rowe, Marina Carr and Enda Walsh, captured the élan of an optimistic era for Ireland that was riding the crest of a wave of what would prove to be an unsustainable property boom. However, just as a number of these new playwrights had originally been forced to leave or circumvent Ireland in order to establish an international career at the turn of the millennium, Polish audiences were more than happy to welcome the plays of these writers as principally universal works that reflected Poland's more pronounced international outlook in the expectant years just prior to EU membership. This was particularly true for the reception of McDonagh's wickedly funny *The Cripple of Inishmaan* (1996) following its premiere performance in Warsaw's People's Theatre on 12 February 1999, with a translation by Małgorzata Semil. It was co-directed by Agnieszka Glińska and Władysław Kowalski, who had instructed the cast to imagine that their characters were from Mars so as to strip them of ethnic baggage.[1] Inspired by the circumstances surrounding the filming of the 1936 American documentary, *Man of Aran,* the play centres on the desperate schemes of crippled Billy, who is trying to get himself cast in the movie so that he may escape both the isolation of the island and the taunts of his crude neighbours. For many Polish reviewers, McDonagh's play could just as well have been set in a fishing village on the Baltic coast.[2] And because of this association, and the play's complex presentation of rural realities, it was appropriated as a Polish theatrical piece and held up as an example to contemporary Polish playwrights. As Tomasz Miłkowski wrote:

> I ask myself why Polish authors can not write such plays. By 'such,' I mean not venting grotesque metaphysics to the skies, but close to the ground, close to people. For playing and for thinking. Close to human experience; not overblown improbabilities, but only full-blooded dramas filled with passion, conflicts and dreams. Perhaps these plays are being written in Poland and the theatres are simply not finding them? […] Fortunately, the Irish have spared us the trouble of looking. […] From Ireland to Poland is a very short distance indeed.[3]

This perception of cultural alterity would be extended to Conor McPherson's banter-filled play *The Weir* (1997) when it was staged by Agnieszka Lipiec-Wróblewska in November of the same year in Warsaw's Studio Theatre, which was based on a translation by Klaudyna Rozhin. Set in the closed world of a rural bar, regulars trade stories, the telling of which reveal their personal sadnesses and tragedies. Described by Ernest Bryll in the programme notes as a pub drama, *The Weir* explores how storytelling can reveal depths of dolefulness. It was the closed world of the bar and the tender treatment of its hollowed-out characters that led reviewers to praise the play for speaking to the human condition, where 'loneliness is oneness'. Indeed, this understanding of the play would thereafter nurture the sense that the world of Irish theatre was as familiar to Polish audiences as it was novel. Perhaps Jacek Wakar put it best when he wrote: 'After fifteen minutes we feel as if we know them well. We treat them like friends, and we'd like to buy the next round of drinks.'⁴ It may even be said that this axiom of 'novel in the familiar and familiar in the novel' had always characterized to one degree or another the reception of Irish drama in Poland. But with the arrival of McDonagh and McPherson a reorientation took place, based simply on a perceptive inkling that soon Polish audiences may also become part of the unfolding story of Ireland. To borrow *The Weir*'s parlance: it would soon be drinks all round.

Notes

1 Joanna Derkaczew (interview with Agnieszka Glińska), 'To nie jest jak w życiu, to są Marsjanie', *Dialog*, 3 (2007), 146–147.
2 Roman Pawłowski, 'Irlandia, czy Polska', *Gazeta Wyborcza*, 38 (1999), 10.
3 'Zadaję sobie pytanie, dlaczego polscy autorzy nie potrafią pisać takich dramatów. "Takich", to znaczy nie ulatujących w metafizyczno-groteskowe przestworza, bliskie ziemi, bliskie człowieka. Do grania i do myślenia. Bliskie ludzkiemu doświadczeniu, a jednak nie bulwarowe sztuczydła, tylko dramaty pełnokrwiste, w których czuje się namiętności, niewymyślone konflikty i marzenia. Nie wiem, może takie sztuki powstają, a tylko teatr ich nie znajduje? […] Na szczęście z kłopotu od czasu do czasu wybawiają nas Irlandczycy. […] Z Irlandii do Polski bardzo blisko.' Tomasz Miłkowski, 'Kaleka, czyli każdy', *Trybuna*, 43 (1999), 13.
4 'Po kwadransie wydaje się, że ich dobrze znamy, traktujemy ich jak przyjaciół, wszystkim chcielibyśmy postawić następną kolejkę', Jacek Wakar, *Życie*, 303 (1999), 8.

Bibliography

Antoniewicz, Grażyna. 'Termos z herbatą, czyli bomba [A Tea Flask, or in Other Words, a Bomb].' *Dziennik Bałtycki*, 57 (2008), p. 25.

Appenszlak, Jakub. 'Scena polska [The Polish Stage].' *Nasz Przegląd* (5 December 1924), p. 3.

Appenszlak, Jakub. 'Wielka satyra polityczna B. Shawa w Teatrze Polskim [Shaw's Great Political Satire in the Polish Theatre].' *Nasz Przegląd*, 164 (1929), p. 9.

Arrington, Lauren. *Revolutionary Lives: Constance and Casimir Markiewicz* (Princeton, New Jersey: Princeton University Press, 2016).

Axer, Erwin. *Sprawy teatralne* [*Theatrical Matters*] (Warszawa: Państwowy Instytut Wydawniczy, 1966).

Bair, Deirdre. *Samuel Beckett: A Biography* (New York: Touchstone, 1990).

Balcerzan, Edward & Rajewska, Ewa (eds). *Pisarze polscy o sztuce przekładu 1440–2005* [*Polish Writers on the Art of Translation 1440–2005*] (Poznań: Wydawnictwo Poznańskie, 2007).

Baliński, Ignacy. 'Rozmowy o Teatrze [Talking Theatre].' *Tygodnik Ilustrowany*, 23 (1914), p. 449.

Belloc. Louise Sw. *Les Amours Des anges et les Melodiés irlandaises* (Paris: Chez Chasseriau, Libraire-Editeur, 1823).

Beckett, Samuel. *En attendant Godot* [*Waiting for Godot*] (Paris: Minuit, 1952). Polish Manuscript (fragments) *Czekając na Godota*. Trans. Rogoziński, Julian. *Dialog*, 1 (1957), pp. 88–98.

Beckett, Samuel. *Fin de partie* [*Endgame*] (Paris: Minuit, 1957). Polish Manuscript: *Końcówka*. Trans. Rogoziński, Julian. *Dialog*, 5 (1957), pp. 36–61.

Beckett, Samuel. *Krapp's Last Tape* (& *Embers*) (London: Faber and Faber, 1959). Polish Manuscript: *Ostatnia taśma Krappa*. Trans. Cękalska, Krystyna, & Błahij, Kazimierz. *Dialog*, 11 (1958), pp. 66–70.

Beckett, Samuel. *Not I* (London: Faber and Faber, 1973). Polish Manuscript: *Nie ja*. Semil, Małgorzata. *Dialog*, 10 (1973), pp. 88–91.

Behan, Brendan. *The Hostage* (London: Methuen, 1958). Polish Manuscript: *Zakładnik*. Trans. Skroczyńska, Maria & Żuławski, Juliusz. *Dialog*, 12 (1960), pp. 49–89.

Behan, Brendan. *The Quare Fellow* (London, Methuen, 1956). Polish Manuscript: *Skazaniec*. Trans. Sinko, Grzegorz. *Dialog*, 11 (1963), pp. 34–70.

Benstock, Bernard. 'Sean O'Casey and/or James Joyce.' [In:] D. Krause & R. Lowery, G. (eds). *Sean O'Casey. Centenary Essays* (Irish Literary Studies) (Gerrards Cross: Collin Smythe, 1980), pp. 41–66.

Beylin, Karolina. 'Czekając na Godota [Waiting for Godot].' *Ekspres Wieczorny* (25 January 1957), p. 6.

Beylin, Karolina. 'Trzy godziny w więzieniu [Three Hours in Prison].' *Ekspres Wieczorny* (29 March 1967), p. 7.

Białoszewski, Miron. 'Ballada o zejściu do sklepu [The Ballad of Going Down to the Shop].' [In:] *Obroty rzeczy* [*The Revolutions of Things*] (Warszawa: Państwowy Instytut Wydawniczy, 1956).

Bidwell, George. 'Sean O'Casey.' *Przegląd Kulturalny*, 41 (1955), p. 2.

Biegański, Wiktor. 'Polska prapremiera *Profesji Pani Warren* [The Polish Premiere of *Mrs Warren's Profession*].' Theatre Programme for *Profesja Pani Warren*. The Theatre of Stefan Jaracz. Olsztyn–Elbląg (1954), pp. 12–14. Available at: http://dlibra.bibliotekaelblaska.pl/dlibra/doc metadata?id=124&dirids=6&ver_id=. Accessed 14 August 2012.

Birmingham, George A. *General John Regan* (London: Hodder & Stoughton, 1913).

Bikont, Anna & Szczęsna, Joanna. *Pamiątkowe rupiecie. Biografia Wisławy Szymborskiej* [*Memories and Oddments. A Biography of Wisława Szymborska*] (Kraków: Znak, 2012).

Bizan, Marian & Hertz, Paweł (eds). *Juliusz Słowacki – Liryki* [*Juliusz Słowacki – Lyrics*] (Warszawa: Państwowy Instytut Wydawniczy, 1959).

Bojanowska, Małgorzata (ed.). *Mieczysław Grydzewski LISTY 1922–1967 Jarosław Iwaszkiewicz* (Warszawa: Czytelnik, 1997).

Bołtuć, Irena. 'Z wrocławskich wspomnień [Wrocław Memories].' *Pamiętnik Teatralny*, 2–4 (1989), pp. 359–367.

Böhme, Margarete. *Tagebuch einer Verlorenen* [*The Diary of a Lost Girl*] (Berlin: F. Fontane, 1905).

Braun, Kazimierz. *A History of Polish Theatre, 1939–1989: Spheres of Captivity and Freedom* (Westport, CT: Greenwood Press, 1996).

Breiter, Emil. 'Teatr Polski. *Święta Joanna* Bernarda Shaw [The Polish Theatre. Bernard Shaw's *Saint Joan*].' *Świat* (13 December 1924).

Breiter, Emil. 'Teatr Rozmaitości, *Marta* Markiewicza [The Variety Theatre. Markiewicz's *Marta*].' *Gazeta Polska* (4 March 1918), p. 3.

Broniewski, Władysław. *Komuna paryska* [*The Paris Commune*] (Warszawa: Księgarnia "Książka", 1929).

Brown, Ivor. '*The Apple Cart*. An initialled notice in the *Manchester Guardian*' (August 1929). [In:] *George Bernard Shaw. The Critical Heritage*.' Tom F. Evans (ed.). (London/New York: Routledge, 1976), pp. 313–316.

Bryll, Ernest. *Wieczernik* [*The Upper Room*] (Warszawa: Instytut Wydawniczy Pax, 1990).

Bułhak, Ewa. 'Zamysł ogólny [A General Idea].' *Dialog*, 12 (1974), pp. 116–119.

Camille, Lucien & Leroux, Gaston. *Alsace* (Paris: 13, rue Saint-Georges, 1913).

Chrobak, Józef & Michalik Justyna (eds). *Tadeusz Kantor i Artyści Teatru Cricot 2*. Vol. I. *Dokumenty i materiały* [*Tadeusz Kantor and the Artists of Cricot Theatre 2*. Vol. I. *Documents and Materials*] (Kraków: Cricoteka, 2009).

Connolly, Leonard W. (ed.), *Bernard Shaw. Mrs Warren's Profession* (Peterborough, Ontario: Broadview Press, 2005).

Conolly-Smith, Peter. 'Shades of Local Color: *Pygmalion* and its Translation and Reception in Central Europe, 1913–1914.' *SHAW: The Annual of Bernard Shaw Studies*, 29 (2009), pp. 127–144.

Cox, J. H. 'Two New Plays.' *Irish Independent* (4 December 1908), p. 4

Craig, Edward Gordon. *On the Art of Theatre* (London: William Heinemann, 1911).

Crawford, Fred. D. 'Shaw in Translation. Part 1: The Translators.' *SHAW: The Annual of Bernard Shaw Studies*, 20 (2000), pp. 177–196.

Csato, Edward. *The Polish Theatre* (Warszawa: Polonia Publishing House, 1963).

Czechowicz, Józef. 'Ranek', *Pion*, 8 (1938).

Ćwiąkała, Jadwiga. 'Joyce in Poland.' *James Joyce Quarterly*, 9 (1971), pp. 93–98.

Czuliński, Jeremi. 'Francuska Awangarda [The French Avantgarde].' *Żołnierz Wolności*, 35 (February 1957), p. 3.

Dean, Joan Fitzpatrick. 'The Riot in Westport: George A. Birmingham at Home.' *New Hibernia Review*, 5(4) (2001), pp. 9–21.

Dębnicki, Antoni & Górski, Ryszard. 'Bernard Shaw na scenach polskich. Okres pierwszy 1903–1913 [Bernard Shaw on the Polish Stage. The First Period 1903–1913].' *Pamiętnik Teatralny*, 2(22) (1957), pp. 227–242.

Degal, Alfred. 'Filozofia pani Warren [Mrs Warren's Philosophy].' *Nowa Kultura*, 4 (1952), p. 8.

Dent, Alan. 'Notice.' *Spectator*, 161 (5 August 1938), p. 232. [In:] Tom F. Evans (ed.). (London/ New York: Routledge, 1976), pp. 357–358.

Derkaczew, Joanna. 'To nie jest jak w życiu, to są Marsjanie [Not as in Life, These are Martians].' *Dialog*, 3 (2007), pp. 146–149.

Dolecki, Zbigniew. 'Godot czeka najdłużej [Godot Waits the Longest].' *Kierunki*, 8 (24 February 1957), p. 3.

Drewnowski, Tadeusz. *Literatura Polska 1944–1989. Próba scalenia. Obiegi – wzorce – style [Polish Literature 1944–1989. An Assessment. Circuits – Patterns – Styles]* (Kraków: Universitas, 2004).

Drozdowski, Bohdan. 'Salto Mortale [A Mortal Leap].' *Teatr*, 4 (1972), p. 9.

Dudzik, Wojciech. *Wilama Horzycy: dramat niespełnienia: lata 1948–1959 [Wilam Horzyca and the Unfulfilled Years 1948–1959]* (Warszawa: Uniwersytet Warszawski, Katedra Kultury Polskiej, 1990).

Eberhardt, Konrad. 'Dramat o klęsce poety [A Drama about the Defeat of a Poet].' *Teatr*, 24 (1955), pp. 17–18.

Eberhardt, Konrad. 'Dramat o ludzkiej bezradności [A Drama About Human Helplessness].' *Sygnały*, 9 (3 March 1957), p. 2.

Eberhardt, Konrad. '*Ulisses* Hübnera [Hübner's *Ulysses*].' *Ekran*, 23 (1970), p. 15.

Eliot, Thomas Sterns. 'Tradition and the Individual Talent [I],' *The Egoist*, 6:4/6:5 (1919), pp. 54–55; 72–73.

Feldman, Wilhelm. *Piśmiennictwo polskie ostatnich lat dwudziestu [Polish Writing of the Past Twenty Years]* (Lwów: Ksiegarnia H. Altenberga, 1902).

Fijałkowski, Mieczysław. *Uśmiechy lat minionych [The Laughter of the Years Gone By]* (Katowice: Śląsk, 1969).

Fik, Marta. 'Bloomsalem.' *Polityka*, 16 (1974), p. 10.

Filipowicz, Halina. 'Tadeusz Różewicz's *The Card Index*: A New Beginning for Polish Drama.' *Modern Drama*, 27(3) (1984), pp. 395–408.

Flach, Józef. 'Teatr Krakowski [Kraków Theatre].' *Literatura i Sztuka*. Supplement to *Dziennik Poznański*, 8 (1914), pp. 117–119.

Fletcher, John. 'Samuel Beckett et Jonathan Swift: vers une étude comparée.' *Littératures X: Annales publiées par la Faculté des Lettres de Toulouse*, 11 (1962), pp. 81–117.

Foster, Roy. *W. B. Yeats: A Life*, Vol. 1. *The Apprentice Mage, 1865–1914* (Oxford: Oxford University Press, 1997).

Friel, Brian. *Dancing at Lughnasa* (London: Faber and Faber, 1990). Polish Manuscript: *Tańce w Ballybeg*. Trans. Semil, Małgorzata. *Dialog*, 4 (1993), 57–103.

Friel, Brian. *The Faith Healer* (London: Faber and Faber, 1980). Polish Manuscript: *Uzdrowiciel* (1996). Trans. Jasińska, Elżbieta (Archive of the Old Theatre, Kraków).

Friel, Brian. *The Freedom of the City* (London: Faber and Faber, 1974). Polish Manuscript: *Obywatelstwo honorowe*. Trans. Skroczyńska, Maria. *Dialog*, 2 (1975), pp. 59–93.

Friel, Brian. *Translations* (London: Faber and Faber, 1981). Polish Manuscript: *Przekłady*. Trans. MacQueen, Angus & Tempska, Urszula. *Dialog*, 5 (1985), pp. 32–69.

Gbr [Gubrynowicz, Bolesław]. 'Z teatru. *Pygmalion*, komedya w 5 aktach Bernarda Shaw'a. Przekład Ryszard Ordyński. [From the Theatre. *Pygmalion*, a Comedy in 5 acts by Bernard Shaw. Translation Ryszard Ordyński].' *Gazeta Lwowska*, 32 (1914), pp. 4–5.

Gerould, C., Zbigniew. (Foreword to) Hübner, Zygmunt. *Theatre and Politics* (Evanston, IL: Northwestern University Press, 1992), pp. vii–xvi.

Gerould, C. Daniel & Lewicki, Zbigniew. '*Ulysses* in Gdańsk.' *James Joyce Quarterly*, 9(1) (1971), pp. 99–116.

Górecki, Antoni. 'Śmierć zdrajcy ojczyzny' ['The Death of the Traitor of the Nation']. *Tygodnik Polski*, 14 (1818).

Górski, Artur (Quasimodo). 'Młoda Polska [Young Poland].' *Życie*, 15 (1898), p. 170.

Greville, Charles. *The Greville Memoirs: A Journal of the Reigns of King George IV and King William IV*, Vol. 1 (London: Longmans, Green, and Co., 1874).

Griffen, Alice. 'The New York Critics and *Saint Joan.' Bulletin (Shaw Society of America)*, 7 (January 1950), pp. 10–15.

Grodzicki, August. 'Jak u nas za okupacji [Recalling our Lives under Occupation].' *Życie Warszawy*, 232 (1955), p. 3.

Grydzewski, Mieczysław & Iwaszkiewicz, Jarosław. *LISTY 1922–1967 [Letters 1922–1967]* (Warszawa: Czytelnik, 1997).

Grzymała-Siedlecki, Adam. *Tadeusz Pawlikowski i jego krakowscy aktorzy [Tadeusz Pawlikowski and His Krakovian Actors]* (Kraków: Wydawnictwo Literackie, 1971).

Hausbrandt, Andrzej. 'Wyrok na *Zakładniku [The Hostage* Has Been Condemned].' *Express Wieczorny* (6 January 1972), p. 6.

Holroyd, Michael. *Bernard Shaw* (London & New York: Vintage, 1998).

Horzyca, Wilam. 'Dyrektor Horzyca obejmuje jutro Teatry Lwowskie: specjalny wywiad *Słowa Polskiego* [Theatre Manager Horzyca Takes Charge of Lwów's Municipal Theatres: A Special Interview with *Słowo Polskie*].' *Słowo Polskie*, 5 (1932), p. 2.

Horzyca, Wilam. 'O Profesji pani Warren. Uwagi reżysera [On *Mrs Warren's Profession. The Director's Observations*].' *Teatr*, 21 (1952), p. 21.

Horzyca, Wilam. *Polski teatr monumentalny [The Polish Monumental Theatre]* (Wrocław: Wiedza i Kultura, 1994).

Hübner, Zygmunt. *Theatre and Politics* (Evanston, IL: Northwestern University Press, 1992).

Hübner, Zygmunt & Rakowiecki, Jerzy. *Rozmowy o teatrze* [*Conversations about Theatre*] (Warszawa: Wiedza Powszechna, 1955).

Hübner, Zygmunt. 'Zygmunt Hübner powiedział.' Available at http://www. zygmunthubner. pl/51_Brendan_BEHAN_-_Zakladnik_1971. Accessed 15 April 2012.

Hutnikiewicz, Artur. *Młoda Polska* [*Young Poland*] (Warszawa: Wydawnictwo Naukowe PWN, 1994).

Huzarska-Szumiec, Magda. 'Entliczek pentliczek [Hickory Dickory Dock].' *Gazeta Krakowska*, 110 (1996). Available at: http://www.e-teatr.pl/pl/artykuly/162463. html. Accessed 14 August 2015.

Huzarska-Szumiec, Magda. 'Wóz Drzymały na irlandzkich łąkach [Drzymała's Caravan on Irish Meadows].' *Gazeta Krakowska*, 143 (1999), p. 4.

Iwaszkiewicz, Jarosław. *Książka moich wspomnień* [*The Book of My Memories*] (Kraków: Wydawnictwo Literackie, 1957).

Iwaszkiewicz, Jarosław. *Stanisława Wysocka i jej kijowski teatr Studya: wspomnienie* [*Stanisława Wysocka and Her Kiev Theatre, Studya: A Memoir*] (Warszawa: Wydawnictwo artystyczne i filmowe, 1963).

Iwaszkiewicz, Jarosław. *Marginalia* [*In the Margins*] (Warszawa: Interim, 1993).

Jarecki, Andrzej. 'Sztuka dla wsi [A Play for the Countryside].' *Sztandar Młodych*, 259 (1960), p. 2.

Jarecki, Andrzej. 'Skazaniec [*The Quare Fellow*].' *Sztandar Młodych*, 71 (1967), p. 3.

Joyce, James. *A Portrait of the Artist as a Young Man* (New York: Hubesch, 1916). Polish Manuscript: *Portret artysty z czasów młodości*. Allan, Zygmunt (Warszawa: Towarzystwo Wydawnicze "Rój", 1931).

Joyce, James. *Finnegans Wake* (London: Faber and Faber, 1939).

Joyce, James. *Ulysses* (Paris: Shakespeare and Company, 1921). Polish Manuscript: *Ulisses*. Słomczyński, Maciej (Warszawa: Państwowy Instytut Wydawniczy, 1969).

Kaestner, Jan. 'Der beste Platz ist an der Theke. Irisches Theater – zwischen der Last der Tradition und der Lust am Spiel.' *Theater heute*, 11 (1978), pp. 47–49.

Karczewska-Markiewicz, Zofia. 'Kukuryku [*Cock-a-Doodle Dandy*'].' *Życie Warszawy*, 258 (1960). Available at: http://www.zygmunthubner.pl/22_Sean_OCASEY_-_Kogut_zawinil_1960. Accessed 14 April 2011.

Karpiński, Maciej. 'Z duchem czasu [With the Spirit of the Time].' *Sztandar Młodych*, 287 (1974), p. 5.

Karpiński, Maciej. 'Gorzkie komedie.' *Sztandar Młodych*, 3 (1971). Available at: http://www. zygmunthubner.pl/51_Brendan_BEHAN_-_Zakladnik_1971. Accessed 20 August 2012.

Kasprowicz, Jan. *Ginącemu światu* [*To a Perishing World*] (Lwów, 1901).

Kasprowicz, Jan. *Salve Regina* (Lwów, 1902).

Kasprowicz, Jan. *Świat się kończy* [*The World is Coming to an End*] (Lwów: nakładem autora, 1891).

Kelly, Ronan. *The Bard of Erin. The Life of Thomas Moore* (Dublin: Penguin, 2007).

Kędzierski, Marek. 'Samuel Beckett and Poland.' [In:] Mark Nixon & Matthew Feldman (eds). *The International Reception of Samuel Beckett* (London: The Continuum International Publishing Group, 2009), pp. 163–187.

Kiberd, Declan. *Inventing Ireland* (Harvard: Harvard University Press, 1997).

Kijowski, Andrzej. 'Koszmar czasu [The Nightmare of Time].' *Teatr*, 7 (1 April 1957), pp. 11–12.

J. Kl. (Kleczyński, Jan). 'Z teatru [From the Theatre].' *Tygodnik Ilustrowany*, 32 (1907), p. 658.

Kłossowicz, Jan. 'Pierwszy z gniewnych [The First of the Angry Men].' *Teatr*, 18 (1967), p. 268.

Knowlson, James. *Damned to Fame. The Life of Samuel Beckett* (London: Bloomsbury, 1996).

Koenig, Jerzy, 'Behan po raz pierwszy [Behan for the First Time].' *Współczesność* (11 April 1967), p. 9.

Kołakowski, Klemens. '*Uczeń Szatana* [*The Devil's Disciple*].' *Dziennik Polski*, 557 (1903), p. 2.

Koneczny, Feliks. 'Teatr Krakowski [Kraków Theatre].' *Przegląd Polski*, 154 (461) (1904), pp. 351–385.

Koropeckyj, Roman Robert. *Adam Mickiewicz: The Life of a Romantic* (New York: Cornell University Press, 2008).

Korzeniewski, Bohdan. 'Shaw dzisiaj u nas [Shaw Today in Poland].' *Pamiętnik Teatralny*, 1 (1956), pp. 247–259.

Kosińska, Maria. '*Zakładnik* z opóźnieniem [*The Hostage* Performed Late].' *Życie Warszawy*, 6 (1972). Available at: http://www.e-teatr.pl/pl/artykuly/63539.html. Accessed 12 April 2012.

Kosok, Heinz. *O'Casey the Dramatist*. Trans. Joseph T. Swan (Irish Literary Studies 19) (Gerrards Cross: Collin Smythe, 1985).

Kowalczyk, Janusz. 'Wymyślne chińskie tortury [Sophisticated Chinese Tortures].' *Rzeczpospolita*, 146 (Supplement A) (1999), p. 11.

Koźniewski, Kazimierz. 'Godot w Warszawie [Godot in Warsaw].' *Przekrój*, 622 (3 March 1957), p. 6.

Krajewska, Wanda. *Recepcja literatury angielskiej w Polsce w okresie modernizmu (1887–1918)* [*The Reception of English Literature in Poland during the Modernist Period (1887–1918)*] (Warszawa: Wydawnictwo Polskiej Akademii Nauk, 1972).

Krasiński, Edward. *Teatr Polski Arnolda Szyfmana 1913–1939* [*The Polish Theatre of Arnold Szyfman 1913–1939*] (Warszawa: Wydawnictwo Naukowe PWN, 1991).

Krechowiecki, Adam. 'Syn Szatana [The Son of Satan].' *Gazeta Lwowska*, 274 (1903), p. 4.

Krechowiecki, Adam. 'Z teatru. *Birbant*. Trywialna komedya w 4 aktach Oskara Wilde'a [From The Theatre. *On The Importance of Being Earnest*. A Trivial Comedy in 4 Acts by Oscar Wilde].' *Gazeta Lwowska*, 244 (1905), pp. 4–5.

Kreczmar, Jerzy. *Stare nieprzestarzałe* [*Old Things with Life in Them Yet*] (Warszawa: Państwowy Instytut Wydawniczy, 1989).

Krzywoszewski, Stefan ('Gordon'). 'Patriotyczna sztuka irlandzka – utwór Polaka [A Patriotic Irish Drama – Written by a Pole].' *Świat*, 35 (1910), reprinted in *Dialog*, 2 (1975), pp. 107–108.

Krzywoszewski, Stefan ('Gordon'). 'Z teatrów warszawskich [From Warsaw's Theatres].' *Świat*, 40–48 (1919), pp. 12–13.

Krzywoszewski, Stefan. *Długie życie. Wspomnienie* [*A Long Life. A Memoir*] (Warszawa: Księgarnia Biblioteka Polska, 1947).

S. K. (Krzyżanowski, Stefan) 'Teatr Polski. *Dzikie Pola* [The Polish Theatre. *Wild Fields*].' Loose-leaf. The Polish Theatre Museum Archive of Warsaw.

Kuchtówna, Lidia. 'Wilam Horzyca (1889–1959): kronika życia i działalności [Wilam Horzyca (1889–1959): A Chronicle of His Life and Career].' *Pamiętnik Teatralny*, 2–4 (1989), pp. 187–284.

Kuciel-Frydryszak, Joanna. *Słonimski. Heretyk na ambonie* [*Słonimski. Heretic in the Dock*] (Warszawa: Fortuna i Fatum, 2012).

Kumor, Stanisława. *Polskie debiuty Bernarda Shaw* [*The Polish Debuts of Bernard Shaw*] (Warszawa: Wydawnictwo Uniwersytetu Warszawskiego, 1971).

Kydryński, Lucjan. 'Skandalik towarzyski. Co robić w Warszawie nocą [A Scandalous Date. What to Do in Warsaw at Night].' *Przekrój*, 1517 (1974). Available at http://www.e-teatr.pl/pl/artykuly/47509.html?josso_assertion_id=0F5ED58F06FA2AD8. Accessed 20 April 2013.

Lasocka, Barbara. 'Joyce'a przypowieść o człowieku [Joyce's Tale about Man].' *Teatr*, 7 (1970), pp. 17–18.

Ławnikowski, Jan. 'W Irlandii Briana Friela [In the Ireland of Brian Friel'].' *Życie Częstochowy*, 134 (1977), p. 8.

Lechoń, Jan. 'O Teatr Polski [On the Polish Theatre].' *Nowa Gazeta*, 287 (1918), p. 4.

Libera, Antoni. 'Beckett i Polska.' *Literatura na Świecie*, 49 (1975), pp. 246–251.

Libera, Antoni (Interview). 'Assistant to the Playwright.' *Irish Times* (15 April 1999).

Libera, Antoni. *W cieniu Godota* [*In the Shadow of Godot*] (Warszawa: Wydawnictwo Znak, 2009).

Limanowski, Mieczysław. '*Pigmalion* [*Pygmalion*].' *Prawda* (13 March 1914), p. 9.

Looby, Robert. 'Looking for the Censor in the Works of Sean O'Casey (and Others) in Polish Translation.' *Translation and Literature*, 17(1) (2008), pp. 47–64.

Lorentowicz, Jan. *Młoda Polska* [*Young Poland*], Vol. I (Warszawa: Księgarnia S. Sadowskiego, 1908).

Lorentowicz, Jan. *Dwadzieścia lat teatru* [*Twenty Years of Theatre*], Vol. II (Warszawa: Nakładem Księgarni F. Hoesicka, 1930).

MacWhite, Eoin. 'A Russian Pamphlet on Ireland by Count Markievicz.' *Irish University Review*, I (1) (1970), pp. 98–110.

MacWhite, Eoin. 'Thomas Moore and Poland.' *Proceedings of the Royal Irish Academy*, 3 (1972), pp. 49–62.

Makowski, Stanisław, Sudolski, Zbigniew & Sawrymowicz Eugeniusz (eds). *W kręgu bliskich poety: listy rodziny Juliusza Słowackiego* [*Juliusz Słowacki's Intimate Circle. Family Letters*] (Warszawa: Państwowy Instytut Wydawniczy, 1960).

Makuszyński, Kornel. 'Jak w romansie Stevensona [Like in a Stevenson Adventure].' *Kurier Warszawski*, 198 (1935). Available at: http://biblioteka.kijowski.pl/makuszynski%20kornel/kartki/jak.htm. Accessed 14 September 2013.

Marczak-Oborski, Stanisław. *Teatr polski w latach 1918–1965. Teatry dramatyczne* [*Polish Theatre in the Years 1918–1965. Dramatic Theatres*] (Warszawa: Wydawnictwo Naukowe PWN, 1985).

Markiewicz, Kazimierz, *Dzikie pola* [*Wild Fields*] (1914). The Polish Theatre Museum of Warsaw, call. no 711.

Markiewicz, Kazimierz (Casimir). *The Memory of the Dead* (Dublin: Tower 1910).

McDonagh, Martin. *The Cripple of Inishmaan* (London: Methuen Drama, 1997). Polish Manuscript: *Kaleka z Inishmaan*. Trans. Semil, Małgorzata. *Dialog*, 5 (1998), pp. 40–81.

McPherson, Conor. *The Weir* (London: Nick Hern Books, 1997). Polish Manuscript: *Tama*. Trans. Rozhin, Klaudyna. *Dialog*, 11 (1999), pp. 51–83.

Michalik, Jan. *Dzieje teatru w Krakowie w latach 1893–1915. Teatr Miejski* [*The History of Theatre in Kraków in the Years 1893–1915. The Municipal Theatre*], Vol. V (Kraków: Wydawnictwo Literackie, 1985).

Mickiewicz, Adam. *Ballady i Romanse* [*Ballads and Romances*] (Wilno: druk Józefa Zawadzkiego, 1822).

Mickiewicz, Adam, *Pan Tadeusz* [*Master Tadeusz*] (Paris: Alexander Jełowicki, 1834).

Mikos, Marek. 'Usypiający uzdrowiciel [The Hypnagogic Faithhealer].' *Gazeta Wyborcza.* Supplement: *Gazeta w Krakowie*, 54 (1996). Available at: http://www.e-teatr.pl/pl/artykuly/162460.html. Accessed 14 August 2015.

Miłkowski, Tomasz. 'Kaleka, czyli każdy [Cripple Applies to Everyone].' *Trybuna*, 43 (1999), p. 13.

Miłosz, Czesław. *The History of Polish Literature* (Los Angeles, CA: University of California Press, 1983).

Moore, Thomas. *Memoirs, Journal and Correspondence of Thomas Moore* (London: Longman, Green, Longman and Roberts, 1860).

Moore, Thomas. *Journal of Thomas Moore: 1836–1842*. [In:] Wilfred S. Dowden (ed.). (Cranbury/London/Ontario: Associated University Presses, 1988).

Moore, Thomas. 'Remember Thee'. *The Irish Melodies* (Dublin: William and James Power, 1807/1808).

Moore, Thomas. *Lalla Rookh* (London: Longman, Hurst, Rees, Orme, and Brown, 1817).

Morash, Christopher. *A History of Irish Theatre 1601–2000* (Cambridge: Cambridge University Press, 2001).

Morawiec, Elżbieta & Vallee, Lillian. 'The Theatre of Grzegorzewski: Between Theatre and Non–Being.' *Performing Arts Journal*, 8(2) (1984), pp. 75–88.

Mościcki, Tomasz. *Teatry Warszawy 1939: kronika* [*Warsaw Theatres 1939: A Chronicle*] (Warszawa: Bellona, 2009).

Mrożek, Sławomir. *Policja* [*The Police*]. *Dialog*, 6 (1958), pp. 55–75.

Mrożek, Sławomir. *Ucieczka na południe* [*Escape to the South*] (Warszawa: Iskry, 1961).

Murphy, Tom. *The Morning after Optimism* (Cork: Mercier Press, 1974).

Naganowski, Egon. 'Odyseja XX wieku. Ulysses [An Odyssey of the 20th Century. *Ulysses*].' Theatre Programme for *Ulysses*. The Coastal Theatre, Gdańsk (1970). Available at: http://www.zygmunthubner.pl/materialy/inne/597.pdf. Accessed 20 August 2013.

Niemcewicz, Julian Ursyn. 'Nieznane utwory [Unknown Works]. Moore's *Melodies* "Remember Thee".' *Pamiętnik Literacki*, 1 (1908), pp. 367–368.

Nowaczyński, Adolf. *Co czasy niosą* [*The Times Ahead*] (Warszawa-Lwów: Księgarnia St. Sadowskiego, 1909).

Nowaczyński, Adolf. *Oskar Wilde. Studium, Aforyzmy, Nowela* [*Oscar Wilde. A Study. Aphorisms. A Novella*] (Warszawa: W. Wiediger, 1906).

Nowaczyński, Adolf. *Szkice literackie* [*Literary sketches*] (Poznań: Nakładem Spółki Wydawniczej Ostoja, 1918).

Nowaczyński, *Nowe Ateny* [*The New Athens*] (Warszawa: Księgarnia Gebethnera i Wolffa, 1913).

O'Casey, Sean. *Cock-a-Doodle Dandy* (London: Macmillan, 1949). Polish Manuscript: *Kukuryku*. Trans. Wojewoda, Cecylia. (*Dialog*, 5 (1960), pp. 47–83).

O'Casey, Sean. *The Bishop's Bonfire* (London: Macmillan, 1955).

O'Casey, Sean. *The Shadow of a Gunman* (London: Macmillan, 1925). Polish Manuscript: *Cień bohatera* (1955). Trans. Hübner, Zygmunt & Pawlik, Bronisław & Żuławski, Juliusz (The Contemporary Theatre, Warsaw, call no. 16).

Ordyński, Ryszard. *Z mojej włóczęgi* [*My Vagabond Years*] (Kraków: Wydawnictwo Literackie, 1956).

Pajączkowski, Franciszek. *Teatr Lwowski pod dyrekcją Tadeusza Pawlikowskiego, 1900–1906* [*Lwów Theatre Under the Management of Tadeusz Pawlikowski, 1900–1906*] (Kraków: Wydawnictwo Literackie, 1961).

Paszek, Jerzy. 'Iwaszkiewicz i Joyce (O dwóch próbach literackiej fugi) [Iwaszkiewicz and Joyce (Two Attempts at Literary Fugue)].' *Twórczość*, 2 (1983), pp. 82–91.

Paszek, Jerzy. *Sztuka aluzji literackiej* [*The Art of Literary Allusion*] (Katowice: Uniwersytet Śląski, 1984).

Pawłowski, Roman. 'Irlandia, czy Polska [Ireland or Poland].' *Gazeta Wyborcza*, 38 (1999), p. 10.

Pewińska, Gabriela. 'Spadkobiercy kawy [The Inheritors of Coffee].' *Polska Dziennik Bałtycki*, 286 (2011), p. 4.

Pieńkowski, Stanisław. 'Z powodu dramatu Synge'a [Responding to Synge's Play].' *Gazeta Warszawska* (18–19 November 1913), p. 5.

Pieńkowski, Stanisław. 'Teatr Polski. *Major Barbara*, komedya w 3 aktach Bernarda Shawa [The Polish Theatre. *Major Barbara*, a Comedy in 3 Acts by Bernard Shaw].' *Gazeta Warszawska*, 299 (1919), p. 5.

Pietrycki, Jan. 'Z teatru [From the Theatre].' *Gazeta Narodowa* (14 February 1914), p. 2.

Płoński, Janusz. 'W środku rzeczy [At the Heart of Matters].' *ITD*, 18 (1974), p. 17.

Podraza-Kwiatkowska, Maria. *Programy i dyskusje literackie okresu Młodej Polski* [*Programs and Literary Discussions of the Young Poland Era*] (Wrocław: Ossolineum, 2000).

Podraza-Kwiatkowska, Maria. *Literatura Młodej Polski* [*The Literature of Young Poland*] (Warszawa: Wydawnictwo Naukowe PWN, 1992).

Polanica, Stefan. 'Czy tylko *Kogut zawinił?* [Shall We Only Blame the Cockerel?].' *Słowo Powszechne*, 260 (1960), p. 4.

Popławski, Wiktor. '*Kresowy Rycerz-Wesołek* [*The Playboy of the Western World*].' *Gazeta Poranna, Dwa Grosze* (21 November 1913), pp. 3–4.

Popławski, Wiktor. 'Teatr Rozmaitości [The Variety Theatre].' *Gazeta Poranna Dwa Grosze*, 810 (352) (1914), p. 3.

Poskuta-Włodek, Danuta. *Trzy dekady z dziejów sceny. Teatr im. Juliusza Słowackiego w Krakowie w latach 1914–1945* [*Three Decades of the Juliusz Słowacki Theatre in Kraków. The Years 1914–1945*] (Kraków: Teatr im. Juliusza Słowackiego w Krakowie, 2001).

W.pr (Prokesch, Władysław). 'Teatr Miejski. *Castus Joseph* dramat Szymona Szymonowica [The Municipal Theatre. *Castus Joseph* a Drama by Szymon Szymonowic].' *Czas*, 25 (1914), p. 4.

Prus, Bolesław. 'Kronika Tygodniowa. Poezja i Poeci [The Weekly Chronicle. Poetry and Poets].' *Tygodnik Ilustrowany*, 23 (1909), pp. 455–457.

Przesmycki, Zenon. 'Po półtoraroczu [After One-and-a-Half Years].' *Chimera*, 6 (1902), pp. 474–475.

Przybylski, Ryszard & Witkowska, Alina. *Romantyzm* [*Romanticism*] (Warszawa: Wydawnictwo Naukowe PWN, 1998).

Przybyszewski, Stanisław. 'Confiteor.' *Życie*, 1 (1899), pp. 1–4.

Quiqley, Patrick. *The Polish Irishman. The Life and Times of Casimir Markiewicz* (Dublin: The Liffey Press, 2012).

R. C. 'Wywiad z polskim tłumaczem sztuki Shaw'a [An Interview with the Polish Translator of Shaw's Play].' *Scena Polska,* 10 (1929), pp. 14–15.

Rabski, Władysław. 'Z teatru. *Nie można przewidzieć* [From the Theatre. *You Never Can Tell*].' *Kurier Warszawski,* 291 (1907), p. 3.

Rabski, Władysław. '*Uczeń Szatana* [*The Devil's Disciple*].' *Kurier Warszawski,* 23 (1912), p. 3.

Rabski, Władysław. *Teatr po wojnie. Premiery warszawskie 1918–1924* [*Theatre after the War. Warsaw Premieres 1918–1924*] (Warszawa: Biblioteka Dzieł Wyborowych, 1925).

Radziwon, Marek. *Iwaszkiewicz. Pisarz po katastrofie* [*Iwaszkiewicz. A Writer after the Catastrophe*] (Warszawa: Wydawnictwo W.A.B., 2010).

Rakowski, Konrad. 'Z teatru. *Bohaterowie,* komedya w 3 aktach Bernarda Shaw'a [*Arms and the Man,* a Comedy in 3 Acts by Bernard Shaw].' *Czas,* 239 (1904), pp. 1–2.

Rakowski, Konrad. 'Z teatru. *Kobieta bez znaczenia,* komedya w 4 aktach Oskara Wilde'a [From the Theatre. *A Woman of No Importance,* a Comedy in 4 Acts by Oscar Wilde].' *Czas,* 19 (1904b), pp. 1–2.

Rakowski, Konrad. 'Z teatru. *Birbant.* Trywialna komedya w czterech aktach Oskara Wilde'a [*On the Importance of Being Earnest.* A Trivial Comedy in 4 Acts by Oscar Wilde].' *Czas,* 218 (1905a), p. 1.

Rakowski, Konrad. 'Z teatru. *Salome,* tragedya w 1 akcie Oskara Wilde'a [*Salome,* a Tragedy in One Act by Oscar Wilde].' *Czas,* 112 (1905b), pp. 1–2.

Rakowski, Konrad. 'Z teatru. *Marnotrawny ojciec,* komedya w czterech aktach Bernarda Shaw'a, przekład T. Konczyńskiego [*You Never Can Tell,* a Comedy in 4 Acts by Bernard Shaw. Translation by T. Konczyński].' *Czas,* 224 (1906), p. 1.

Rakowski, Konrad. 'Z teatru. *Profesja pani Warren,* komedya w 4 aktach Bernarda Shawa [From the Theatre. *Mrs Warren's Profession,* a Comedy in 4 Acts by Bernard Shaw].' *Czas,* 230 (1907a), p. 1.

Rakowski, Konrad. 'Z teatru. *Mąż idealny,* sztuka w 4 aktach Oskara Wilde'a' [From the Theatre. *An Ideal Husband,* a Play in 4 Acts by Oscar Wilde].' *Czas,* 289 (1907b), p. 3.

Rakowski, Konrad. 'Z Teatru Miejskiego w Krakowie. *Pygmalion.* Komedya w 5 aktach Bernarda Shaw'a [From the Municipal Theatre. *Pygmalion.* A Comedy in 5 Acts by Bernard Shaw'].' *Czas,* 18 (1914), p. 4.

Rittner, Tadeusz. 'Przed premierą *Candidy* – Bernard Shaw [Before the Premiere of Bernard Shaw's *Candida*].' *Świat,* 9 (1906), p. 5.

Rocco-Bergera, Niny. '*Ulysses* by Joyce in a Modern Performance at Palazzo Grassi in Venice.' *James Joyce Quarterly,* 9 (1972), pp. 397–399.

Z. R. [Rosner, Zygmunt] '*Castus Joseph* Szymonowica [*Castus Joseph* by Szymonowic].' *Gazeta Poniedziałkowa,* 5 (1914), p. 3.

Różewicz, Tadeusz. *Kartoteka* [*The Card Index*] (Warsaw: Państwowy Instytut Wydawniczy, 1961).

Sardou, Victorien. *Madame Sans-Gêne* (Paris: Albin Michel, 1893).

Schiller, Leon. *Teatr ogromny* [*Monumental Theatre*] (Warszawa: Czytelnik, 1961).

Schuchard, Ronald. *The Last Minstrels. Yeats and the Revival of the Bardic Arts* (Oxford: Oxford University Press, 2008).

Semil, Małgorzata & Hussakowski, Bogdan. 'Uwagi o tekście [About the Text].' Theatre Programme: *Tancząc w Ballybeg* [*Dancing at Lughnasa*]. The Juliusz Słowacki Theatre (1993), pp. 2–3.

Sempoliński, Ludwik. *Wielcy mistrzowie małych scen* [*Great Masters of Small Stages*] (Warszawa: Czytelnik, 1968).

Shaw, George Bernard. '*Arms and the Man*' [In:] *Plays Pleasant and Unpleasant* (London, Constable, 1898). Polish Manuscript: *Bohaterowie* (1904). Trans. Rakowski, Konrad (The Juliusz Słowacki Theatre, call no. 3335).

Shaw, George Bernard. '*Candida*' [In:] *Plays Pleasant and Unpleasant* (London, Constable, 1898). Polish Manuscript: *Kandyda* (*Candida*) (1906). Trans. Błeszyński, Jan (The Silesian Digital Library, call no. BTL 3606).

Shaw, George Bernard. *Geneva* (London: Constable, 1939). Polish Manuscript: *Genewa* (1939). Trans. Sobieniowski, Florian (The Polish Theatre Museum of Warsaw, call no. 711).

Shaw, George Bernard, *Major Barbara* (& *John Bull's Other Island*). (London: The Times Book Club, 1907). Polish Manuscript: *Major Barbara* (1910). Trans. Ordyński, Ryszard (The Juliusz Słowacki Theatre, call no. 1461); Trans. Wołowski, Zygmunt (1919) (The Polish Theatre Museum of Warsaw, call. no. 229).

Shaw, George Bernard. *Mrs. Warren's Profession* [In:] *Plays Pleasant and Unpleasant* (London, Constable, 1898). Polish Manuscript: *Profesja Pani Warren* (1907). Trans. Popławski, Wiktor (The Polish Theatre Museum of Warsaw, call no. 1338); Trans. Unsigned (The Juliusz Słowacki Theatre, call no. 2032); Trans. Sobieniowski, Florian (1951) (The Contemporary Theatre, Warsaw, call no. 6).

Shaw, George Bernard. *Pygmalion* (London: Constable, 1913). Polish Manuscript: *Pygmalion* (1914). Trans. Sobieniowski, Florian (The Polish Theatre Museum of Warsaw, call nos. 34 & 36); Trans. Ordyński, Ryszard (1914) (The Juliusz Słowacki Theatre, call no. 3147).

Shaw, George Bernard. *Saint Joan* (London: Penguin, 1924). Polish Manuscript: *Święta Joanna* (1924). Trans. Sobieniowski, Florian (The Polish Theatre Museum of Warsaw, call. no. 2457).

Shaw, George Bernard. 'Statement to the Press.' *The Star*. London (30 September 1929).

Shaw, George Bernard. *The Apple Cart* (London: Constable, 1930). Polish Manuscript: *Wielki Kram* (1929/1930). Trans. Sobieniowski, Florian (The Polish Theatre Museum of Warsaw, call no. 530).

Shaw, George Bernard. *The Devil's Disciple* [In:] *Three Plays for Puritans* (London: Richards, 1901). Polish Manuscript: *Uczeń diabła* (1903). Trans. Beaupré, Barbara (The Silesian Digital Library, call no. 3441).

Shaw, George Bernard. *You Never Can Tell*. [In:] *Plays Pleasant and Unpleasant* (London, Constable, 1898). Polish Manuscript: *Marnotrawny ojciec* (1906). Trans. Konczyński, Tadeusz (The Silesian Digital Library, call no. 3531; The Juliusz Słowacki Theatre, call no. 1082).

Shaw, George Bernard. 'Sardoodledom.' *The Saturday Review* (1 June 1895).

Sieradzki, Jacek. 'Beckett: zagęszczanie materii [Beckett: A Compaction of Matter].' *Polityka*, 34 (1985), p. 9.

Sieradzki, Jacek. 'Tańcząc w Ballybeg [Dancing at Lughnasa].' *Dialog*, 9 (1993), pp. 117–125.

Sinko, Grzegorz. 'Kłopoty i Niespodzianki [Problems and Surprises].' *Nowa Kultura*, 46 (1960), p. 3.

Sinko, Grzegorz. 'Stara i młoda Anglia [Old and Young England].' *Dialog*, 4 (1961), pp. 89–102.

Słomczyńska-Pierzchalska, Małgorzata. *Nie mogłem być inny. Zagadka Macieja Słomczyńskiego* [*I Could Never Have Been Different. The Conundrum of Maciej Słomczyński*] (Kraków: Wydawnictwo Literackie, 2003).

Słomczyński, Maciej. 'Circe.' *Twórczość*, 7–8 (1958), pp. 40–56.

Słomczyński, Maciej. 'Przedmowa [Foreword].' *Dialog*, 12 (1964), pp. 20–24.

Słomczyński, Maciej. 'Point of View.' *James Joyce Quarterly*, 4 (1967), p. 236.

Słomczyński, Maciej. '*Ulisses* na scenie [*Ulysses* on Stage].' Theatre Programme for *Ulisses*. The Coastal Theatre, Gdańsk (1970). Available at: http://www.zygmunthubner.pl/materialy/inne/597.pdf. Accessed 20 August 2013.

Słonimski, Antoni. '*Wielki Kram* [*The Apple Cart*].' *Wiadomości Literackie*, 25 (1929), p. 4.

Słonimski, Antoni. '*Genewa* w Teatrze Polskim [*Geneva* in the Polish Theatre].' *Wiadomości Literackie*, 33 (1939a), p. 5.

Słonimski, Antoni. 'Kronika Tygodniowa [The Weekly Chronicle].' *Wiadomości Literackie*, 33 (1939b), p. 5.

Smollett, Tobias. *The Adventures of Peregrine Pickle* (London, 1751).

Sobieniowski, Florian. 'Wspomnienia tłumacza [The Recollections of a Translator].' *Teatr*, 9–10 (1936), pp. 17–18.

Stempowski, Jerzy. '*Ulisses* Joyce'a jako próba psychoanalizy stosowanej [Joyce's *Ulysses* as an Attempt at Applied Psychoanalysis].' *Wiadomości Literackie*, 6 (1932), p. 2.

Synge, John Millington. *The Playboy of the Western World* (Dublin: Maunsel & Co., 1907). Polish Manuscript: *Kresowy Rycerz-Wesołek* (1913). Trans. Sobieniowski, Florian (The Polish Theatre Museum of Warsaw, call no. 28; The Silesian Digital Library, call no. 4360).

Synge, John Millington. *The Well of the Saints* (London: A.H. Bullen; Dublin: The Abbey Theatre, 1905). Polish Manuscript: *Cudowne źródło* (1908). Trans. Wysocki, Alfred (The Silesian Digital Library, call no. 3776).

Szczawiński, Józef. 'Na barykadach Paryża [On the Barricades of Paris].' *Słowo Powszechne*, 49 (1982), p. 4.

Szczepański, Jan Alfred. 'Na przykładzie: *Czekając na Godota* [On the Example of: *Waiting for Godot*].' *Trybuna Ludu*, 36 (1957), p. 6.

Szczepański, Jan Alfred. 'Z dalekiego kraju [From a Far-off Country].' *Trybuna Ludu*, 13 (1972), p. 6.

Szczepański, Ludwik. 'Sztuka narodowa [The National Theatre].' *Życie*, 9–10 (1898), pp. 97–98, 109–110.

Szczepański, Ludwik. 'Teatr Krakowski [Kraków Theatre].' *Życie,* 21 (1898), p. 247.

Szmydtowa, Zofia. *Mickiewicz jako tłumacz z literatur zachodnioeuropejskich* [*Mickiewicz as a Translator of Western European Literature*] (Warszawa: Państwowy Instytut Wydawniczy, 1955).

Szturc, Włodzimierz. '*Końcówka* Becketta [Beckett's *Endgame*].' *Echo Krakowa*, 208 (1981), p. 2.

Szydłowski, Roman. 'Profesja burżuazyjnego wyzyskiwacza [The Profession of a Profiteer].' *Trybuna Ludu*, 352 (1951), p. 4.

Szydłowski, Roman. 'Bohaterowie i tchórze [*Heroes and Cowards*].' *Trybuna Ludu*, 269 (1955), p. 8.

Szydłowski, Roman. 'Kogut z podciętymi skrzydłami [A Cockerel with Clipped Wings].' *Trybuna Ludu*, 300 (1960), p. 6.

Szydłowski, Roman. 'Bunt, gniew i rozpacz [Rebellion, Anger and Despair].' *Trybuna Ludu*, 79 (1967), p. 5.

Szydłowski, Roman. '*Ulisses* w Teatrze Wybrzeże [*Ulysses* in the Coastal Theatre].' *Trybuna Ludu*, 72 (1970), p. 6.

Szyfman, Arnold. *Moja wojenna tułaczka* [*My War-Time Exile*] (Warszawa: Wydawnictwo Ministerstwa Obrony Narodowej, 1960).

Szyfman, Arnold. *Labyrint teatru* [*The Theatre Labyrinth*] (Warszawa: Wydawnictwo Artystyczne i Filmowe, 1964).

Szymonowic, Szymon. *Castus Joseph* (Kraków, 1578).

Taborski, Roman. *Warszawskie teatry prywatne w okresie Młodej Polski* [*Private Warsaw Theatres in the Era of Young Poland*] (Warszawa: Wydawnictwo Naukowe PWN, 1980).

Tarn, Adam. 'Lekcja warsztatu scenicznego [Lessons from a Theatre Workshop].' *Teatr*, 1 (1951), pp. 65–67.

Tenner, Juliusz. 'Teatr Lwowski [Lwów Theatre].' *Krytyka*, II (1906), pp. 471–477.

Thullie, M. 'Tumult w Teatrze Miejskim we Lwowie [Tumult in the Municipal Theatre in Lwów].' *Przegląd Powszechny*, 101 (1909), pp. 482–483.

Treugutt, Stefan. 'Godot.' *Przegląd Kulturalny*, 7 (1957), p. 6.

Trotter, Mary. *Modern Irish Theatre* (Cambridge: Polity Press, 2001).

Tuwim, Julian. 'Mieszkańcy [The Dwellers].' *Biblia cygańska* [*The Gipsy Bible*] (Warszawa: J. Mortkowicz, 1933).

Tyson, Brian. *The Story of Shaw's St. Joan* (Quebec: The McGill-Queens University Press, 1982).

Wakar, Jacek. 'Taniec jest życiem [Dancing is Life].' *Teatr*, 7(8) (1993), p. 29.

Wakar, Jacek. 'Każdy ma swoją opowieść [Everyone has their Own Story].' *Życie*, 303, (1999), p. 8.

Warmiński, Janusz. 'W sprawie *Ulissesa*. List otwarty do Macieja Słomczyńskiego' [On *Ulysses*. An Open Letter to Maciej Słomczyński].' *Życie Literackie*, 11 (17 March 1974). Available at: http://www.e-teatr.pl/pl/artykuly/94145.html. Accessed 20 April 2013.

Wasilewski, Zygmunt. 'Demonstracja w teatrze miejskim we Lwowie [Demonstration in Lwów's Municipal Theatre].' *Słowo Polskie*, 84 (1909), p. 3.

Webersfeld, Edward. *Teatr Miejski we Lwowie za dyrekcji Luwika Hellera 1906–1918* [*The Municipal Theatre in Lwów under the Management of Ludwik Heller 1906–1918*] (Lwów: Drukarnia W. A. Szyjkowskiego, 1917).

Weintraub, Stanley. 'GBS and the Despots.' *The Times Literary Supplement* (22 August 2011). Available at: . Accessed 14 July 2014.

Wells, Warre B. *Irish Indiscretions* (London: George Allen & Unwin Ltd. Ruskin House, 1922).

Wickstrom, Gordon M. 'The Heroic Dimension in Brendan Behan's *The Hostage*.' *Educational Theatre Journal*, 22 (4) (1970), pp. 406–411.

Wierzyński, Kazimierz. 'Dziennik poety [A Poet's Diary].' *Tygodnik Powszechny*, 42 (1983), pp. 6–7.

Wilde, Oscar. *An Ideal Husband* (Leonard Smithers, 1899). Polish Manuscript: *Mąż idealny*. Trans. Rakowski, Konrad (Warszawa: Feliks West, 1908).

Wilde, Oscar. *A Woman of no Importance* (London: John Lane, 1894). Polish Manuscript: *Kobieta bez znaczenia*. Trans. Beaupré, Barbara (Warszawa: Feliks West, 1908).

Wilde, Oscar. *Lady Windermere's Fan* (London: John Lane, 1893). Polish Manuscript: *Wachlarz lady Windermere*. Trans. Trzciński, Teofil (Warszawa: Feliks West, 1907).

Wilde, Oscar. *Salome* (Boston: Copeland & Day; London: Elkin Mathews & John Lane 1894). Polish Manuscript: *Salome*. Trans. Fromowicz, Władysław (Kraków, Gebethner i Wolff, 1904); Trans. Gąsowska, Jadwiga (Monachium: J. Marchlewskii Co, 1904).

Wilde, Oscar. 'The Critic as Artist.' [In:] *Intentions* (London: Osgood, McIlvain, 1891).

Wilde, Oscar. *The Importance of Being Earnest* (London, Leonard Smithers, 1899). Polish Manuscript: *Birbant* (1905). Trans. Unknown. The Silesian Digital Library, call no. BTL 4931.

Wilde, Oscar. *The Portrait of Dorian Gray* (London: Ward Lock, 1891). Polish Manuscript: *Obraz Doriana Graya*. Trans. Feldmanowa, Maria (Warszawa: Przegląd Tygodniowy, 1905); Jaroszyński, Tadeusz (Warszawa: S. Orgelbrand, 1916).

Winch, Antoni. 'Mrożek robi sceny [Mrożek Makes a Scene].' *Dialog*, 2 (2012), pp. 150–163.

Winiarski, Leon. 'Estetyzm - Oskar Wilde: *Wachlarz Lady Windermere* i *Kobieta małej wartości*. [Aestheticism - Oscar Wilde: *Lady Windermere's Fan* and *A Woman of No Importance*].' *Prawda*, 27 (1893), pp. 316–317.

Winiarski, Leon. 'Czynniki etniczne w sztuce i poezji z drugiej połowy naszego stulecia [Ethnic Elements in the Theatre and Poetry from the Second Half of Our Century].' *Prawda*, 10 (1894), pp. 111–113.

Wiśniewska, Marzena. 'Anatomia Upadku [Anatomy of the Fall].' *Sztandar Młodych*, 70 (1982), p. 9.

Wojdowski, Bogdan. 'Rzecz dzieje się w Nyadnanawe [A Play Set in Nyadnanave].' *Współczesność*, 22 (16 November 1960), p. 10.

Wroczyński, Kazimierz. 'Kresowy Rycerz [*The Playboy*].' *Tydzień Teatralny*, 43 (1913), p. 12.

Wróbel, Zdzisław. 'Gdański rekonesans. Teatr, do którego nie można dostać biletów [Gdańsk Reconnaissance. A Theatre to Which You Can't Get a Ticket].' *Pomorze*, 21 (1970). Available at: http://www.zygmunthubner.pl/48_James_JOYCE_-_Ulisses_1970. Accessed 20 April 2013.

Wróblewski, Andrzej. 'Dzień Powszedni Pana Bloom [An Ordinary Day for Mr Bloom].' *Panorama Północy*, 14 (1970), p. 12.

Wróblewski, Andrzej. 'Irlandczycy zawsze wymyślą coś, żeby sie bić [The Irish Always Find a Reason to Fight with One Another].' *Dialog*, 2 (1975), pp. 103–106.

Wysińska, Elżbieta. 'Konfrontacje: w obronie Sean'a O'Casey [Confrontation: In Defence of Sean O'Casey].' *Dialog*, 12 (1960), pp. 135–137.

Wysińska, Elżbieta. 'Teatralny wstęp do Joyce'a [A Theatrical Introduction to Joyce].' *Teatr*, 7 (1970), pp. 19–20.

Wysińska, Elżbieta. 'Teatry dramatyczne powojennego pięćdziesięciolecia [Post-War Dramatic Theatres].' [In:] M. Fik (ed.). *Teatr. Widowisko* (Warszawa: Instytut Kultury, 2000), pp. 59–98.

Wysocki, Alfred. '*Candida* Shawa [Shaw's *Candida*].' *Gazeta Lwowska*, 216 (1906), p. 4.

Wysocki, Alfred. 'Tadeusza Pawlikowskiego czasy lwowskie [Tadeusz Pawlikowski and His Time in Lwów].' *Pamiętnik Teatralny*, 1(5) (1953), pp. 153–160.

Wysocki, Alfred. 'Z teatru. *Cudowne źródło* J. M. Synge'a [From the Theatre. J. M. Synge's *The Well of the Saints*].' *Gazeta Lwowska*, 262 (1908), p. 4.

Wysocki, Alfred. *Sprzed pół wieku* [*Looking Back on Half a Century*] (Warszawa: Wydawnictwo Literackie, 1974).

Wyspiański, Stanisław. '*Klątwa* [*The Curse*].' *Życie*, 15/16 (1899), pp. 272–294.

Wyspiański, Stanisław. '*Warszawianka* [*The Varsovian Anthem*].' *Życie*, 45/46 (1898), pp. 590–598; 610–612.

Wyspiański, Stanisław. *Wesele* [*The Wedding*] (Kraków: Uniwersytet Jagielloński, 1901).

Wyżyńska, Dorota. 'Godot w garnizonie [Godot in a Garrison].' *Gazeta Stołeczna*, 216 (2001), p. 4.

Yeats, William Butler. '*The Countess Cathleen*.' [In:] *Poems* (London: Unwin, 1895). Polish Manuscript: *Księżniczka Kasia*. Trans. Kasprowicz, Jan. *Chimera*, 7 (20/2) (1904), pp. 17–84.

Yeats, William Butler. 'To Ireland in the Coming Times.' [In:] *The Rose* (London: Unwin, 1892).

Yeats, William Butler. *The Land of Heart's Desire* (London: Unwin, 1894).

Zamoyski, Władysław. *Jenerał Zamoyski* [*General Zamoyski*], Vol. III, 1832–1837 (Poznań: Nakładem Biblioteki Kórnickiej, 1914).

Zawistowski, Witold. '*Święta Joanna* [*Saint Joan*].' *Kurier Polski* (19 January 1925), p. 3.

Zborowski, Stanisław. 'Poeta i jego klęska [The Poet and His Defeat].' *Dziś i Jutro*, 39 (1955), p. 6.

Zielińska, Ewa. 'Świat kobiet [The World of Women].' *Kurier Polski*, 86 (1993), p. 3.

Żmij-Zielińska, Danuta. 'Z młodości *Dialogu* [From the Early Days of *Dialog*].' *Dialog*, 2 (2009), pp. 162–166.

Unnamed Reviews

— From Our Special Correspondent. 'Poland's Long Connexion with Shaw's Plays.' *The Times* (31 December 1956).

— Unsigned. 'Count Markievicz's New Play.' *Irish Times* (3 December 1908), p. 6.

— Unsigned. 'Ruch artystyczno-literacki. Z teatru. *Cudowne źródło*, legenda irlandzka w 3 aktach J.M. Synge'a. [The Art-Literary Movement. From the Theatre. *The Well of the Saints*, an Irish Legend in 3 Acts, by J.M. Synge]', *Gazeta Narodowa*, 262 (1908).

— Unsigned. 'Z teatru. *Pygmalion*. Komedya w 5 aktach Bernarda Shaw'a. Z oryginału przełożył Ryszard Ordyński [From the Theatre. *Pygmalion*. A Comedy in 5 Acts by Bernard Shaw. Translated from the Original by Ryszard Ordyński].' (1914) Loose-leaf. The Juliusz Słowacki Theatre Archive.

— Unsigned. 'Nekrologia.' *Kurier Warszawski*, 334 (1900), p. 6.

— Unsigned. 'Stragan z jabłkami i atmosfera polska [A Cart with Apples and the Polish Atmosphere].' *Express Poranny* (22 May 1929).

— Unsigned. 'Genialny Kpiarz [An Ingenious Joker].' *Kurier Czerwony* (16 May 1929).

— Unsigned. 'The Theatre: New Play in Dublin.' *Time* (14 March 1955). Available at: http://content.time.com/time/magazine/article/0,9171,807100,00.html. Accessed 12 August 2012.

— "Zastępca" (stand-in anonymous reviewer). '*Marnotrawny ojciec*, komedya w 4 aktach Bernarda Shawa [*You Never Can Tell*, a comedy in 4 acts by Bernard Shaw].' *Głos Narodu*, 455 (1906), pp. 3–5.

— "Zastępca" (stand-in anonymous reviewer). '*Profesja pani Warren* [*Mrs Warren's Profession*].' *Gazeta Lwowska*, 88 (1937), p. 3.

Index